The Mawddwy, Van & Kerry Branches

by
Lewis Cozens,
R.W. Kidner & Brian Poole

THE OAKWOOD PRESS

© Oakwood Press 2004

British Library Cataloguing in Publication Data
A Record for this book is available from the British Library
ISBN 0 85361 626 4

Typeset by Oakwood Graphics.
Repro by Ford Graphics, Ringwood, Hants.
Printed by Pims Print, Yeovil, Somerset.

First Edition 1972
Second Edition 2004

A Collett '14XX' class 0-4-2T with the branch goods at Dinas Mawddwy station on 27th June, 1950. *W.A. Camwell*

Front cover: Captured in a beautiful sylvan setting, 'Dean Goods' class 0-6-0 No. 2538 returns from Kerry with a goods train on 4th April, 1956. *G.F. Bannister*

Rear cover, top: Railway Clearing House map showing the branches to Mawddwy, Van and Kerry.

Rear cover, bottom: Drawing of the Kerry Tramway's 0-4-0 wing tank *Excelsior*.
Roy C. Link

Published by The Oakwood Press (Usk), P.O. Box 13, Usk, Mon., NP15 1YS.
E-mail: oakwood-press@dial.pipex.com
Website: www.oakwood-press.dial.pipex.com

Contents

Introduction to the Second Edition

Eminent authors on the minor railways of North and Mid-Wales, Lewis Cozens (*left*) and James Boyd (*right*), use a gangers' trolley to propel themselves along the Mawddwy Railway at Aberangell in May 1953.   *G.C.J. Lockhart*

I knew Lewis Cozens in the 1930s, and admire his perseverance in his studies of little railways. I was therefore glad, 40 years later, to republish three of his booklets in collected form. Since then I have on frequent visits seen their decay; they were not for this present world, and Brian Poole's hard work enables readers to see them as they once were.

R.W. Kidner
Llandre
July 2002

In the summer of 1967 I had come to Newtown to start my teaching career at the Agricultural Section of the then Montgomery College of Further Education. I stayed in digs for about four weeks prior to finding a flat. One week, Lewis Cozens stayed, while he was revising his book on the Mawddwy, Van and Kerry lines. I found this Londoner interesting, but maybe a little eccentric, not knowing I would be joining the same tribe some 35 years later.

Lewis Cozens had begun his series of booklets on minor railways 'to give him something to do on holiday'. By the time he was preparing the Mawddwy book in 1954 he had become assiduous in searching local and county records, and had also become especially interested in the less successful branch lines of the former Cambrian Railways. In 1972 Oakwood published a new edition of his three Cambrian booklets in one volume, at the same time updating what little was left.

In May 2002 I walked the length of the Kerry branch to find much intact within woodland or grazing land. I could not really find much reference to this railway so I wrote to Oakwood Press saying I would attempt to research a revised volume. They already had the original history manuscript, which had been revised by Roger Kidner, but the addition of local people recalling their part could be another valuable section. I set out to add the Van and the Mawddwy lines also.

I did not think that there would be too many people able to recall these three branch lines. I would contact one of my ex-students' dads and, from there on, a web would pass me from one witness to another. Please note they are recollections so they are subject to error of recall; an example is the considerable confusion over siding use on the Van railway. Some photographs have come to light which are new but photography would not have been a popular hobby within the family farm or with railway workers of the 1930s. The interviews took place between May and November 2002.

The college farmed at Newtown and on the Kerry Ridge. I do not know how many times I must have passed Kerry station in a car, a Landrover, a tractor, a minibus or a lorry. I could not understand how a capital-intensive structure had been built to serve such a small potential freight and passenger loading before the 1890s when some financial help (subsidy) was available, and I suppose the question remains unanswered.

Powys contains many abandoned railways. Towards the end of my career, I travelled and visited many farms from Ystradgynlais in the south to Llanrhaeadr in the north and saw these relics slipping back into the countryside. The Mid Wales line* ran through the length of the county yet there is little trace now of Moat Lane Junction. Some other examples are the Llanfyllin branch, a line to New Radnor, and the Brecon line out to Hay and on to Hereford. Head Offices of the previous companies of the Cambrian at Llanidloes, Welshpool, Machynlleth and Oswestry are now listed and restored buildings for other uses except the Oswestry building which needs help. There is something haunting about them, the ghosts of services past. Of all these the Mawddwy, Van and Kerry were the first to expire, their loading was so light that lorry and bus soon reduced their revenue. The collection of these reminiscences has been most enjoyable; I have been welcomed with much hospitality so I hope readers will also treasure them. I thank everyone for their valued contributions, and apologise that some items could not be used as the volume must be contained within a limit.

Brian Poole,
Newtown,
2004

---

* See *The Mid Wales Railway* by R.W. Kidner, Oakwood Press (OL79), 2003 for more details.

Chapter One

The Mawddwy Railway

The Mawddwy Railway, which was of standard gauge, latterly formed part of British Railways (Western Region) and ran between Cemmes Road (Montgomeryshire) - 5 miles 10 chains east of Machynlleth - and Dinas Mawddwy (Merioneth), a distance of 6 miles 63 chains.

The railway had a chequered career. Constructed at the instance of Mr (later Sir) Edmund Buckley in 1866/1867 it led a hand-to-mouth existence before falling into disuse in 1908. Under Cambrian Railways auspices and the drive of Mr Davies of Llandinam (later 1st Baron Davies of Llandinam) it was re-opened in 1911 for all traffic, only to expire in 1951 - 20 years after the last regular passenger trains had run.

The village of Dinas Mawddwy with its 400 inhabitants gives little indication of its proud past. Quite early it laid claim to being a Borough though it is doubtful whether a Charter was ever granted by the Crown: it was disenfranchised in 1886 when it ceased to be a Corporation due to passing of the Municipal Corporations Act of 1883.

In 1894 the parish of Mallwyd, of which Dinas Mawddwy forms part, became an Urban District Council and finally passed in 1934 to its present status as the parish of Mallwyd, part of the area governed by the Dolgelley Rural District Council.

The upper reaches of the Dovey valley contain considerable slate deposits. Such deposits have been worked intermittently since the middle of the last century and probably much earlier; no quarry is now operating in this valley. George Borrow, with his wife and daughter, passed through Dinas Mawddwy in October 1854 and in his *Wild Wales* relates that he found many houses letting lodgings to miners.

The Lordship of the Manor of Mawddwy passed to Sir Edmund Buckley, Bart at this period. His seat was Plas Dinas, and the mansion, with its extensive grounds, attracted much attention until its destruction by fire in 1917 - only the shell now remains.

Sir Edmund was born on 19th April, 1834, and was married on 14th March, 1860, to Miss Sarah Rees, daughter of Mr William Rees, of Tonn, Llandovery (a well-known Welsh family of publishers). There were five children, namely:

Edmund, born 7th May, 1861, died 20th January, 1919
William, born 10th January, 1863, died 1909
Sarah, born 18th December, 1864, died 5th April, 1870
Mary, born 16th June, 1870, died 8th September, 1879
Sybil, born 11th July, 1872, died May 1947

The Baronetcy was created on 11th December, 1868. Lady Buckley died on 21st April, 1883, and Sir Edmund later married Miss Sara Mysie Jackson (a cousin of his first wife); there was no issue.

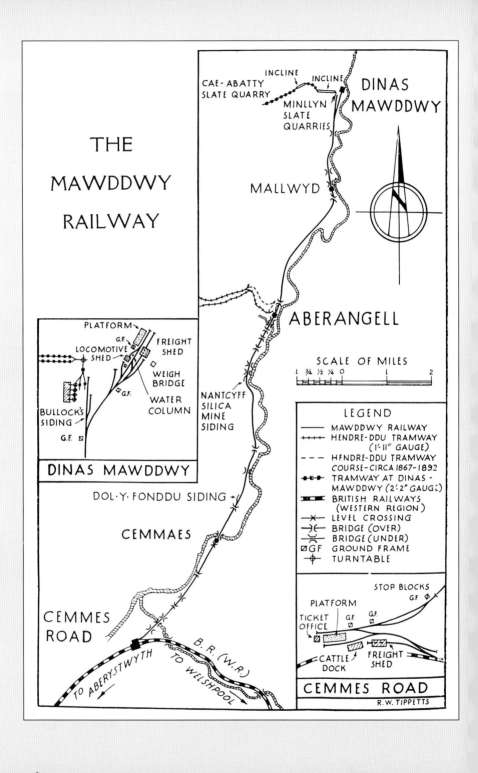

THE ACT OF INCORPORATION (1865)

Preamble

An Act for making a railway from the Cemmes Road Station on the Cambrian Railway to near the Town of Dinas Mowddwy [*sic*], and for other Purposes (5th July, 1865).

Whereas a Railway from at or near the Cemmes Road Station on the Cambrian Railway in the Parish of Darowen in the County of Montgomery to near the Town of Dinas Mowddwy in the County of Merioneth would be of public Advantage, and the persons in this Act named, with others, are willing to form a Company and carry the Undertaking into effect: And whereas it is expedient that Provision should be made to enable the Company incorporated by the Act (herinafter called 'The Company') to have the use of the said Cemmes Road Station upon certain terms and conditions, and that the Company and the Cambrian Railways Company should be authorised to enter into Working and Traffic Agreements . . .

[The following extracts of sections and parts have been made from the Act: they would appear to be those sections of most popular interest. The Act, in addition to the Preamble, contains 43 sections.]

Company Incorporated

Section 3. Edmund Buckley senior, Edmund Buckley junior, William Rees, and all other Persons and Corporations who have already subscribed or may hereafter subscribe to the Undertaking, and their Executors, Administrators, Successors, and Assigns, respectively, are by this Act united into a Company for the purpose of making and maintaining the Railway, and for other the Purposes of this Act and for those Purposes are by this Act incorporated by the name of 'The Mowddwy Railway Company' . . .

[The corporate seal was of the following form: Diameter 2¼ in., with the words 'Seal of the Mawddwy Railway Company 1865' appearing within the perimeter. Centrally a shield per pale. Dexter side: Double-headed eagle displayed. Sinister side: A chevron indented between two shields each charged with a bull's head caboshed. The Prince of Wales' Feathers above a coronet surmounted the shield. In this connection it is interesting to recall the Arms granted to Sir Edmund Buckley (vide *Burke's Peerage*, 1874): – Arms: Sa. a chevron indented between three shields. Arg. each charged with a bull's head caboshed, all within a bordure wavy of the first. Crest: On a mount in front of a bull's head sable, two fern branches, ppr. over all a bendlet, sinister wavy or. Motto: *Nec temere nec timide*.]

Capital

Section 4. The Capital of the Company shall be Twenty One Thousand pounds in Two Thousand One hundred Shares of Ten Pounds each.

First Meeting

Section 7. The First Ordinary Meeting of the Company shall be held within Three Months after the passing of this Act.

Number of Directors and Quorum

Section 8. The Number of Directors shall be Six but the Company from Time to Time may reduce or increase the Number of Directors within the Limits of Six as the Maximum and Three and the Quorum of the Meeting of the Directors shall be Three, except when the Number of Directors is Three and then the Quorum shall be Two.

Qualification of Directors

Section 9. The Qualification of a Director shall be the Possession in his own Right of Shares to the aggregate nominal amount of Three hundred Pounds.

First Directors

Section 10. Edmund Buckley senior, Edmund Buckley junior, and William Rees shall be Three of the first Directors.

POWER TO BORROW ON MORTGAGE

Section 13. The Company may from Time to Time borrow on Mortgage such Sums as they think fit, not exceeding in the whole Seven Thousand Pounds . . .

DEBENTURE STOCK

Section 14. The Company may create and issue Debenture Stock . . .

POWER TO MAKE A RAILWAY

Section 16. The Company may make and maintain the following Railway, with all proper Stations, Approaches, Works, and Conveniences connected therewith; (that is to say,)

A Railway to commence at or near the Cambrian Railway at the Cemmes Road Station thereof in the Parish of Darowen in the County of Montgomery and to terminate near the Town of Dinas Mowddwy in the County of Merioneth.

GAUGE

Section 22. The Company may construct the Railway of such Gauge as they think fit, provided that it not be wider than Four Feet Eight Inches and a Half, or narrower than Two Feet Three Inches, and if the Gauge be narrower than Four Feet Eight Inches and a Half it shall not be lawful for the Company to allow any Train to be drawn on the Railway at a rate exceeding Fifteen Miles per Hour.

MAXIMUM RATES OF CHARGES FOR PASSENGERS

Section 27. Rate for each First Class Passenger . . . . .3*d*.   per mile
Rate for each Second Class Passenger . . . . .2*d*.   per mile
Rate for each Third Class Passenger . . . . .1*d*.   per mile

PASSENGERS LUGGAGE

Section 29. Each Passenger's Ordinary Luggage without charge:
1st class . . . . .not exceeding 120 lbs.
2nd class . . . . .not exceeding 100 lbs.
3rd class . . . . .not exceeding 60 lbs.

TOLLS FOR SMALL PARCELS AND SINGLE ARTICLES OF GREAT WEIGHT

Section 32   Parcels not exceeding 7 lbs. in weight . . . . .4*d*.
Parcels 7 lbs. but not exceeding 14 lbs. . . . . .6*d*.
Parcels 14 lbs. but not exceeding 28 lbs. . . . . .1*s*.
Parcels 28 lbs. but not exceeding 56 lbs. . . . . .1*s*. 6*d*.
Parcels 56 lbs. but not exceeding 500 lbs. –
such sum as the Company may think fit.

AS TO USE OF CEMMES ROAD STATION

Section 36. The Company for the Purposes of their Traffic may have the Use of the Cemmes Road Station of the Cambrian Railways Company jointly with that Company, or the separate Use of a Portion of such Station and the Booking and other Offices, Buildings, Works, and Conveniences as may be mutually agreed upon between the Said Two Companies or in case of difference, as may be settled by Arbitration in manner provided by 'The Railways Companies Arbitration Act, 1859'.

POWER TO COMPANY AND CAMBRIAN RAILWAYS COMPANY TO MAKE AGREEMENTS

Section 37. The Company and the Cambrian Railways Company may from Time to enter into such agreements as they may from Time to Time think fit . . .

Physical Description (as when open)

Most travellers approach the Dovey valley from the East. After leaving Moat Lane Junction the scenery becomes increasingly grand as the climb to Talerddig is made. Dropping at 1 in 52/56 through the cutting beyond the diminutive station, the line is carried past Llanbrynmair and Commins Coch to Cemmes Road station (Montgomeryshire). The rocky River Twymyn, which has kept company on the left-hand side, passes under the railway shortly before Cemmes Road - it is at this point that we have our first sight of the Mawddwy Railway, the bridge by which it formerly crossed the Twymyn, just above that river's confluence with the Dovey, being visible a short distance downstream.

On entering Cemmes Road the main line splits to form a passing loop. Before entering the Cambrian station, a connection to a freight shed is continued to connect with the Mawddwy Railway and into a dead-end beside the passenger platform. The layout obliged a train to back out to a loop for running round.

The former booking office and waiting room of the original Mawddwy Railway were for some years occupied by a civil engineering firm, previous to which they were utilised by the Dinas Mawddwy Coal and Lime Company.

The station stands on a shelf at approximately 153 feet above sea level with the Dovey lying in the valley ¼ mile to the north. Rather more than a locomotive length beyond the further points of the passing loop stop blocks have been erected but the single track continues. The railway drops at 1 in 41 through a grass-grown cutting before easing as it emerges into the open and reaches the Twymyn river bridge.

A short embankment followed, with a lane passing below the railway to give access to Dol-Twymyn Farm - the bridge has now been removed. Pushing north-westerly in open country with the River Dovey in close attendance the railway climbed at 1 in 83 to Cemmaes (1 mile 41½ chains). Immediately before reaching this station a short siding, entered by facing points and protected by a ground frame, was thrown off right-handed close to a lane leading to the village ¼ mile distant.

On leaving this station the railway at once crossed the River Dovey by a low timber bridge of nine spans. The line passed under a bridge near Dol-y-fonddu and just beyond was the site of a short private farm siding - entered by facing points it lay on the left of the railway and was out of use when the railway closed in 1908; it was not relaid when the railway was reconditioned.

The Dovey was now flowing to the right (east) of the line and to avoid its sinuous course the railway turned in a northerly direction. The valley contracts and shortly beyond the third mile post severe reverse curves secured a course west of the river. Here, at Nantcyff, a silica mine operated from late 1928 until May 1935. A siding, entered by trailing points and situated on the left of the railway, was constructed in 1929, with accommodation for three trucks, and survived until 1937. The locomotives of the original company were replenished from a wayside tank at this point.

Leaving Nantcyff the railway struck north-westerly for Aberangell (4 miles 5½ chains, 156 feet above sea level). Immediately before entering the station occur two fine stone bridges - the first over the Angell (where the railway entered

A 1909 view of the nine-span timber viaduct that carried the Mawddwy Railway over the River
Dovey just north of Cemmaes station.

0-6-0T *Mawddwy* and carriage No. 4 are just visible in this scene from 1904. In the foreground is
Pont Minllyn which was built by Dr John Davies at the start of the 17th century to assist the
export of wool and finished cloth using Welsh ponies and donkeys.   *R.W. Miller Collection*

Merioneth), the second over the main road into the village. This station had a stone waiting room upon its platform, immediately to the north and to the left-hand side of the railway. This latter platform was served by a siding, seven chains in length, which could be entered from either end and thus formed an emergency loop. Two ground frames gave the necessary protection and the station yard boasted a crane. The Hendre-ddu slate tramway (*see Chapter Five*) had a single line with wagon table on the exchange platform and climbed away northwards at a gradient of 1 in 20.

On passing the points at the northern end of the siding the railway ran in a cutting below a bridge at 4 miles 13 chains. Leaving the cutting the line crossed a footpath from Gwastadgoed to the foot of Pen-y-clipiau (586 feet). The railway was now running just below the 200 feet contour line with the Dovey carving its tortuous path in the nearby valley. An open stretch followed and passing Camlan-Isaf Farm (just before the 5th mile post) the Dovey was again close at hand. At 5¼ miles there occurred a short cutting and the line turned due north under a bridge at Camlan-Uchaf to come alongside a lane running up the valley. On leaving it Mallwyd (5 miles 55½ chains) is reached, with its short platform on the left-hand side of the line. This station at one time boasted a waiting shed but was without a siding. Public access was by a gate off the lane above referred to. The river is particularly beautiful in this neighbourhood as it dashes through a rocky gorge with falls at nearby Pen-y-bont. Soon the outlying houses of Dinas Mawddwy, with the Minllyn Quarry on the mountainside to the left of the line, came into view and passing Quarry Cottages a siding, known as Bullock's, ran forward to a terminus below a slate wharf carrying the trans-shipment line of the quarry's 2 ft 2 in. system, which by means of two inclines transported slates over its bridge rails from the 1,000 ft level and rather over ½ mile from the lower terminus. This quarry ceased to function in 1935. At one time this tramway extended to the Cae-Abatty Quarry, a further ½ mile south-west and also at 1,000 ft, but both this quarry and section of tramway had closed before 1900. Bullock's siding was removed in September 1933.

Returning to the Mawddwy Railway we find that the line fell from the Bullock's siding junction to its terminus at Dinas Mawddwy (6 miles 63 chains and 267 feet above sea level). The siding entered by facing points, and leading to stop blocks backing the locomotive shed, was removed subsequent to 1939. The station house with booking office and waiting room, attached, and platform, rather longer than those at intermediate stations, are still in being as a café.

The station is situated at Minllyn, an outlying part of Dinas Mawddwy, and as one leaves the station, with its impressive stone gateway, a walk of half a mile is required to bring us to the village itself with its bodyguard of mountains.

Mawddwy posing with the branch train about 1900. The first carriage is first/second composite No. 4 and the other third brake No. 5.

Operation 1866-1901

In 1865 Mr R.S. France was engaged at Llanymynech (Montgomeryshire) on the construction of the Potteries, Shrewsbury and North Wales Railway. Mr Edmund Buckley secured his services as Contractor to the Mawddwy Railway, work commencing in 1866. The silver trowel used in that year in connection with the setting of the keystone of the Twymyn River bridge is a worthy memento of the occasion. Its blade is 5⅝ in. in length and of maximum width of 3⅜ in.: the inscription reads 'Presented by Mr G.T. Taylor to William youngest [in fact younger] son of Edmund Buckley, Esquire, MP, for setting the keystone of the Railway Bridge over the River Twymyn, Montgomeryshire, 1866'.

Construction costs were about £41,000 of which Mr Buckley gave £20,000 without security.

The opening to all classes of traffic was effected on 1st October, 1867, and, so far as can be traced, was carried through without the celebrations then customary on such occasions. Dinas Mawddwy was known as Dinas by the railway during the opening years, the full title being attained in the 1870s. The railway, from its earliest years, did much to assist the district, quarry owners and farmers alike benefiting.

The 0-6-0 Manning, Wardle tank locomotive *Mawddwy* worked the first trains and was joined by a similar, though slightly larger, locomotive from the same makers in 1868 - this second locomotive received the name *Disraeli*. At all periods trains were run 'mixed' if freight offered, and the struggle to secure adequate revenue was early apparent. Throughout the life of the railway two events made their annual contribution to the scanty returns, viz: the combined Dovey Valley Sunday Schools trip to Aberystwyth and, secondly, the 'specials' which removed the sheep from the mountains in late September in order that animals might winter on the lowlands of the Cambrian coast (around Dyffryn, Pensarn, Harlech and Criccieth in particular); the return to the mountains was made in late March or early April.

As early as 1882 local traders agreed to pay 1s. 2d. per ton extra rate, and a few years later 1s. 6d., as subsidy for carriage.

The timetable for the period 1st April to 30th June, 1887, was as follows:

	am	am	pm
Dinas Mawddwy	5.35	8.40	4.05
Aberangell	5.50	8.55	4.20
Cemmes	6.05	9.10	4.35
Cemmes Road	6.10	9.15	4.40

	am	am	pm
Cemmes Road	6.20	9.25	4.50
Cemmes	6.25	9.31	4.55
Aberangell	6.40	9.43	5.15
Dinas Mawddwy	6.55	10.00	5.25

During the late 1890s Dinas Mawddwy was contracted to Mawddwy simply, to revert to its full title at the 1911 re-opening, Cemmes was not altered to its correct spelling Cemmaes until 1911.

Mawddwy with the branch train at Cemmes Road station.   *Philip Griffiths Collection*

An early view of Dinas Mawddwy station; note the unusual bay window on the first floor.

Mawddwy Railway.

(Change at Cemmes Road on the Cambrian Railways.)

CHEAP THROUGH FARES TO DINAS MAWDDWY.

During the Summer Months cheap Week-day Return Tickets are issued from Aberystwyth, Borth, Towyn, Aberdovey, Barmouth and Dolgelley, to

DINAS MAWDDWY

The nearest Railway Station to Aran Mawddwy,

The next highest mountain to the Snowdon range in Wales, it being 2,972 feet in height, the distance from Dinas Mawddwy being only 4 miles to the foot of same ; also to LAKE VYRNWY, the distance being 12 miles from the north-west end.

The Railway runs alongside the RIVER DOVEY for some miles, and the well-wooded hills and scenery along the various walks and drives form a very

PICTURESQUE VIEW,

and is considered by competent judges to be unsurpassed by any in Wales.

Special Train Service for July, August, and September.

Time Tables at the Railway Stations.

"We believe that Dinas Mawddwy will be one of the most popular places in the district for Day Trips now that the difficulty of getting there has been removed."—*Cambrian News.*

Cann Office is 12 miles distant ; Bala, 18 miles ; Vyrnwy Lake (north-west end), 12 miles ; Cross Foxes Pass, 5 miles ; Bwlchygroes (the most rugged and difficult Pass in Wales), 7 miles ; and Dolgelley, 10 miles.

For further particulars and information see Handbills and Time Tables, or apply to the Station Agent, Dinas Mawddwy, or to

CHAS. E. WILLIAMS,

Dinas Mawddwy, R.S.O.   Secretary and General Manager.

Publicity for through fares was published each summer to attract tourists to Dinas Mawddwy.

CELYN BRITHION, DINAS MAWDDWY,

Overlooking beautiful scenery.   Close to the River Dovey.

Comfortable Apartments for Tourists.

Terms moderate.   Apply, MRS DAVID JONES.

LEWIS EDWARDS,

Maengwyn St., Machynlleth,

Saddlery, Harness, Horse Clothing,

And a large variety of other articles always in stock.

GUIDES.

The services of the following Persons can be obtained at any time upon two days' notice being given, either to the Persons direct or to MR. O. M. NICHOLSON, *the Station Agent at Dinas Mawddwy :—*

DAVID HUMPHREYS, Ty'nyfedw, Cowarch, near Dinas Mawddwy,

Guide to Aran Mawddwy, by Cwm Cowarch route.

WILLIAM HUMPHREYS, Ty'nymaes, Cowarch, near Dinas Mawddwy,

Guide to Aran Mawddwy via Cowarch.

HUGH EVANS, Perthyfelin, Cowarch, near Dinas Mawddwy,

Guide to Aran Mawddwy via Cowarch,

DAVID REES, Llanymawddwy, near Dinas Mawddwy.

Guide to Aran Mawddwy via Llaethnant.

ROWLAND HUGHES, Dinas Mawddwy,

JOHN LEWIS, Minllyn, Dinas Mawddwy,

General Guides to the neighbourhood.

Extract from a tourist guidebook. Shown here is an advertisement for accommodation and details of guides available through the station agent at Dinas Mawddwy.

Mallwyd was working from 1896, or possibly from the opening, and merely not quoted in this table. It had no buildings.

In 1889 Mr C.E. Williams, of Oswestry, became the Secretary and Registrar (later amended to 'Secretary and Manager').

Maes-y-gamfa Quarry was opened about 1892 and sent much slate over the Hendre-ddu Tramway, but by this date the railway was becoming increasingly dilapidated. Its rails were worn and its carriages, which were acquired by now second-hand from the London & North Western and North London railways, the object of derisive remarks.

The slump continued despite the introduction of excursion rates and extensive advertising - the railway's posters were exhibited as far afield as Snow Hill station, Birmingham. It comes as no surprise therefore, when the decision was made to close the railway to passenger traffic as from 17th April, 1901. The timetable for April 1901, showed four trains in each direction on Mondays to Fridays inclusive with an additional (evening) train operating on Wednesdays and Saturdays only. Journey time was 30 minutes at this date.

Traffic had never attained the promoters' expectations and it is recorded that only 842,493 passengers were carried during the years 1871 to 1900 (receipts £17,838), whilst freight for the same period totalled but 183,000 tons. The average annual gross receipts for the four years 1897 to 1900 inclusive, as shown in the Railway Returns, were £1,572, and for 1900 alone £1,427 - the worst of the four years.

No dividend was paid at any date!

In Limbo 1902-1909

This was a particularly bleak period in which the condition of the railway became progressively worse - if possible! The overall picture was sombre for the slate industry was involved in one of its depressions and the carriage of freight of all descriptions, viz: slate, coal, lime, sheep, etc., was continued only by the assistance of subsidies from the railway's customers - an unhealthy state of affairs which soon encountered trouble.

A daily return freight train was worked until the total closure in April 1908. In July 1904, this train left Dinas Mawddwy at 4.30 pm, arriving at Cemmes Road at 5.30 pm. After shunting, it returned to Dinas Mawddwy. Bradshaw's comment for would-be passengers at this period was 'Service discontinued pending repairs'. The cessation of passenger trains caused the mail to be carried on a manually-operated trolley which Mr Abiah Williams (a fireman) worked over the length of the line each weekday morning and evening.

The district soon became conscious of the restricted use of the railway and on Wednesday 30th September, 1903, an enquiry was held at the Town Hall, Machynlleth, before Col Boughey, RE, CSI, and Mr Henry Allen Stewart (two Light Railway Commissioners) - with Mr E. Welby Everard as Acting Secretary, into an application of the Mawddwy Railway Company, under the Light Railways Act of 1896, for £13,000 as a free grant and partly as a loan for the purpose of repairing the permanent way, bridges, culverts, etc., and providing locomotives and rolling stock for the Mawddwy Railway.

A view of (the then) Cemmes station on 25th July, 1904 looking towards Dinas Mawddwy.

Mallwyd station on the same day, looking twards Cemmaes Road.

Included amongst those at this well-attended meeting were:

Lord Henry Vane-Tempest
Sir Edmund Buckley, Bart (Chairman of the Mawddwy Railway).
Mr Charles E. Williams, Oswestry (Secretary and Manager of the Mawddwy Railway).
Mr R. Burton, Wrexham (Engineer to the Mawddwy Railway).
Mr Woosnam, Solicitor, Newtown (for the promoters of the scheme to work the railway as a light railway).
Mr Bullock (Minllyn Slate Co., Dinas Mawddwy).
Mr John Rowlands, Solicitor, Machynlleth (Mallwyd Urban District Council).
Mr A.J. Hughes (Inhabitant of Dinas Mawddwy).
Mr Kenrick Minshall, of Messrs Minshall, Parry-Jones and Pugh, Oswestry (for the Cambrian Railways Company).
Mr W.R.M. Wynne, Lord Lieutenant of Merioneth.
Mr C.S. Denniss, Secretary and General Manager of the Cambrian Railways Company.
Mr W.H. Gough, Superintendent, Cambrian Railways Company.
Col Norton
Revd R.H. Jones
Revd R. Richards, Cemmaes.

Mr Woosnam gave the early history of the company, and explained that £13,000 would be required to put the line in order and it was proposed that the Cambrian Railways Company should work the railway for them on terms to be agreed.

Mr Williams stated their railway was at a disadvantage compared with the larger companies such as the Cambrian in locomotives and track maintenance. The condition of the track due to lack of maintenance had caused the abandonment of passenger services. He said that the promoters asked for 100 per cent increase in the rates for carriage of minerals.

The terminus station at Dinas Mawddwy in 1904. *F.E. Fox Davies*

In reply to a Commissioner, Mr Williams said that the original Act of 1865 was amended by an Act of 1891 under which some rates were reduced and others raised. He explained that the Agreements signed by traders under which they paid extra rates to subsidise carriage were not in force at the date of the meeting, but several persons paid the rate voluntarily and they thought it hard lines that the remainder did not assist similarly.

Col Boughey said that if the increased rates were granted it would be on the ground that the Board of Trade would have the power to reduce them at any time if it was thought necessary - to which Mr Woosnam concurred.

Mr Williams passed next to the question of passengers and asked for the following increases:

First class: from 3*d*.   to 4*d*. per mile.
Second class: from 2*d*.   to 3*d*. per mile.
Third class: from 1½*d*.   to 2*d*. per mile.

The rate for Parliamentary trains, of which there had been two daily, was to remain at 1*d*. a mile.

Mr Richard Burton, Engineer to the company, gave his estimate for putting the line in order as £13,013 18*s*. 0*d*. Mr Rowlands observed that £575 was set apart in the estimate for improving the track layout at Dinas Mawddwy. It was not proposed to increase the siding accommodation at Aberangell or to build a warehouse there.

Mr C.S. Denniss, Secretary and General Manager of the Cambrian Railways Company, said that his company was interested in the Mawddwy Railway because of the considerable tourist traffic which passed off the Cambrian on to it. The slate traffic was also an attraction and, in the event of the line being closed, the cost of cartage to Cemmes Road station - about 10*s*. per ton - would be prohibitive.Traffic would decrease with subsequent loss to the Cambrian. He added that he had the authority of his Board to state that the Cambrian was prepared to enter into an agreement to work the line for 65 per cent of the gross receipts (70 per cent was later agreed).

In reply to a question from Mr Stewart, Mr Denniss said it would mean a loss to the Cambrian to work the railway on the old maximum charges, whilst in reply to Col Boughey he said it was a question of the working expense. For the same cost of working the Mawddwy company could carry four or five times the amount of traffic that they did.

Mr Hughes said that he would much like to see the draft agreement. Mr Woosnam said personally he was quite willing to show Mr Hughes the draft agreement - which prompted the latter to enquire whether the working agreement would include the provision of rolling stock by the Cambrian Railways Company.

Mr Denniss replied that he could not say at present. His company had agreed to work the Tanat Valley Railway and to provide rolling stock, but that railway was double the length of the Mawddwy and traversed a richer district.

Sir Edmund Buckley, Bart, Chairman of the Mawddwy Railway, stated that he was substantially in agreement with what Mr Williams had said. He was anxious to facilitate the working of the line and added that neither the Chairman nor Directors had ever received a shilling for their labours.

Mr John Jones, Manager of the Dinas Mawddwy Coal and Lime Co., spoke of the advantage the railway was to him. If the line were to be closed, the cartage rates for coal and lime would rise from 3s. per ton to 7s. or 8s.

Mr Bullock said that the rate for coal was heavy enough already. Had it not been for Sir Edmund Buckley's plantations, many people would have been without fires in the winter. On being asked by Mr Stewart whether the slate slabs would be put off the market if the line were closed and, if they would not, how could they be sent to Cemmes Road station, Mr Bullock replied that they would haul them on the railway by means of horses (laughter) to which Mr Charles Williams retorted 'Oh no!' (further laughter).

Mr Woosnam said that the reopening of the line to passengers was dependent on the grant from the Treasury. No attempt had been made to raise the money locally. Col Boughey said that efforts of the promoters to raise money must be shown. When this had been done the promoters must submit the details together with the working agreement with the Cambrian to the Board of Trade, and when the rates were definitely put before them, an order would be framed.

Mr Woosnam said the promoters relied on the Treasury for help, as the district was a very poor one. He thanked the Commissioners for a courteous hearing and the enquiry closed.

The railway struggled on until by 1908 the track was in such poor condition that even the daily return freight train could not operate safely any longer. The mails continued to be conveyed over the railway by manually-operated trolley during the period of 'Freight only working'. On 8th April of that year complete closure was effected.

Now without rail communication of any kind, attempts were made to carry freight over the valley road, a step which early threatened heavy expenditure to the ratepayers. By the autumn of 1908 the inconveniences incurred were making themselves felt and provoked much comment in the contemporary Press. The *Cambrian News* recorded how Sir Edmund Buckley had done everything a reasonable, generous man could do but had met with no adequate response:

> The question is whether the inhabitants of Dinas Mawddwy and the district are capable of doing anything to help themselves, or whether it is possible that some rich man may be found to spend money in trying to run a dead horse for their benefit . . . We do not suppose for one moment that the inhabitants of Dinas Mawddwy and the district are prepared to do anything to help themselves in reference to railway communication, but, if they are, we have no doubt they will be met reasonably and even generously. We should like to see Dinas Mawddwy awake.

The same issue contained a lengthy letter over the nom-de-plume 'Dovey Valley' which expressed 'the state of deep despair and gloom caused by the absence of railway communications with the outer world' and contained the following paragraph:

> As a rule a district wanting facilities loses trade to a district possessing them. For instance, there are insufficient quarries in the Corris district to supply all the requirements of the British markets. It therefore follows that if our quarries in Aberangell and Dinas Mawddwy are closed, the trade will simply shift to Corris and Machynlleth owing to the greater conveniences provided there for merchants and

quarry owners. It therefore follows that if we want to keep our trade we must fight to keep it. Providence, it is said, helps those that help themselves, and I am convinced that unless we bestir ourselves, and that promptly, we shall never again obtain a chance of competing with the rest of the World upon equal terms.

Mr John Humphreys, of Cemmes Road, conveyed the mails to and from Dinas Mawddwy as from 4th January, 1909 by means of pony and van. The fight was truly joined and the hour produced the man in the the person of Mr David Davies of Llandinam, Montygomeryshire. He was soon at work in the manner typical of a family which has done so much for Montgomeryshire, indeed for Wales. Mr Davies caused two notices to be printed and circulated in May 1909 - both were issued from his residence, Llandinam Hall. The first was dated 3rd May and headed 'Mawddwy Railway' and was a personal appeal to the various local authorities. It referred to the old railway and went on to say that it had been

> . . . laid with flat bottom iron rails, which are now very badly worn and damaged and will have to be entirely renewed. The sleepers are, taken as a whole, completely destroyed, and the line will have to be re-ballasted . . . The hedge fences are in good condition except that they are overgrown. Three of the bridges require to be entirely renewed, and some others will need new superstructure. The only buildings of any consequence are at Dinas Mawddwy, and the timber buildings here will have to be rebuilt. The rolling stock will have to be entirely renewed.
>
> It will therefore be seen that the line will have to be practically rebuilt before it can be opened for Passenger and Goods Traffic. Three estimates by different Engineers have been obtained for the cost of placing the line in thorough working order. From a comparison of these it may be reasonably assumed that the probable cost will be approximately £14,500, and it is possible that the Cambrian Railways Company might be prepared to undertake the work of reconstructing the line. There would have to be added to the sum mentioned about £3,500 for rolling stock.
>
> When negotiations were opened with Sir Edmund Buckley, it was found that certain debentures existed which have been purchased for £300, and by paying an agreed sum I have received the option to purchase the whole of the existing undertaking within six months at the price of £4,000. Adding to this figure of £4,000, £1,000 for the cost of the debenture referred to, the cost of the negotiations, and other expenses incidental to the formation of the Company, it would appear that the capital actually required before a Light Railway Company can be formed with any prospect of success is £23,000, although it is possible that this might be somewhat reduced. The capital of the new Company would be made up as follows:

> Purchase of old undertaking and expenses connected therewith
>   and with the formation of a new Company   £5,000
> Reconstruction of the line   £14,000
> Rolling stock, etc.   £3,500

> The total share and loan capital paid up to the Old Company was £25,745.

It referred then to Section 5 of the Light Railways Act under which

> H.M. Treasury is authorised under certain circumstances to make special advances, either by way of grant or loan, to Light Railway Companies . . . Assuming that the Treasury would be willing to make a few grants, it is certain that the greater part of the

capital required would have to be found elsewhere, and the question to be settled is from what sources, if any, this money can be drawn.

First, there are Local Authorities whose duty it is to consider the interests of the localities with which they are concerned, and the financial advantages to themselves likely to result from the opening of the line, e.g., the costs of maintaining the roads. It is understood that the average annual cost to the Montgomeryshire County Council of maintaining the main road from Mallwyd to Cemmes Road has increased very largely since the line was closed, and it may be assumed that there has also been very considerable increase of cost to the Merioneth County Council. These two Councils would, therefore, benefit financially by the re-opening of the line and should be expected to give substantial financial assistance to the proposed new Company. It is understood that the other Local Authorities concerned are:

The Dolgelley Rural District Council
The Dinas Mawddwy Parish Council
The Mallwyd Urban District Council
The Trefcaereinion Fechan Parish Meeting
The Cemmes Parish Council
The Machynlleth Urban District Council and
The Machynlleth Rural District Council

Apart from any question of convenience, the benefit to trade likely to accrue from the re-opening of the line is considerable, and those local authorities which have power to borrow money for such a purpose therefore should find a considerable sum between them.

Secondly, there are landowners, traders, and other individuals concerned and it should be expected that these would give the proposed new Company financial support by taking either debentures or preference stock . . . Personally I should be prepared to take shares, half debentures and half ordinary, to the extent of the purchase money £4,000 plus any other expenses to which I might be put, but I should have to impose the condition that the Local Authorities must take debentures and not insist upon their loans taking precedence over debentures.

As stated above, the capital required immediately is about £23,000 and of this sum about £8,500 would have to be found locally before the Treasury would entertain an application for a grant.

The Treasury has not yet been approached but it is hope that the Capital would be made up as follows:

Free Grant from Treasury	£10,000
Debentures to Local Authorities and Mr David Davies, say	£8,250
Preference Stock of which, say, £2,250 would be held by	
Mr David Davies	£4,750
	£23,000

and it is suggested that any balance, after paying dividends, etc., should be used to pay off debentures. It is assumed that at least £2,500 Preference Stock would be taken up by individuals, but if this should not be the case, the only alternative would be for Local Authorities to make up the difference in Debentures.

Before agreeing to make a grant the Treasury would require an existing Railway Company to execute an agreement to construct the light Railway and work it for 99 years. The Cambrian Railways Company would, it maybe assumed, provide staff, etc., and execute renewals and repairs. It might be found desirable to pay the Cambrian an increased percentage of gross receipts, and allow that Company to provide the rolling stock, but this point will receive consideration later.

Assuming that the annual gross receipts of the new railway would be no more than £1,400 and deducting, say, sixty-five per cent. for working expenses, viz, £910, an annual sum of £490 would be left for payments of interest, etc. The figure of £1,400 is not a high one and works out at only £4 per mile per week - a lower rate than that of either the Llanfair Railway or the Tanat Valley Railway or the Corris Railway. The £490 would be disposed of as follows:

	£	s.	d.
Interest at 3% on £8,250 - Debentures	247	10	0
Interest at 4 % on £4,750 - Preference Stock	190	0	0
Balance	52	10	0

It is proposed that the Directorate should consist of a Chairman, a Deputy Chairman, and six others, one of whom should be appointed by the Merioneth County Council, and one by the Montgomeryshire County Council, or one by an Urban District Council in Merioneth and one by a similar body in Montgomery.

If the Line were thoroughly well started the receipts might increase, especially if the railway rates were re-adjusted, and tourists to Dinas Mawddwy and the surrounding district were catered for. In any case it is desirable to secure authority to obtain further capital by way of debentures or preference or ordinary stock in the future, and the 'authorised' capital of the Company should therefore be, say, £30,000 which would enable the Company to raise a further £7,000 for future development should the circumstances warrant such a course. The 'authorised' capital of the old company was £29,648.

[The notice concluded by asking if each of the Local Authorities named and addressed would undertake to take certain sums specified and added:] It is probable that the whole of this sum will not be required.

It would be necessary to give notice this month of intention to apply for a light Railway Order. The matter is therefore very urgent, and it is absolutely essential that I should have the replies of all the local authorities by Saturday, 15th May, at the latest.

In conclusion, I must make it quite clear that unless the replies of the Local Authorities are favourable, and are received by me by the date mentioned, I shall be unable to proceed any further with the proposal, and a good opportunity of acquiring the old undertaking and of reconstructing the line will be lost.

Believe me to be,
Yours faithfully,
DAVID DAVIES

The second notice was headed:

MAWDDWY RAILWAY
Scheme for the Formation of a Light Railway Company

This notice was dated 5th May. Similar to the first, except that it was not over the signature of David Davies, it appealed to individuals to play their part in taking Preference Shares and asked them to write to Mr W.J. Evans, Llandinam Hall, 15th May at the latest, mentioning the amount of shares they would take. These notices caused many public meetings to be held forthwith in the districts covered by the project, including a special meeting of the Montgomery County Council held at Newtown on Thursday 13th May.

The Chairman, Captain Mytton, presided. Amongst those present were:

Mr Hugh Lewis (Vice-Chairman)
Mr G.R.D. Harrison (Deputy Clerk)
Mr Hutchins (County Surveyor)
Mr W.J. Evans
Colonel Pryce-Jones
Mr W. Forrester Addie
Mr Richard Jones
Mr William Jones
Mr J.E. Poundley

After the Chairman had opened the discussion Mr Richard Jones rose to endorse the expression of deep gratitude to Mr Davies for this truly philanthropic movement. He felt that so far as Montgomeryshire was concerned their interest in the re-opening of the line was mainly as a road authority. They had six miles of road running up the valley - expenditure on that road for the 12 months ending 30th June next would have been £1,316 17s. 9d. Of that sum, part was on account of extraordinary traffic. He referred to the timber growing in the locality which would be ripe for felling in about 20 years' time. Damage done by traction engines led him to observe that if that timber was to come over those roads they would not know where they should be and where their liabilities would end. He thought that £4,000 was rather a large sum to take in debentures, and that Merionethshire ought to have done more.

Col E. Pryce-Jones moved that the County Council agree to subscribe a sum not exceeding £4,000 in debentures to the proposed Mawddwy Light Railway Company subject to sufficient free grant being obtained from the Treasury and the remainder of the necessary share capital being provided, and that a small committee be appointed to draw up the details. Mr W. Jones seconded the motion.

The Chairman said that he thought £14,500 was a very large sum to put the line in order. He felt that some special engineer should watch their interests rather than a committee.

Col Pryce-Jones said that the railway would be worked by a company to which Mr W.J. Evans added that the company would be like the Llanfair Light Railway.

After further discussion the resolution was put to the meeting and carried unanimously, and a vote of thanks passed to Mr Davies for his efforts to open the line.

The Committee appointed was the Chairman, Vice-Chairman, Chairman of Main Roads Committee, Mr W. Forrester Addie and Mr R. Jones.

The inventory for Dinas Mawddwy and Aberangell stations, dated 12th June, 1909, which follows, is included in full to show what even a minor railway company gathers around itself over the years:

Dinas Mawddwy

Booking Office contains:
Telephone Instrument No. 1 with Battery complete - Telephone Instrument No. 2 with Battery complete, belonging to Mr T. Stedman, Peniarth Arms, Mallwyd - Telephone No. 3 belonging to Dr Walker, Plas, Dinas Mawddwy - Telegraph Instrument with 3 Batteries and Stand the property of the Postmaster General - 3 Ticket Cases - 1 Hand

Ticket Case - 1 Booking Office fixture with 7 Drawers and book rack containing Telegraph Stores and unused tickets - 1 Cupboard with postal telegraph stores - 3 Boxes containing type for dating stamp - 1 Ticket Dating Stamp - 1 Copying press - 1 Letter rack - 1 Desk fixture - Office Books belonging to Traffic Department.

General Waiting Room
1 Weighing Machine complete - 1 Clock fixture - 1 Fender - 3 Hand Lamps - 3 Oil Lamps - 3 Oil Tins.

Station Master's Office
1 Shelf containing Goods Department Books - 1 Writing Table - 1 Desk - 2 Maps - 1 Lamp - 2 Chairs - 1 Safe.

Ladies' Waiting Room
1 Table - 4 Chairs - 1 Ticket Box - 1 Ticket Case - 1 Rat Trap (wire) - 1 Hand Truck.

Old Carriage
1 Wheelbarrow - 1 Box containing carriage handles - Quantity Oak keys - 2 Trespass notice boards - 1 Station name board.

Lamp Room
Containing Carriage Roof Lamps (12).

Weighing Machine House and Office
1 Weighing Machine complete - Furniture belongs to tenants, Dinas Mawddwy Coal & Lime Co.

Locomotive Shed
1 Kalamazoo Car propelled by manual power (has been used for carrying Mails) - 1 Locomotive Engine No. 268 complete with tool box containing Spanners etc. - Head Light Lamp - 1 Locomotive No. 140 complete with Tools etc. - 2 Smith's Anvils - 1 Work bench with 2 iron vices fixed - Drawer in bench containing various nuts, bolts etc. - 1 Set of locomotive Wheels (3 pair) belonging to Engine No. 140 - 6 spare Brass Tubes belonging to Locomotive No. 140 - 1 Grind Stone and frame - 1 Passenger Carriage No. 2 containing: - 1 Small bundle loco packing - 1 Crosscut Saw - Quantity Cotton waste - 1 Mallet.

Quantity old Tallow Casks (empty) - Quantity old Carriage fittings - Iron chairs (for Permanent Way) - 2 Point Boxes - 10 Bridge Planks - 1 Trespass Board - Quantity Platelayers tools - Quantity Hedging Tools - 2 Scythes - 1 Cask loco oil (part full) - 1 Cylinder belonging to Vacuum brake - 2 Screw Jacks - 1 Jim Crow - 3 old Engine Springs - 2 empty Oil Casks - 1 Workman's Trolley with pulley handle and wheels - 1 Platelayers Trolley.

Lime Shed
2 Oak Gates posts - 1 Third class Compo Coach with Guard's Compartment and Brake No. 1140 - Vacuum Brake attached, contains 1 short Ladder - 1 Parcel rack - 1 Box unused tickets - 1 Date Stamp - 1 Passenger Coach No. 4 with Vacuum Brake attachment - 1 Compo Guards Van and Passenger Coach No. 5 contains 1 empty oil cask and part of pipe belonging to Vacuum Brake fittings.

Warehouse
1 Compo First and Second class Carriage No. 1022 - 1 Cask with glass burner screens and gas burners belonging to carriages Nos. 1140 and 1022 - 1 Cask wagon grease (part full) - 21 Time table boards - 6 empty oil casks - Quantity Vacuum Brake fittings - 1 Bundle Hay Forks - 2 Scythes - 1 Compo Third class Carriage.

Aberangell Station
Crane - Sack Truck - Tramways Rails on Wharf.

The May meetings did much to quicken the tempo of events and early in July the following deputation waited upon The Chancellor of the Exchequer in London in connection with the application for the Treasury Grant:

Mr David Davies (MP for Montgomeryshire)
Mr Edward Powell (for Montgomeryshire County Council)
Sir A. Osmond Williams (Merioneth County Council)
Mr E. Gillart (Machynlleth Council)
Mr Roberts (Mallwyd Council)
Mr G. Pryce (Dolgelley Rural District Council)
Mr G.D. Harrison, Solicitor, and
Mr W.J. Evans

The application was successful and led to the Mawddwy Railway (Light Railway) Order of 2nd March, 1910: meanwhile Mr Davies had completed the purchase of the undertaking on 25th August, 1909, for the sum of £4,300.

Fares and Tickets 1867-1901

Booking offices were provided at Dinas Mawddwy and Cemmes Road: passengers at intermediate stations were booked by the guard.

Mr Williams and Mr Aslett, General Manager of the Cambrian Railways, arranged that as from the summer of 1893 there should be cheap day return tickets to Dinas Mawddwy from Aberystwyth, Borth, Towyn, Aberdovey and Barmouth during the summer months. At the same period excursion rates were introduced on Mondays, Wednesdays and Fridays from Machynlleth to Dolgelley (and vice versa) via the Cambrian Railways to Cemmes Road, thence by Mawddwy Railway to Dinas Mawddwy, with the journey beyond covered by coach. The fares were 7s. 6d. and 5s.

Cheap day tickets were issued from Dinas Mawddwy to Machynlleth. Normal fares included the following:

Cemmes Road to Dinas Mawddwy:	1st Class Single 1s. 3d., Return 2s. 3d.
	2nd Class Single 1s., Return 1s. 11d.
	3rd Class Single 10d.
Aberangell to Cemmes:	3rd Class Single 4d.
Dinas Mawddwy to Mallwyd:	3rd Class Single 1d.

On certain tickets the name of the railway was shown in full, whilst on others the initials sufficed.

Dinas Mawddwy was referred to in varied forms, viz: Dinas, Dinas Mawddwy, Dinas Mawddy and Mawddwy; Cemmes was so spelt and not as Cemmaes.

Four main classes of tickets were issued, viz: first, second, third and Parliamentary, and the railway was not a party to the Railway Clearing House.

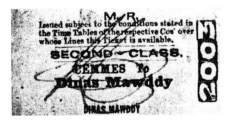

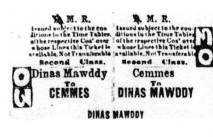

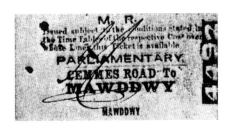

Some unused Mawddwy Railway tickets from the collection of the late W.E. Hayward. Firsts were white, seconds - pink, thirds -blue and Parliamentary - buff.

Chapter Two

A New Beginning

The Mawddwy Railway (Light Railway) Order, 1910 under Section 10 of the Light Railways Act of 1896, authorised the Mawddwy Railway Company to construct a Light Railway on the site of the disused Mawddwy Railway. The Preamble is here quoted in full and is followed by such sections or parts of sections from the Act as would appear to be of most popular interest. There were two Schedules, the first of which is quoted.

PREAMBLE

Whereas the Mawddwy Railway Company (hereinafter called 'the Company') were incorporated by the Mawddwy Railway Act 1865 (hereinafter called 'the Act of 1865') and were authorised to construct and work the railway (hereinafter called 'the old railway') in the said Act described in the counties of Montgomeryshire and of Merioneth:

And whereas the Company constructed the old railway but they have for some years ceased to work the same and it has fallen into such a state as to be wholly unfit for traffic and it is necessary and expedient that the Company should be authorised to construct a new railway (hereinafter called 'the railway') as hereinafter provided:

And whereas an application was in May 1909 duly made to the Light Railway Commissioners by the Company in pursuance of the Light Railways Act 1896 (hereinafter called 'the principal Act') for an Order to authorise them amongst other things to construct the railway as aforesaid and to work the same as a light railway under the principal Act:

And whereas the capital of the Company as authorised by the Act of 1865 is twenty-one thousand pounds in two thousand one hundred shares of ten pounds each of which the Company have raised and issued twenty-one thousand pounds (hereinafter called 'the existing capital'):

And whereas the Company are by the Act of 1865 authorised to borrow on mortgage seven thousand pounds and to create and issue debenture stock in respect thereof and the amount of four thousand seven hundred and forty-five pounds (hereinafter called 'the existing debentures') is now due and outstanding:

And whereas it is expedient that the existing debentures should be cancelled on the terms and conditions hereinafter contained and that the unexercised powers under the Act of 1865 of raising money should also be cancelled and the Company authorised to raise capital as hereinafter provided:

And whereas the local authorities hereinafter mentioned have in pursuance of special resolutions respectively passed in manner directed by the First Schedule of the principal Act applied to be authorised by this Order to advance for the purposes of the railway sums not exceeding in the case of the County Council of Montgomery the sum of four thousand pounds(,) in the case of the County Council of Merioneth the sum of two thousand pounds(,) in the case of the Machynlleth Urban District Council the sum of five hundred pounds(,) in the case of the Mallwyd Urban District Council the sum of five hundred pounds(,) in the case of Dolgelley Rural District the sum of four hundred pounds and in the case of Machynlleth Rural District the sum of six hundred pounds:

And whereas the Treasury have agreed subject to the fulfilment of certain conditions that the railway shall be aided under Section 5 of the principal Act by a free grant not exceeding nine thousand pounds:

And whereas the railway will be either wholly or partly outside the area of each of the said local authorities and the Board of Trade are satisfied that in the case of each such authority the amount of the expenditure of the authority for the purpose of the advance is so limited by this Order as not to exceed such amount as will in their opinion bear due proportion to the benefit which may be expected to accrue to the area of the authority from the working of the railway:

Now we the Light Railway Commissioners being satisfied of the expediency of granting the said application do in pursuance of the principal Act and by virtue and in exercise of the powers thereby vested in and of every other power enabling us in this behalf Order as follows:

SHORT TITLE

This Order may be cited as 'The Mawddwy Railway (Light Railway) Order 1910' and shall come into force on the date on which it is confirmed by the Board of Trade [in fact, 2nd March, 1910].

DIRECTORS

6. David Davies and two other persons to be nominated by him and consenting to such nomination shall be directors of the Company and shall continue in office until the first ordinary meeting held after the commencement of this Order.

APPOINTMENT OF DIRECTOR BY CAMBRIAN COMPANY

8. (1) If and so long as the Cambrian Company work the railway they may appoint one director of the Company.

(2) Any director appointed by the Cambrian Company as aforesaid shall at the time of his appointment be either a director or an official of the Cambrian Company and may be appointed by the Cambrian Company in such manner and for such period and subject to such conditions as the Cambrian Company may subject to the provisions of this section determine and shall be subject to the provisions regulating the term of office and retirement and qualification and election of the ordinary directors of the Company but except as aforesaid shall be in the same position as an ordinary director of the Company:

(3) If by reason of any such appointment of a director by the Cambrian Company the total number of directors of the Company would exceed the maximum number of six prescribed by Section 8 (Number of directors and quorum) of the Act of 1865 that in such case one of the directors elected by the shareholders of the Company in accordance with the provisions of the section of this Order of which the marginal note (here heading) 'Directors' shall retire so as to reduce the total number of the directors to six and the individual so to retire shall be determined as provided by Section 88 of the Companies Clauses Consolidation Act 1845 in the case of retirement by rotation.

WORKS

Power to construct and work new railway as light railway.

10. Subject to the provisions of this Order the Company may on and within the limits of the lands and property acquired the Act of 1865 construct a new railway on the site and in the lines and according to the levels of the old railway and with all proper rails plates sidings junctions turntables bridges culverts drains viaducts stations approaches roads yards buildings and other works and conveniences connected therewith and work the same as a light railway under the principal Act: Provided that if the Company under this Order construct or build any bridge to carry the railway over any road or any road over the railway they shall make the same such dimensions as were prescribed or authorised in relation thereto under the Act of 1865.

GAUGE OF RAILWAY AND MOTIVE POWER

11. The railway shall be constructed on a gauge of four feet eight and a-half inches and the motive power shall be steam or such motive power as the Board of Trade may approve. Provided that nothing in this Order shall authorise the Company to use electrical power on the railway.

PROVISIONS AS TO WORKING
Restriction of weight on rails on speed

10. (1) The Company shall not without the previous consent in writing to the Board of Trade use upon the railway any engine carriage or truck bringing a greater weight than twelve tons upon the rails by any one pair of wheels: Provided that if at any time the rails weigh not less than sixty four pounds per yard the Company may use upon the railway any engine carriage or truck bringing a weight not greater than fourteen tons upon such rails by any one pair of wheels and that if and when rails weighing not less than seventy pounds per yard are used the said weight may be increased to sixteen tons;

(2) The Company shall not run any train or engine upon the railway at a rate of speed:

(A) exceeding at any time twenty-five miles per hour;

(B) exceeding twenty miles an hour when such train or engine is passing over any gradient steeper than one in fifty feet;

(C) exceeding fifteen miles an hour when such train or engine is passing over any gradient steeper than one in forty feet;

(D) exceeding ten miles an hour when such train or engine is either passing over any curve the radius of which is less than nine chains or within the distance of two hundred yards from a level crossing over a public road where no gates are erected and maintained across the railway;

(E) exceeding any less maximum speed fixed by the Board of Trade for any part of the railway where the Board consider such further restrictions necessary for public safety.

Charges for small parcels.

27. For the conveyance on the railway of small parcels not exceeding five hundred pounds in weight by passenger trains the Company may demand and take any charges not exceeding those authorised by Section 32 of the Act of 1865.

Maximum rates for passengers.

28. The maximum rate of charge to be made by the Company for the conveyance of passengers upon the railway including every expense incidental to such conveyance shall not exceed the following; (that is to say)

For every passenger conveyed in a first-class carriage threepence per mile;

For every passenger conveyed in any other class carriage twopence per mile;

Provided that the Company shall not charge more than one shilling for each passenger conveyed in such carriage for only one journey upon the railway;

For every passenger conveyed on the railway for a less distance than three miles the Company may charge as for three miles and every fraction of a mile beyond three miles or any greater number of miles shall be deemed a mile.

Workmen's trains.

29. A failure by the Company to comply with any order with respect to the railway under Sub-section (2) of Section 3 of the Cheap Trains Act 1883 shall be deemed to be a failure to comply with the provisions of this Order.

FIRST SCHEDULE

Permanent Way: The rails used shall weigh at least fifty-eight pounds per yard.

On curves with radii of less than nine chains a check rail shall be provided.

If flat-bottom rails and wooden sleepers are used -

(a) The rails at the joints shall be secured to the sleepers by fang or other through bolts or by coach-screws or by double spikes on the outside of the rail with a bearing plate; and

(b) The rails on curves with radii of less than nine chains shall be secured on the outside of the outer rail to each sleeper by a fang or other through bolt or by a coach-screw or by double spikes with a bearing plate; and

Cemmes Road station c.1912 the two lines centre left form a loop before a single line continues on to Dinas Mawddwy. The line on the right links the M____ ____ R____y ____ with the Cambrian Railways' main line.

R.W. Miller Collection

(c)   The rails on the curves with radii of less than nine chains shall be tied to gauge by iron or steel ties at suitable intervals or in such a manner as may be approved by the Board of Trade.

Turntables: No turntables need be provided but no tender engine shall be run tender foremost at a rate of speed exceeding at any time fifteen miles an hour.

Electrical Communication: If the Board of Trade require means of electrical communication to be provided on the line the Company shall make that provision in such manner as the Board of Trade direct.

Signals: At places where under the system of working for the time being in force trains may cross or pass one another there shall be a home-signal for each direction at or near the entrance points. If the home-signal cannot be seen from a distance of a quarter of a mile a distance-signal shall be erected at that distance at least from the entrance points. The home-signals and distance-signals may be worked from the station by wires or otherwise.

Every signal-arm shall be so weighted as to fly to and remain at danger on the breaking at any point of the connection between the arm and the lever working it.

Precautions shall be taken to the satisfaction of the Board of Trade to ensure that no signal can be lowered unless the points are in proper position and that two conflicting signals cannot be lowered simultaneously.

Platforms, &c. – Platforms shall be provided to the satisfaction of the Board of Trade unless all carriages in use on the railway for the conveyance of passengers are constructed with proper and convenient means of access to and from the same from and to the level of the ground on the outside of the rail.

There shall be no obligation on the Company to provide shelter or conveniences at any station or stopping-place.

Operating 1911-1930

Reconstruction of the railway proceeded apace under the direction of the Cambrian Railways Engineer, Mr G.C. MacDonald, and his assistant, Mr James Williamson. Standard type bull-headed rails secured second-hand from that railway's main line were utilised, and ballast was secured from the Van mines as weedkiller. Cambrian Railways 0-4-0ST locomotive No. 22 was put to work, and three bridges were strengthened or rebuilt: that over Twymyn and two over the Dovey; a hand-wound pile-driver was used to sink piles. The entire fabric was greatly strengthened.

Saturday 29th July, 1911, saw the re-opening of the railway, to the general delight of the Dovey valley residents. The stopping of the services had caused much inconvenience, and the closing, or partial closing, of the slate quarries had brought misery to a countryside from which many had moved to the coalfields of South Wales or emigrated to the Canadian wheat prairies.

The opening ceremonies proved both enjoyable and successful. In response to the invitation of Mr David Davies, Chairman of Directors, a considerable company gathered for the special train from gaily decorated Cemmes Road station. The company included:

Mr John Conacher (Deputy Chairman)
Mr R.C. Anwyl (Director)
Mr Edward Powell, JP (Director)

Dinas Mawddwy station on 29th July, 1911 decked out in flags and bunting to celebrate its reopening.

The Dovey Valley Brass Band led the procession on on the day of reopening. Here they are, still having a good blow, for the jubilee of King George V in 1935. He reigned longer than the restored passenger service!   *Maggie Edwards Collection*

Major F.J. Walton, JP (Director)
Mr W.J. Evans (Secretary)
Mr Alfred Herbert (Director of the Cambrian Railways Company (CR))
Mr S. Williamson (Secretary of the CR)
Mr C.L. Conacher (Traffic Manager of the CR)
Mr Herbert Williams (Chief Assistant of the CR)
Mr W. Finchett (Accountant of the CR)
Mr G.C. Macdonald (Engineer of the CR)
Mr J. Williamson (Assistant Engineer of the CR)
Mr Herbert E. Jones (Locomotive Superintendent of the CR)
Mr Hugh Lewis (Chairman of the Montgomery County Council)
Mr G.R.D. Harrison (Clerk to the Montgomeryshire County Council)
Mr G.A. Hutchins (Surveyor to the Montgomeryshire County Council)
Col Pryce-Jones, MP
Mr William Owen (Chairman of the Merioneth County Council)
Mr H. Jones (Chief Constable of Merioneth)
Col Norton
Mr E. Humphreys (Chairman of the Machynlleth Urban District Council)
Mr R. Ll. Jones (Vice-Chairman of the Machynlleth Urban District Council)
Mr E. Gillart (Clerk to the Machynlleth Urban District Council)
Mr E. Evans (Chairman of the Dinas Mawddwy Urban District Council)
Mr Meredith Roberts (Clerk to the Dinas Mawddwy Urban District Council)
Mr John Evans, Welshpool (Secretary of the Llanfair Light Railway Company), and
Representatives of the Machynlleth and Dolgelley Rural District Councils

Mr David Davies and Mr Herbert E. Jones took their places on the rebuilt 0-6-0 Cambrian Railways freight locomotive and to the reports of detonators the train of five saloons and four composite six- and eight-wheeled carriages (all Cambrian) left for Dinas Mawddwy. All along the line crowded platforms greeted the passengers. Dinas Mawddwy was in particularly happy mood and the schoolchildren of that village, together with those from Aberangell and Cemmaes, from their vantage point on a nearby knoll vied with the local residents in a lively demonstration of goodwill as the train reached the terminus. The station premises were decorated with streamers supported by tall Venetian poles bearing heraldic shields.

With the Dovey Vale Brass Band at their head the company proceeded through the station entrance to a large marquee which had been erected nearby. The catering was in the hands of Mr Evan Bebb, of Newtown; the luncheon guests - over 300 - are said to have been fully satisfied! Mr David Davies presided and was supported by his co-Directors, Col Norton and others.

Following the loyal toast given from the Chair, the toast 'Success to the Mawddwy Railway' was submitted by Col Norton, a prominent shareholder, in vigorous speech. He expressed satisfaction at seeing so many distinguished public men in the assembled company and compared the smooth running of the special train with the state of things that had existed previously. He referred to the scenic beauties of the area, its mineral wealth and the possibility of tapping the lead and other minerals believed or be in the Cowarch valley. He concluded by stating that he considered the shareholders would see the railway a success, and that it would remain a success (applause).

This poor quality image shows Cambrian Railways 2-4-0 No. 43 with a passenger train made up of 4-wheel coaches at Dinas Mawddwy.   *R.W. Miller Collecton*

A splendid portrait of Cambrian Railways 2-4-0 No. 43 on the turntable at Machynlleth on 2nd July, 1909. This engine regularly worked trains to Dinas Mawddwy.   *R.W. Miller Collection*

It would be ungracious to conclude the account of a great day in the Dovey valley's history without mentioning the fine singing of the local schoolchildren. Their reward was a free trip to Cemmes Road, followed by tea, cakes and selections on Mr H. Robertson-Sherby's gramophone. The sports were cancelled due to a thunderstorm breaking over the valley.

In the reconstruction of Dinas Mawddwy station the wooden freight shed was pulled down and a new shed erected a few yards to the south.

The full public service opened two days later (Monday 31st July, 1911) with the following timetable:

Down	am	pm	pm	pm
Dinas Mawddwy	8.30	12.15	3.55	6.10
Mallwyd	8.34	12.19	3.59	6.14
Aberangell	8.40	12.25	4.05	6.20
Cemmaes	8.52	12.37	4.17	6.32
Cemmes Road	9.00	12.45	4.25	6.40
Up				
Cemmes Road	10.40	1.20	5.30	6.50
Cemmaes	10.47	1.27	5.37	6.57
Aberangell	11.00	1.40	5.50	7.10
Mallwyd	11.06	1.46	5.56	7.16
Dinas Mawddwy	11.10	1.50	6.00	7.20

It will be noted that Dinas Mawddwy and Cemmaes stations had reverted to their correct postal designations.

The services were worked by *Mawddwy* and a variety of Cambrian Railways 2-4-0 locomotives (including No. 28). The booking office at the Mawddwy Railway's Cemmes Road terminus was closed; henceforth passengers were booked at the main line office. The intermediate stations' passengers were booked by the guards.

With the outbreak of World War I in August 1914, came the closing of Maes-y-gamfa Quarry, Minllyn following in 1915. The added loss of tourist traffic was countered by the heavy timber traffic resulting from war requirements, and the carriage of explosives to HM Magazine, Dinas Mawddwy (housed in the buildings formerly occupied by the Minllyn Slate Quarry Company). The timber hauliers found the entrance to the yard at Dinas Mawddwy too narrow and it was widened without delay.

Early 1915 saw the arrival of Cambrian Railways 2-4-0 tank locomotive No. 59 *Seaham*. This locomotive was recalled to Oswestry within a few months to work further branch lines. Cambrian 2-4-0 locomotives Nos. 44 and 56 followed, and gave excellent service.

In June 1918, the services had deteriorated to three trains daily in each direction. Journey time was 30 minutes except for the 12.35 and 4.05 pm trains ex-Dinas Mawddwy, both of which were allowed five minutes extra. The cessation of hostilities caused the demand for timber to slacken and brought about the closure of HM Magazine, the huts, office furniture, etc., of which were disposed of by auction on 22nd December, 1920.

Cambrian Railways 2-4-0 No. 53 hauls the 8.30 am Dinas Mawddwy-Machynlleth train tender-first into Machynlleth on 15th August, 1913.   *LCGB/Ken Nunn Collection*

GWR '517' class 0-4-2T No. 1155 with the Mawddwy branch train *circa* 1926. The first and second class coaches immediately behind the engine are of Great Western origin, the third class coach at the rear of the train is ex-Cambrian Railways.   *R.W. Miller Collection*

The Mawddwy Railway was absorbed by the Great Western Railway (GWR) as from 1st January, 1923. It will be appreciated that although the Cambrian Railways Company was acquired by the GWR in 1922, the Mawddwy Railway was 'worked and maintained' by the Cambrian and was therefore the subject of special legislation. The debenture holders were lucky to receive £27 per £100; however, the company had somehow managed to pay a dividend of 4 per cent each year from 1914 to 1920.

For many years certain trains were virtually 'Specials' for children bound for Machynlleth County School, locomotives and carriages working through to Machynlleth from Mondays to Fridays inclusive during term. Such trains in October 1923, were as follows:

		am	pm
Dinas Mawddwy		8.20	3.00
Mallwyd		8.24	3.09
Aberangell		8.30	3.20
Cemmaes		8.42	3.32
Cemmes Road	arr.	8.50	3.40
	dep.	9.10 MF	3.55 MF
Machynlleth		9.20 MF	4.05 MF
Machynlleth		9.50 MF	5.00 MF
Cemmes Road	arr.	10.00 MF	5.10 MF
	dep.	10.45	5.35
Cemmaes		10.52	5.42
Aberangell		11.05	5.55
Mallwyd		11.11	6.01
Dinas Mawddwy		11.15	6.05

MF - Mondays to Fridays inclusive during Machynlleth County School term only.

The early 1920s saw rural districts everywhere being opened up by bus services and the Dovey valley was invaded by the vehicles of both the GWR and the Corris Railway. This narrow-gauge railway, which was operated at this date by the Bristol Tramways & Carriage Co. Ltd, had road depots at Corris and Machynlleth and headed its relative handbills 'Corris Railway Road Services'. The Corris Railway was purchased by the GWR under an Act dated 4th August, 1930. It would appear from *The Merioneth County Times* of 31st July, 1948, that the GWR had acquired and was working the route Machynlleth to Dinas Mawddwy prior to 1930, and had already extended to to Dolgelley. The issue in question contained the following:

In August, 1930, the GWR took over the (Corris) Railway and the buses . . . All the Corris Railway bus services, together with the GWR Machynlleth to Aberystwyth and Machynlleth to Dolgelley routes were handed over to The Wrexham Transport Co., with whom the Railway Company had half shares. This Company was renamed The Western Transport Co., but was soon taken over by the Crosville Co., another railway-owed bus company. All bus services are run as in 1930, except the former GWR Machynlleth-Dolgelley route. Instead of this, we find buses running between Machynlleth, Corris and Aberllefefenni, on the old Corris Railway route, with connections at Corris as in Corris Railways days, with Dolgelley, Tal-y-llyn and Towyn.

A mixed train at Dinas Mawddwy in 1928, with GWR 0-4-2T No. 846, which was shedded there for several years.   *Revd B.B. Edmonds*

An up mixed train crossing the River Dovey on the approach to Cemmaes station.
                                                                   Revd B.B. Edmonds

The first buses to serve Dinas Mawddwy from Machynlleth started about 1924. The Mawddwy Railway passenger services were now fighting for their very existence.

The services for January 1930, are appended:

Down	am	am	pm	pm	pm
Dinas Mawddwy	8.25	10.00	12.40	3.05	6.30
Mallwyd	8.29	10.04	12.44	3.09	6.34
Aberangell	8.34	10.09	12.49	3.13	6.39
Cemmaes	8.43	10.18	12.58	3.29	6.48
Cemmes Road	8.48	10.23	1.03	3.40	6.53
Up					
Cemmes Road	9.00	10.40	1.20	5.05	7.10
Cemmaes	9.05	10.45	1.25	5.10	7.15
Aberangell	9.16	10.57	1.36	5.21	7.26
Mallwyd	9.22	11.09	1.42	5.27	7.32
Dinas Mawddwy	9.25	11.13	1.45	5.30	7.35

Passengers services persisted until the running of the last regular trains on Wednesday 31st December, 1930, when Dinas Mawddwy locomotive shed ceased to be used. Normally the trains were made up of a locomotive, two carriages and brake van and, if required, up to 10 wagons.

The figures for 1930 include:

		Receipts £
Dinas Mawddwy:		
Passengers on the branch	15,007	862
Parcels on the branch	1,976	107
Tonnage of goods	2,922	1,498
Aberangell:		
Tonnage of goods	2,447	1,432

The stoppage produced the usual flood of objections, but all to no avail. Thereafter 'freight only' was the order, with the annual Sunday Schools' special passenger excursion to prove the exception.

When the Cambrian Railways commenced working the railway they booked passengers at their main line booking office at Cemmes Road, the Mawddwy Railway's booking office passing to other uses. For local journeys the guards were supplied with perforated tickets and bell punch for booking third class passengers *en route*. Paper tickets were issued for first class local-booked passengers: two classes only were carried during the years 1911-1930, with third class accommodation sufficing for the Sunday Schools' specials of 1931 to 1939 inclusive.

For a short period, 1929-1935, a silica mine at Nantcyff (between Cemmaes and Aberangell) added to the revenue. A short siding was laid in, the points of which faced Aberangell.

The railway was operated by one locomotive in steam or two locomotives coupled together. The wooden train staff was painted red, with a straight black

Aberangell station looking north.

Aberangell station site in 1971. The loop and exchange siding were just beyond.   *R.W. Kidner*

handle. The narrow brass plate on each side was lettered 'Cemmes Road and Dinas Mawddwy'; attached to the staff was a key for operating the following points:

Cemmes Road station
Cemmaes station
Timber siding near Dol-y-fonddu   }   In use for limited period
Nantcyff silica mine siding   }   points lever and locking lever
Aberangell: Freight siding, with points connected with main line at each end, thus forming a loop for emergency use only under proper authority.
Bullock's siding (Minllyn Quarry): points lever and locking lever
Dinas Mawddwy: all yard sidings

It is believed that on the original Mawddwy Railway (1867/1908) all points were worked by ground frames, which system prevailed to the final closure.

Neither signals nor turntables were provided. Platform lighting was by means of oil lamps, those at Cemmaes, Aberangell and Mallwyd being removed by the guard to Cemmes Road for cleaning and trimming as required.

Trains were subjected to a speed limit of 25 mph, with a further reduction to 15 mph on the reverse curves between Cemmaes and Aberangell. Mile posts and gradient posts were provided, though the latter had disappeared before the end.

Freight Only - 1931-1954

The railway now relapsed into a condition calling for freight trains worked from Machynlleth on Mondays, Wednesdays and Fridays only. The question of the continuance of even this slender service was receiving attention at the close of 1938 and early 1939.

With the cessation of regular passenger services the canopy on Dinas Mawddwy station platform covering the angle in the station house, and the relative seats, were removed in 1931, together with the waiting shed at Mallwyd. The similar shed at Cemmaes was not removed until several years later.

Due largely to the efforts of Sir Robert Vaughan, Mr Hugh J. Owen (the Clerk to the Merioneth County Council), Mr Rowlands (Deputy Clerk) and Messrs J. Breese Davies (on behalf of the in the inhabitants of Dinas Mawddwy and district) and Hugh Morris (Chairman, Mallwyd Parish Council), it was learnt in February 1939 that the GWR would maintain freight services until the end of the summer of that year. In the summer service timetable of 1939 these services were as follows:

Up		am	Down		am
Cemmes Road	dep.	9.38	Dinas Mawddwy	dep.	10.50
Dinas Mawddwy	arr.	10.10	Cemmes Road	arr.	11.20

Stops were made at Cemmaes and Aberangell if required.

Cemmaes station looking north in 1934. Note the wagon in the siding, beside a track which led up to the village. The shallow bridge in the foreground still exisits.   *R.W. Kidner*

Cemmaes station in March 1952. The siding to the right had been recently lifted. Track materials salvaged lay alongside the line.   *J.I.C. Boyd*

The combined Dovey Valley Sunday Schools' trip to Aberystwyth which ran annually on the last Monday in June operated for the last time on 26th June, 1939. No doubt many of the older travellers were in reminiscent mood as the train of six- and eight-wheeled carriages came down the valley, and, crossing the Twymyn, climbed the 1 in 41 bank to Cemmes Road, there to join the similar main line trip which had started from Llanbrynmair.

The GWR maintained a camping coach at Dinas Mawddwy.

With the outbreak of World War II on 3rd September, 1939, the remaining quarries served by the Hendre-ddu Tramway soon ceased production, but the plan to close the railway was shelved, temporarily at least. Timber again provided much traffic and, with the use of Hendre-ddu Quarry for storing explosives, daily trains were re-introduced, with Sunday workings on occasion. It should be noted that late in 1939 the tramway was lifted and a rough road laid over the greater part of its length.

As in World War I women were again recruited for railway service and it was to Dinas Mawddwy station that Mrs N. Williams was appointed on 3rd March, 1942, as a porter (grade I).

The war over, the need for the railway at once lessened and henceforth freight trains ran on Tuesdays and Fridays only as follows:

Up		pm	Down		pm
Cemmes Road	dep.	12.25	Dinas Mawddwy	dep.	1.45
Dinas Mawddwy	arr.	1.10	Cemmes Road	arr.	2.15

Stops were made at Cemmaes and Aberangell if required.

On 1st January, 1948, the railway became part of British Railways (Western Region) under the Nationalisation Act, 1947.

The freight trains run on Tuesday 5th September, 1950, proved to be the last. Heavy rainfall followed and on the morning of the 7th it was discovered that the Dovey, by then in full spate, had displaced the bridge immediately to the north of Cemmaes station. On several previous occasions the flooded Dovey had caused temporary cessation of services. It is interesting to recall that this was the second railway closed by the Dovey in a little over two years - the last freight trains ran on the nearby Corris Railway on 20th August, 1948.

Faced with the outlook of decreasing receipts and considerable reconstruction, the Railway Executive, by public advertisement, on 23rd June, 1951, stated that the railway would be closed as from 1st July following. In fact a special train, comprising locomotive and van, ran on 4th July.

The local councils protested on the grounds that the agricultural population's needs could not be adequately met by road transport as regards the carriage of coal, lime and other heavy merchandise.

Early in 1952 it was stated in the local Press that the track was to be lifted and that in addition to 1,060 tons of steel thus secured, there would be obtained 11,000 sleepers, 31 tons of long timber, 2 tons of iron from weighbridges, and a quantity of other materials. Messrs Rhodes of Sheffield bought the track as it stood and employed local labour to dismantle it and load up. This work was commenced on 26th January, 1952, and was completed on 26th May following.

There were 18 railway bridges between Cemmes Road and Dinas Mawddwy, all have now gone. A 2002 view of the remains of the ill-fated bridge on the Aberangell side of Cemmaes station which was damaged by floods in September 1950. British Railways decided to close the line rather than carry out repairs. The remains of the wooden support posts can still be seen.

B. Poole

The most substantial ruin of any of the 18 bridges is at Dol-y-fonddu. This view is looking towards Aberangell in 2002. This was a farm bridge for access to fields. *B. Poole*

Certain of the bridges were removed by British Railways (Western Region) under the direction of the Bridge Inspector T.H. Edwards. The locomotive used in the demolition work was 'Dean Goods' class 0-6-0 No. 2323, the bridge at Cemmaes being specially shored up for its passage at low speed.

Today

Unlike many contemporaries, the Mawddwy was not allowed to decay gracefully. By 26th May, 1952 track lifting was completed, except for the sidings at Cemmes Road. The only large building on the line, Dinas station, became a residence and later a café.

It was a peaceful scene for more than a decade, but then adjacent to the locomotive shed a largish factory, Meirion Mills, was set up manufacturing woollen goods. A shop was there also, and the station yard was cleaned up for car parking. In 1977, 600 yards of 2 ft gauge track was laid from the shop to a picnic site at Maescalan, worked by a 'Simplex' locomotive and two carriages, as an attraction for visitors to make a longer visit to the Mills, which has been considerably extended. Unfortunately this was given up two years later, though a short piece of track and some old wagons were left at the shop end of the car park.

The course of the branch remains visible, though the Cemmaes site is somewhat altered by the lane to the goods yard having been extended across the line and on to join a minor road to Machynlleth.

Dinas Mawddwy station yard weighbridge in 2002. Many of the railway facilities can still be observed within the car park of the retail outlet of Meirion Mills. The weighbridge is now a craft shop.   *B. Poole*

A portrait of Manning, Wardle 0-6-0ST *Mawddwy*.

The second and larger Manning, Wardle 0-6-0ST *Disraeli*, unusual in having a round-topped tank.   *F.E. Fox-Davies*

Chapter Three

Mawddwy Locomotives and Rolling Stock

Locomotives 1867-1908

Mawddwy

This Manning, Wardle type 'F' locomotive (Works No. 140) was built in 1864 and delivered in 1865 to Mr R.S. France at Llanmynech (Montgomeryshire) where he was engaged on the construction of the Potteries, Shrewsbury & North Wales Railway. During its brief stay there it was named *Alyn* and is believed to have worked on that railway before passing in the same year to the Mawddwy Railway, of which Mr France was also the contractor and where it was renamed *Mawddwy*. It was rebuilt in 1893, when it was fitted with the vacuum brake, and was further rebuilt in 1911.

Dimensions
Cylinders: 12 in. diameter x 17 in. stroke
Diameter of wheels: 3 ft 0 in.
Wheelbase: 10 ft 9 in. (5 ft 5 in. leading to driving wheels, 5 ft 4 in. driving to trailing wheels).

Disraeli

Built in 1868 by Manning, Wardle type 'M' (Works No. 268), this was a slightly larger locomotive and was fitted with hand brakes, the blocks operating on driving and trailing wheels only.

Dimensions
Cylinders: 13 in. diameter x 18 in. stroke
Diameter of wheels: 3 ft 6 in.
Wheelbase: 11 ft 6 in. (5 ft 10 in. leading to driving wheels, 5 ft 8 in. driving to trailing wheels).

Rolling Stock 1867-1908

The company could not afford new carriages, and second-hand ones in 1867 were clearly rather grim. However, No. 1, a short first/second composite from the London & North Western Railway (LNWR) had some luxury. Some time after 1900 the LNWR authorities discovered that one of its early coaches still existed, and sent a party with fullplate camera to Dinas Mawddwy to record it. By this time one compartment was unglazed and seems to have been used as a third. Regrettably the LNWR did not purchase it and the body was later grounded.

Coaches at Dinas Mawddwy with No. 4 on the right.

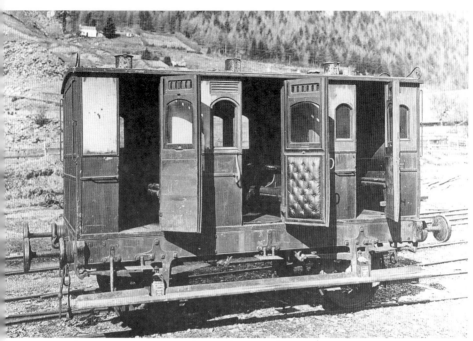

Two views of Mawddwy Railway coach No. 1 (*see page 51*). *(Both) J.A. Peden*

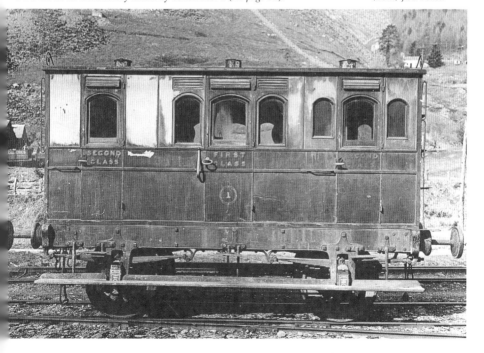

Machynlleth shed on 13th August, 1913 with *Mawddwy* after its rebuilding and now in the guise of Cambrian Railways No. 30.   *LCGB/Ken Nunn Collection*

Cambrian Railways 2-4-0 No. 28 at Machynlleth in July 1909, a regular engine on the Mawddwy branch.   *H.L. Hopwood*

The inventory of 12th June, 1909, already cited, shows that the railway closed in 1908 with the following six carriages in service:

No. 2   Third class. Five compartments.
No. 4   First class, second class, third class smoking. One compartment of each.
No. 5   Third class (2 compartments) and brake.
No. 1022   First and second class.
No. 1140   Third class and brake.
And one further, third class and brake.

Details of carriages:

No. 2 – This carriage was open from end to end. The unfortunate travellers sat on narrow wooden seats, their backs supported by a wooden bar placed about 1 ft 6 in. above the seats. Apart from the windows in the upper part of the five doors only four small windows were in evidence on each side of the carriage. Three oil lamps gave indifferent lighting.

No. 4 – The first class compartment was furnished in blue cloth, which had become very shabby at the close. The second class was sparsely upholstered whilst the third was innocent of all comforts. The carriage was fitted with vacuum brake.

No. 5 – This carriage was in very poor condition at the close.

Nos. 1022 & 1140 – These carriages bore numbers given them by their previous owners, the North London Railway (NLR). They were open from end to end and were without upholstery.

Carriages Nos. 2, 4 and 5 had at one time been painted red. An iron step was placed below each compartment door: an arrangement common-place in the early years of railways.

It has been rumoured that a third brake body grounded at Nesscliff station, Shropshire & Montgomeryshire Railway, came from Mawddwy. This could have been No. 2 with one end compartment altered for a guard. It carried a Manchester, Sheffield & Lincolnshire maker's plate.

Locomotives 1911-1952

Mawddwy was rebuilt in 1911 (becoming CR No. 30) but *Disraeli* was at once scrapped.

Cambrian Railways 2-4-0 locomotives were put to work on the railway, No. 28 being regularly on trains.

The heavy timber traffic of World War I proved too much for *Mawddwy*. To give relief 2-4-0 No. 59 arrived early in 1915; formerly named *Seaham* it was built by Messrs Sharp, Stewart & Co. in 1866 (Works No. 1683). It was rebuilt in 1894 at Oswestry, when a new boiler was fitted, whilst under the GWR a new chimney, top feed arrangement, safety valves covers and larger bunker were installed. Principal dimensions were:

Cylinders: 14 in. diameter x 20 in. stroke
Coupled wheels: 4 ft 6 in. diameter
Boiler pressure: 150 lb. per sq. in.
Weight in working order: 29 tons

Men line up for this photograph in front of 2-4-0 No. 28 at Dinas Mawddwy in 1913.
Gwynedd Archives, Dolgellau

2-4-0T No. 59 *Seaham* at Oswestry.   *R.W. Miller Collection*

After a few months' stay No. 59 returned to Oswestry for branch duties elsewhere, and was succeeded by 2-4-0 locomotives Nos. 44 and 56; both were built by Messrs Sharp, Stewart & Co.: No. 44, built 1864 (Works No. 1488), GWR No. 1190; No. 56, built 1865 (Works No. 1656), GWR No. 1191.

Meanwhile *Mawddwy* had slipped quietly away to the Van Railway, where, as GWR No. 824, it carried on until it was scrapped when that railway ceased to function in November 1940.

Cambrian livery: Black, lined with yellow and red.

Under the GWR their 0-4-2 side tank No. 846 regularly worked the passenger trains until their cessation at the end of 1930.

In the motley collection of locomotives which followed appeared 0-6-0T No. 819, 0-4-2T No. 1434, 4-4-0 *Tre Pol and Pen* (in 1941), whilst 'Dean Goods' 0-6-0 No. 2323 was employed on the demolition train.

Liveries: Great Western Railway, green and black; British Railways (Western Region), black.

Rolling Stock 1911-1952

The Cambrian Railways at once scrapped the coaching stock of the old company except for one ex-NLR vehicle which became a service vehicle, and provided six-wheeled gas-lit carriages. Two classes of passenger accommodation only were provided, first and third.

Cambrian saloon No. 10 - a favourite with football teams on main line journeys - was in use for some years on the Mawddwy Railway. With the removal of its tables the booking by the guard of passengers from intermediate stations was greatly facilitated.

The Great Western Railway introduced electrically-lit carriages and continued to supply both first and third class accommodation until the cessation of regular passenger services.

Private Owners' Wagons

So far as can be traced the only private owners' wagons operating were four to six of 10 tons capacity belonging to the Dinas Mawddwy Coal & Lime Co. This firm, which was operating prior to 1893 and ceased business about 1924, had depots at Dinas Mawddwy, Aberangell, Cemmes Road(utilising the former ticket office and waiting room) and Kerry.

Engines of a small class of 4-4-0 built by Sharp, Stewart for the Oswestry & Newtown Railway in 1863/4 were used on the branch in 1911. The Cambrian was very short of tank engines; Nos. 44 and 56 of this class were rebuilt as 2-4-0Ts in 1907.

Cambrian Railways 2-4-0T No. 56 at Machynlleth, as rebuilt from an Oswestry & Newtown Railway 4-4-0.   *LCGB/Ken Nunn Collection*

Two views at Oswestry of *Mawddwy*, by now in its final guise as GWR No. 824.

(Below) R.W. Miller Collection

Cambrian Railways 4-4-0 No. 64 at Cemmes Road with the 10.55 am from Aberystwyth in July 1909.   *H.L. Hopwood*

A general view looking west towards Cemmes Road station in the 1960s. A Shrewbury-bound train headed by an Ivatt 2-6-0 pulls away from the station.

Chapter Four

Mawddwy Memories

Harold Morgan trained as a signalman at Caersws and Moat Lane Junction. His daughter, Maureen, was four years old when the family moved to Cemmaes village. Dad was transferred to be one of the signalmen at Cemmes Road. They had a house at Cemmaes so Maureen went on all or most of the Sunday School trips. Dad was moved to Talyllyn near Brecon around 1939 but could not get housing so the GWR brought him back to the area, where he worked at Machynlleth through the war. Dad would cycle to his shift on his bike. In 1947, Dad moved to Welshpool and the family moved to Forden. Now Maureen is back in the village of her birth, Caersws.

Maureen would often walk, either a summer evening or summer holiday to spend time with Dad in the Cemmes Road box. The main line was a place of thundering noise as trains with bankers set off to tackle the long haul up to Talerddig. The Dinas train only ran two or three times a week before the war; it was so quiet with only a few trucks, which would be mainly coal in and slate from Aberangell out. Maureen can clearly remember Dad giving the ground frame key [and train staff] to the fireman; the train would then pass through the station almost to the old bridge, then reversing back into the north side of the Mawddwy platform, it could proceed up the valley. Cemmaes station would often be flooded. There had been a small shelter but as far as Maureen could remember, it was falling down.

The Welsh spelling is Cemaes; one 'm' only but it is often spelt with two so the main line station would often be known as Cemmaes Road. The Cambrian Railways and GWR timetables show Cemmes Road. Cemaes refers to the flat river field where the river edge keeps altering due to flood, a very good description where the river continually erodes one bank and builds another section. So the Dyfi (Dovey) did a cemmaes (bank erosion) at Cemmaes and caused the rail line to be shut down.

The Station Maintenance Man

Oswald Davies was born at Cemmes Road in 1922; he was from a railway family. His grandfather was a ganger and he had three uncles and two cousins working on the line. On leaving school, he worked for the Co-op but his career was interrupted by war service including the traumatic experiences of the Normandy Landings. On demobilisation, he joined the railway, first as a ganger and then in the maintenance section of masons and carpenters and finally was the supervisor. The work was maintaining stations from Welshpool to Aberystwyth, plus the coast line and the Rheidol branch and he served 38 years for the GWR and BR. The depot was at Machynlleth and liaison took place with the bridge section, which was on the truncated Van line at Caersws. Father died of tuberculosis when Oswald was only five so mother worked hard to bring up three children. She took in board and lodgings for the railway company and one man was Harry Morgan, ex-Caersws signalman, who stayed until he was allocated a Cemmaes house. Another was the Criccieth inspector who, twice a year, supervised the loading etc. of the 'away wintering' train.

Oswald would travel most Saturdays to see Nain (granny) and the fare was 1½d. return to Aberangell. Cemmes Road Junction was a railway creation, the Welsh name is Glantwymyn. The village school, the parish and church were centred at Cemmaes. Usually both he and his two sisters would walk to school but when it was very stormy, Mam would find the 3d. for them to go on the train. Oswald is a deeply religious man, yet once he sinned. On one of the trips to Nain, he was given some bananas. He was so hungry, they looked so delicious and so all had been consumed before the train got to Aberangell. He had not foreseen that, next week, Mam would ask Nain if she enjoyed the bananas, and so he was found out. Oswald is a Knight of the Order of St John of Jerusalem; he has a British Rail Certificate of Merit for first aid services given and his first aid work has made a significant contribution to the area.

Until 1931, a senior ganger called William Evans plus four men looked after the branch line. After passenger closure, one man remained as patrolman. He was Henry Shepherd y Sais (the Englishman) and he would walk the line repairing boundaries and track as needed.

There was no trailing junction into the main line at Cemmes Road. It really was a clumsy 'z' shape still using the old separate company station track. It was not a great problem for the passenger train and the light goods. Both the 20-plus livestock wagons of 'away wintering' and the Sunday school trip train had to be broken into up to four shunts on to the main line and could occupy this single line on the Commins Coch side for up to a half hour. The Sunday school trip could be up to 14 bogie coaches with 700-plus passengers. It was always a weekday trip to Aberystwyth and Oswald can remember the thrill of the newly-opened Woolworths. So Oswald went on most trips in the 1930s. The train was far in excess of the length of the platforms and a certain section was for Cemmaes people, then Aberangell, then Mallwyd and finally Dinas.

Another special in the area would be for the free church Gymanfa Ganu (hymn singing festival) and one year the venue was Capel Ebenezer at Dinas Mawddwy, so the chapel was full as also were the special trains.

After passenger closure, there was no longer a station master at Dinas Mawddwy; maybe a yardman was retained. The station master at Cemmes Road became responsible for invoicing etc. on the branch. There was a flourish of munitions and forest traffic in World War II but afterwards it was obvious that such a lightly used freight line could not compete with lorries. For example, there were only livestock pens at Dinas and Cemmes Road so fatstock were driven to either until the late 1920s, then lorry collection at the farm became far more convenient and cheaper.

The Hill Farmer

Dafydd Wyn Jones, Blaenplwyf, Aberangell has lived and farmed in this valley and surrounding hills for 78 years. Dafydd is well skilled in the art of englynion; a poetic form of a single stanza with set syllables not unlike a Japanese haiku, covering virtually any topic. Over the years, the farm made use of the branch line. There are still traces of the line along the ystrad (flood plain) and reminders of early optimism as one of the inns in Dinas Mawddwy is named after Sir Edmund Buckley, the financier behind the first railway company.

The line had a purpose; there were substantial quarries of which Minllyn was the largest. The workings can be seen clearly from Dinas station. There was a lead mine at Cwm Cywarch but this had ceased operation before the railway came. Dafydd can remember the Hendre-ddu and the Hendre-feredydd narrow gauge tramway going up the Nant Angell. This tramway continued until 1939. One branch, that of Maes-y-gamfa, is on some of their hill land, this quarry produced slab slate, some of which can be seen on the local chapel. This slab was used in Victorian and Edwardian times for billiard and snooker tables so there must have been Maes-y-gamfa slate in many an officers mess around the British Empire. This was before Dafydd's time but this slate was carefully loaded on a flat truck with three or four wooden slats underneath. The Hendre-ddu railway was worked by a small internal combustion engine and one of the last drivers was a John Breese.

The farm would take horses and carts to the siding at Aberangell and unload coal and lime directly from the rail wagon to the cart. Farm machinery would also be delivered to the station. Dafydd can remember a Cambridge Roll coming in 1940. The line was only carrying full loads after passenger closure. Sundries were delivered on certain days, probably from Machynlleth, in a GWR lorry.

The important livestock movement until the 1940s was 'away wintering'. Ewe hoggs would leave the valley in mid-October and return in April. A hill farm wanted the ewe hogg replacements to grow strongly so these sheep were sent to a lowland area for 'tack' or away wintering. It is important that the breeding sheep pass on knowledge of the mountain from generation to generation. This is cynefin in Wales and a heft in England and Scotland. Each hill area would send their sheep to a certain lowland area. Montgomeryshire sheep went to Shropshire, Cardigan coast and in the case of Dafydd's valley, to Criccieth on the Lleyn peninsular. The sheep were collected and penned between the walls of the quarry manager's house and the cemetery. A temporary ramp at the end enabled sheep to be quickly loaded at the siding; it was far more difficult at Criccieth where the sheep had to be driven through the town from the station.

Dafydd's father helped with local forest felling in the early part of World War I until called up. Two steam traction engines took the larger trunks down to Cemmes Road where there was a larger loading crane and more space. The pit props were loaded at Aberangell siding. Father served in the appalling trenches and survived. One of his friends was Hedd Wyn and Dad had the story that he and others would write home while Hedd Wyn would be writing poetry. (Hedd

Wyn from Trawsfynydd won the Eisteddfod chair posthumously and this chair is known as Cadair Ddu Penybedw or the Black Chair of Birkenhead because the chair was draped in black, as the bard could not be chaired.)

The family would make use of the passenger service for shopping in Machynlleth and his mother-in-law would have travelled daily to the County School (Grammar) at Machynlleth. Dafydd attended Ysgol Dolgellau as a scholarship student. By the time he was 11, the passenger service had closed and the education authority provided a bus on Monday and Friday and he resided with other Dinas children in Dolgellau during the week. Blaenplwyf could be translated as the last farm in the parish as the farm straddles Montgomeryshire and Merionethshire.

Robert Jones looked after the railway interest at Aberangell; he had the village store which was next to the station. He looked after the waiting room and storeroom and continued helping with goods after passenger closure. Dafydd cannot remember if tickets were issued here or by the guard.

The line came to life again during World War II. The old quarry and the buildings around Hendre-ddu became a munitions stores. The tramway had closed so lorries carried munitions up and down as required. The narrow lane acquired the nickname of 'the Burma Road'. Timber extraction also took place in some volume and much again left from the siding. Once the war ceased, traffic became light to non-existent, finally there were only two trains a week going up to Dinas around lunch time. It was little surprise that it closed after the Cemmaes bridge had been damaged by flood.

The Coal Merchant

Ifan Price (Ifans y glo) has been a coal merchant for 56 years in the Cemmaes area. Ifan was brought up in Cwmlline and now lives in Aberangell. The coal yard is at Cemmaes. Ifan was a very young boy when the passenger service ceased; it was already more convenient to use the bus as the walk from Cwmlline to Cemmaes station was well over a mile. However Ifan travelled on many of the Sunday School trips including the final one in 1939.

The coal during the early part of his career was delivered by rail to Cemmes Road; they would then take it by road to the depot in Cemmaes. The pick-up goods stopped in 1964 and lorry transport was then used direct from colliery or wholesaler. The area was in the National Coal Board North West Region so coal came from the Stoke and Cannock coalfields. The wholesaler would provide specific requests, such as anthracite, coke or smokeless for customers.

A very enjoyable afternoon was spent with Ifan travelling the roads close to the Mawddwy line. There were 18 bridges excluding culverts, over, under the road and river bridges. Ifan has a story that one of his friends answered a tourist enquiry for directions. Thinking in Welsh, and thinking the person knew the area he replied, 'Turn left and go straight on underneath the bridge that is not there'. He felt a bit of a fool when he realised the problem in his answer. Anyhow, let us proceed along the valley of the 18 bridges that are not there.

The A470T proceeds along the east side of the valley. On the west side of the

Dyfi, a lane runs close to the track for the length of the old line. Far more of the track has been absorbed back into the farmland compared with the Kerry and the Van railways and the track would be impossible to traverse. Many traces of the bridges within the farmland can still be seen as filled-in cuttings or grass-covered mounds. Nature has quickly taken over in this high rainfall area.

At Cemmes Road Junction a veterinary surgeon's practice is now on the site of the Mawddwy platform. The yard and other buildings can only be imagined including the trackwork where the line faced up to join the main line where a now road bridge has been built. The line quickly curved north over the first farm/field access bridge and there was a large bridge over the River Twymyn. There were four further access bridges until Cemmaes station. There was a siding which curved to be close to the lane which was then owned by the railway with an entrance gate at Cemmaes village; a distance of about 400 yards across the flat valley floor. There was a ford and a footbridge across the Dyfi to the back lane; there is now a steel trellis bridge marked Rhyd-y-gwial, 1963. The station platform was just above the level crossing; the platform is now the line of a fir hedge. The ford has a little history because one of the farmers decided to risk taking his horse and cart through when the river was in flood and his two pigs jumped out and swam away. Traces of the only bridge across the Dyfi can still be seen; both the stone work and the remains of the wooden stanchions are visible. This is the bridge that received flood damage causing the railway to close the line. The local consensus is that damage was not too great and repair could have been done.

The next rail bridge was just before Dol-y-fonddu siding, which had been used for timber loading. This was one of several bridges with a severe hump over the track and even in the late 1940s, lorries could get stuck on the crest. There were two other farm access bridges prior to Nant-y-cyff siding close to the adjacent quartz or silica quarry which closed around 1935.

The approaches and village of Aberangell had a succession of rail bridges over and under the back road as the lane swings east and then west of the track, crosses the River Angell and then a low arch went over the road that leads to the A470T. This bridge was demolished in 1966 so that buses and lorries could enter the village from the shortest route from the A470. The station was convenient for the village.

The triangle of the station yard is still *in situ* with two picnic tables. The platform edge can be found within the overgrowth. The only building still standing is the warehouse within a private garden. A crane stood in one corner with '3 ton maximum, single chain, 5 ton maximum twin chain' written on it. There was a wide entrance gate with a plaque stating 'The penalty for leaving this gate open is forty shillings'. The transfer sidings for the Hendre-ddu tramway were within this triangle.

The line then proceeded towards Mallwyd; a side lane went over the track to Camlan Uchaf. The river is now very close to the west steep sides and the track squeezed between the river and the road, which precluded the provision of a siding. The same flood that damaged the Cemmaes bridge, caused a landslip here. Part of the remains of the bridge at this T-junction can still be seen. The right turn and lane is about 1,000 yards to Mallwyd. Mallwyd church is on a foundation of a far older site, North Montgomeryshire and this corner of Merioneth still sing the

The Hendre-ddu loading platform at Aberangell at the site of the (by now truncated) loop in March 1952. The Hendre-ddu tramway ran along the road curving away to the right.

Trackwork from the Hendre-ddu Tramway can just be made out in the foreground in this view of the site of the exchange sidings at Aberangell in March 1952.

The bridge over the Afon Angell at Aberangell in 1971. *R.W. Kidner*

The site of Mallwydd station, looking towards Dinas Mawddwy on 13th August, 1951.

G.F. Bannister

Advertisements included in a booklet published by the Cambrian Railways to promote the railway *circa* 1912.

Maggie Edwards Collection

older alliterative carols, usually without instrumental accompaniment, known as 'Y Plygain' around Christmas. The Mallwyd plygain is well known. The line now heads to Dinas. There was one very low bridge over the lane on a sharp bend where the stonework can still be clearly seen on the west side.

The bus service started in 1924 from Machynlleth to Dinas and was far more convenient for Cemmaes, Cwmlline, Mallwyd and Dinas Mawddwy. Only the school train ran direct to Machynlleth; all others had to change at Cemmes Road and, by 1930, only 1,500 passengers used the service from Aberangell, a mean of five per day or less than two for each train, yet over 2,500 tons of goods went through the station. In 1939, 218 adults (3s. 8d. each) and 129 children (1s. 10d. each) joined the Sunday school trip from the four stations. The goods trains would just glide down the gentle gradient from Dinas; it was said that it was so quiet that cats would sleep on the rails in warm weather and be killed, as they were so unaccustomed to any traffic.

Ifan fully understands that many bridges were too low or too weak for modern traffic but regrets that the entire 18 have all gone; it truly is the valley of bridges that are not there. Now the full cycle has taken place and the private car has taken over from the bus.

The Terminus at Dinas Mawddwy

The line on from Mallwyd would not have posed any construction problems. No one with detailed knowledge on the station operation such as that of Rex Bound of Kerry (*see Chapter Nine*) can now be found but two of the older people of the village have recalled very interesting memories.

Maggie Edwards was born in 1914 but lived at Cywarch about three miles from the station. She cannot remember travelling on the passenger service prior to closure in 1930 but travelled on many Sunday School specials throughout the 1920s and 1930s. She had a memory of going with her father to collect foods from the station with his farm horse and cart.

Maggie has a copy of the Cambrian Railways *Pocket Guide to Dinas Mawddwy* (1911) and a number of postcards of the same period. The branch is the only one of the three where railway companies actively promoted tourism. Dinas is set in spectacular scenery and walks; walks with guides, horse-drawn excursions and fishing were promoted. The 10 shops of groceries, clothes, shoes, etc. are now reduced to just the post office. The whole edifice of the tourist trade can be seen in the little promotion with apartments and accommodation close to the station; hire of pony and trap and walking sticks for tourists a speciality. Again, Maggie can remember the goose pudding dumplings. Her face showed some horror at the memory. She can also remember peat fires in the farmhouses.

When she was a little girl, she can remember older people telling her that an area by the river was used for 'pedoli gwartheg'. This was the placing of two small iron shoes on cattle hooves by the drovers before the long walk to London or Birmingham. One of several routes could have been chosen but they may have taken the route from Cemmaes over Dylife and crossed both the Trannon Valley and climbed up over the Kerry Ridgeway.

Dinas Mawddwy in its final years with the engine shed on the left and goods shed on the right.

Dinas Mawddwy station looking south from the platform towards the corrugated iron goods shed on 30th March, 1958.   *R.J. Leonard*

William Robert Edwards (no relation) moved from Ty'n Twll, Cywarch to Bryn Siôn in 1921 when eight years of age. Again William travelled on many of the specials but also travelled on the pre-1930 passenger service to Cemmes Road and changed for Machynlleth and would also travel to see a relative who lived at Nantcyff, walking from Aberangell station. Coal, flour, lime and sundries all came in by rail. Timber would have been the only goods leaving on a regular basis as the Minllyn quarries had closed during the World War I. The then all-age school was close to the station and the inclines of the quarry could be easily seen. William's dad used to watch from the school window the tram trucks being hauled up and down. This would have been around 1885. There was a siding to the old quarry shed. This quarry shed became a wool merchant's depot and many bales of wool would have left from here. The old railway goods shed was of corrugated iron and stood until the late 1960s. A friend can remember unloading bacon sides here. The current site of Meirion Mills was the store for finished items of the slate quarry waiting to be shipped out and then became a timber mill. William can remember the mill hooter at midday also telling the school children lunchtime was near.

The horses of the valley were tough, hardy beasts and a Mr Hughes of Llangurig would purchase some and they would be taken away in a cattle wagon. There were livestock loading facilities and the pens would be full of sheep on the day of the 'away wintering' train. The passenger trains could be heard from the school and helped to time the day; one arrived about 11 in the morning and departed back to Cemmes Road during the school lunch break.

Dinas Mawddwy station before its conversion to a café. Earlier, there had been a shelter and lamp in front of the right-hand portion, and a frame of notices to the right of the left window.   *R.W. Kidner*

Neither Maggie nor William can remember the fire at Plas yn Dinas but this was part of the story of the village and the hulk of the burn-out mansion was a clear memory of the village prior to World War II. Maggie was aware that a small section of narrow gauge line was laid from the station to the old quarry siding in the 1970s as an additional tourist attraction but only operated for one or two seasons as it could not have been financially viable,

Eurwyn Francis was present with William during the interview. Eurwyn can only recall the railway in the last few years after World War II but added two extras from within the family memories. Representatives of companies such as Osmond's of Grimsby would visit the farms and collect orders for sheep dip chemicals, molasses, minerals, Stockholm tar for foot rot, pitch for marking sheep and worm drenches. This would be priced to the nearest station and collected by the farmers from the station within several weeks of placing the order. The agricultural merchant based at the yard was G. Griffith & Son and sold cakes and meals from Merseyside and this would all have used rail transport in the 1930s. Travel would have been rare for his parents but there is a story that one lad went with his dad to Amwythig (Shrewsbury) which seemed a huge distance. How the concept of travel could alter so quickly within a lifetime.

The Hotel Keeper at the Railway Junction

Maurice Davies, The Dovey Valley Hotel, Cemmes Road can remember travelling when the service was goods only somewhere around 1939 to 1940. He was friendly with the station master's children so he knew the railway staff well. The train would arrive from Machynlleth, move onto the branch and leave for Dinas about 1.15 pm. The train would stop at Aberangell, there was still a covered van that would have goods for Mr John Disley. It then went on to Dinas and again unloaded village goods. There were coal trucks to put down and empties to collect. By this time Maurice thought that the Aberangell quarries had closed. The train would stop about an hour in Dinas. The children would walk into the village and return within an hour. The wagons of pit props were added and the train would be back at Cemmes Road by 4.00 pm and then on to Machynlleth. There were only three trains per week.

Dovey Valley Hotel advertisement *circa* 1912.   *Maggie Edwards Collection*

The station at Dinas was looked after by a Mrs Williams. Both she and her husband lived in the station house and Mr Williams worked as one of the signalmen at the junction. Another signalman was Harold Morgan from Caersws. The guard who gave them the lift was Mr Edwin Jones. They would go up once or twice each holiday. The journey was delightful; the children all stood at the rear of the brake van; the train was really slow and it would rattle over the bridges. In summer the line could be a little overgrown and sometimes branches could be heard on the roof and leaves fluttered down behind. There were no trips later in the war for the children because ammunition was being transported to Aberangell. Maurice went on to the County School at Machynlleth and the now well known Welsh railway historian, Gwyn Briwnant Jones, was in the same class sitting about two desks away. Gwyn would always use any spare moment to sketch bridges, stations and trains.

The Cemmes Road signal box was rebuilt in the late 1930s replacing a smaller unit. The builders, maybe from Oswestry, stayed in the hotel. Cemmes Road had a large food store for agricultural merchants and also had much trade in loading cattle and sheep. The railway had been an important source of trade for the hotel. People coming for a walking holiday etc. would arrive late in the evening after a long journey from Manchester, London etc. They would book into the hotel and catch the first train up to Dinas. The reverse happened when they came down on the last train, stayed in the hotel then caught the early train east. Also commercial travellers and dealers were still travelling by train and would use the hotel. Again if people had an hour to wait they would come to the hotel for food and refreshments. Maurice took over the hotel from his mother nearly 40 years ago and Cemmes Road, essentially a community created by the railway, has seen many changes since then.

The Abermule Hotel was once called the Railway Hotel. It is likely that it had a similar trade for the Kerry branch.

The Mawddwy branch platform at Cemmes Road in 1934. Only the left side of the 'island' could be used by passenger trains.   *R.W. Kidner*

The Farm Worker's Story

John Lewis Davies, born in 1907, has lived in Cemmaes all his life working on various farms but much of the time with the Breese family at Rhyd-y-gwiail Isaf close to Cemmaes station. The ford (rhyd) had only a wooden footbridge for pedestrians and horses and carts had to wade through. A narrow concrete bridge was built in the late 1920s for vehicles, but this was swept away in floods and replaced with a steel trestle bridge in the early 1960s.

The station had a siding, which curved towards the village parallel to the railway road. There was a coal merchant there when John was a child and the coal was sold round the village by a Mr David Foulkes. There were allotments by the siding and Dad had one so John spent much time there. The station had a shelter with a wooden bench but the shelter gradually fell down after passenger services ceased in 1930. There were no staff at Cemmaes; any ticket was purchased from the guard. The road and adjoining field from the village was owned by the railway company.

John can remember the trains of World War I. There was much timber taken out from higher up the valley and the trains were long with each truck full of pit props or long timber. John would often watch the train from the cottage. It usually had two coaches and some goods trucks. There was also a goods train and this one did the shunting at Cemmaes. John must have been on every Sunday school trip over a period of 25 years. They were huge events especially in the early 1920s before the recession and people starting to leave the valley. A large crowd would walk from Cwmlline to join the Cemmaes people. The station platform was full and others had to queue on the road. It was always on the Monday after the summer term had been completed. It was organised by all the chapels and churches and each child was given some spending money, maybe a swllt (shilling).

The 'away wintering' sheep were loaded at Dinas, Aberangell and Cemmes Road. John would go to Criccieth on the train the day before to sort and deliver sheep on arrival. The 'away wintering' sheep were grouped from the three areas. When they returned, the Cemmaes ewe hoggs were all mixed up from various farms. They were unloaded into a field and John had to sort them into the various flocks both by appearance and checking on the ear notch. The sheep were then walked back to the various farms in Cemmaes and Cwmlline. The same procedure must have taken place in Aberangell and Dinas. John's wife, Martha Elin, would go back to see her family at Staylittle. She would catch a train from Cemmaes, change at Cemmaes Road for Llanbrymnair and then walk up the Twymyn Valley past Pennant and over the watershed to Staylittle; maybe a distance of eight miles in a high rainfall valley. Martha would have to arrange for someone else to do her work and she would do the reverse trip home on the Monday.

For many years, John supplemented his income by using ferrets to catch rabbits. Two local dealers would purchase these. A Mr Howells took his to the train at Cemmes Road for delivery to Birmingham while a Mr Townsend went to Dolgelley for delivery to Liverpool. Fresh rabbits were in the city shops less that 24 hours after being caught.

John joined the railway as one of the lengthmen between Ty Brics and Talerddig summit in the 1950s until retiring. The rail bridge that caused the Dinas line to shut was close to the cottage. The bridge had been skewed. The problem was and still is that the floods carry trunks, branches and debris which block across the bridges making pressure even worse. A number of trains crossed the bridge after official closure and they proceeded over at snail's pace. This was to collect stranded wagons and goods and there was also the train used by the contractors who lifted the line. Then over the years, it has all reverted and now can be difficult to trace.

The Fireman and Driver on the Mawddwy Branch

Archie Fleming is now 81; he retired in the early 1980s after a career in the railway industry that started in 1937. From greaser, he moved to cleaner to fireman, to driver and relief foreman. Although much time was spent at Machynlleth, he also spent periods of time at Shrewsbury, Hereford, Llanidloes, Worcester, Brecon and Tyseley (Birmingham). Archie may not only be the last person to have driven on the Mawddwy, he has also done some other duties where there may be few, if any, others with such experience. When the regular driver, Wmfre Humphreys, was unwell Archie would drive the Corris narrow gauge engine before the flood cut the bridge. He spent two months as emergency cover because of illness working the Kington branch from Leominster with engine No. 3574, an 0-4-2T forerunner of the '1400' series. This duty also worked back to Worcester via Bromyard. Archie was exempt from call up during World War II because he received special training for all duties, guard, fireman and driver on ammunition trains. The main duty was working the ICI gunpowder trains from Penrhyndeudraeth through to munitions factories. He became a driver at a younger age than others did because of these war duties. Archie has written several sheets of his memories of the Dinas branch. This now follows, it does contain some duplication but it may be the last account from anyone with direct experience.

By 1947 the branch was nearing the end. A freight train ran to and from Machynlleth on three days per week, taking about 1¼ hours to complete the journey on the six miles of the branch. Double heading was allowed. Speed on the branch was not to exceed 25 mph and certain sections were restricted to 15 mph. The '1400' class tank engines usually operated the short freights on the branch. Closure was caused by the floods of the Dyfi weakening the bridge situated on the Aberangell side of Cemmaes station where the line was inclined at 1 in 83. Speed on the bridge was 5 mph. The train operated for regular goods until 1950.

The sheep specials carried ewe lambs for 'away wintering' to Criccieth. These specials were worked by 'Dean Goods' engines and this was the only working that Archie had with double-heading on the branch. 'Dean Goods' were rostered because they had plenty of water in the tenders and would work the train through to Criccieth. The branch conveyed a lot of wagons of timber stakes, coal, wool and lime. Very occasionally cattle were loaded. The wool sheds were at Dinas and the graded wool bales went forward to Bradford. The warehouse at Cemmes Road was also busy with wool traffic after the branch closure for a few more years. Sheep and cattle straying on the line could be a problem. There was a permanent way member travelling with the train from Cemmes Road to Dinas and often he had a difficult task of trying to put the sheep back in the fields.

In 1948, Huw Morgan and John Wynne were loading some timber on to a 'Macaw' wagon. It was hard work loading large trees by hand crane. It could take up to three hours to complete the job and to ensure all the chains were secured. Guard Morris gave orders to back these on to the goods brake but unfortunately, in going forward from the sidings, the 'Macaw' was derailed. The problem was that the curvature of the exit from the siding was such that the engine could not be uncoupled from the 'Macaw'. It took over an hour with warm language before the wagon could be uncoupled. Morris was shouting that couplings should be made of elastic. The derailed wagon was left there. The next day the men went back with the brake van and several fitters to re-rail the timber wagon. The work was very hard because of the length of the 'Macaw' and its weight with five or six big trunks chained on it. The track on the little used siding at Dinas was in poor condition that made both walking and getting purchase with jacks difficult.

The Cemmes Road section of the branch was difficult in winter working in the dark with no lights. A sheep special had to go from Dinas to Shrewsbury. The Traffic Inspector wanted this to leave Cemmes Road before the mail, which could then pass the sheep wagon train somewhere like Caersws or Newtown. The guard Trevor Jones was doing his best under difficult circumstances when the Traffic Inspector told him to start running a bit. A reply came from the gloom that his mum thought it was a miracle that he had even learnt to walk. Shunting could be both dangerous and hard work. Once they were shunting with guard Lewis at Cemmes Road after coming down from Dinas. It was dark and they were following the movements of his handlamp. Archie was fireman that day and the driver stopped and said he had lost sight of the lamp. Archie found that guard Lewis had slipped and his foot was wedged underneath the rail so that he was stranded across the track. The lantern had broken when he stumbled. They got him out and on to his feet. They completed the shunting movements using the gauge lamp off the engine. At the end of the shift, guard Lewis showed signs of shock. It was a little miracle that he lived to tell the story just because the driver sensed that the lantern was not in view.

Dinas Mawddwy station had a very good lady looking after the goods called Mrs Williams. Her husband was one of the signalmen at Cemmes Road. She would always have the kettle boiling for the traincrew. Tea and a slice of cake would be most welcome and her kindness will always be appreciated. Machynlleth was allocated two 0-4-2 locomotives, Nos. 1434 and 1465, for working either the auto train from Barmouth to Dolgelley or the Mawddwy. Both had the necessary equipment for auto working. If one were in for repair, the Mawddwy would use one of the 'Dean Goods' engines. At the end of the turn the ticket would be given in at Machynlleth and another duty day had been completed.

The tank engines would sometimes not have enough water for the round trip. There was a water tank at Dinas. It was very slow. There was no problem with driving the engine to Dinas, no severe gradients and no excessive curves; the

Kerry branch was the opposite. The main problem was excessive growth of branches in the late summer and sheep straying on the line. This contrasts with the main line where the engine was eased from Machynlleth to Cemmes Road so that maximum pressure and power would then be available to lift the train up the severe gradient to Talerddig. The engine driver, fireman and guard were allocated to the Dinas working as rostered.

Both the Aberangell siding and Cemmaes siding were still in use until the end. The use of the Cemmaes siding was not very frequent, being only for unloading lime or slag for farmers. Timber was loaded at Aberangell. This siding was used frequently during the war period for unloading and loading ammunition etc. that was stored at Hendre-ddu quarry. Certain sections especially around the ystrad (flood plain) at Cemmaes would be flooded and certainly Archie has taken a train through where the lower spokes would be covered in water.

Permission was given by the Cemmes Road signalman to enter the branch. It was a most awkward system. The train was drawn through the station to stop under the now demolished old road bridge. The branch had been unlocked so the train was backed down into the siding by the old Dinas company station and then the train went forward across another set of points. Finally the train was on the branch line and could proceed to Dinas. Archie cannot remember fully but there were some stop blocks so the train could not get back on to the main line until the controls from the signal box altered these. Archie took trains over the ill-fated Cemmaes bridge after the flood. Instead of 5 mph, the engine just inched over. So sometime in 1951 or early 1952, Archie would have driven 'Dean Goods' No. 2323 back from Dinas being one of the last drivers to use the line.

A view along the nine-arch timber viaduct over the River Dovey towards Cemmaes station on 13th August, 1951.

G.F. Bannister

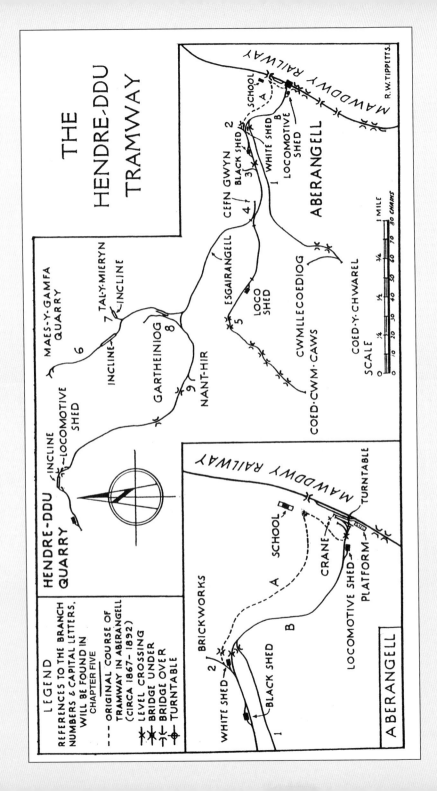

THE
HENDRE-DDU
TRAMWAY

R.W.TIPPETTS.

LEGEND

REFERENCES TO THE BRANCH
NUMBERS & CAPITAL LETTERS
WILL BE FOUND IN
CHAPTER FIVE

‒ ‒ ‒ ORIGINAL COURSE OF
TRAMWAY IN ABERANGELL
(CIRCA 1867-1892)

LEVEL CROSSING
BRIDGE UNDER
BRIDGE OVER
TURNTABLE

HENDRE-DDU
QUARRY

INCLINE
LOCOMOTIVE
SHED

MAES-Y-GAMFA
QUARRY

TAL-Y-MIERYN
INCLINE

INCLINE
7
6

GARTHEINIOG
8

NANT-HIR
9

ESGAIRANGELL

CEFN GWYN

BLACK SHED 2
WHITE SHED
3
1
LOCOMOTIVE
SHED

SCHOOL
A
B

MAWDDWY RAILWAY

ABERANGELL

4

5
LOCO
SHED

CWMLLECOEDIOG

COED·CWM·CAWS

COED·Y·CHWAREL

SCALE

0   10   20   30   40   50   60   70   80 CHAINS
    ¼   ½   ¾   1 MILE

MAWDDWY RAILWAY

BRICKWORKS

SCHOOL
A

B

WHITE SHED
2
BLACK SHED

CRANE
LOCOMOTIVE SHED
PLATFORM
TURNTABLE

1

ABERANGELL

Chapter Five

The Hendre-ddu Tramway

The exact date of the construction of this tramway from Aberangell to Hendre-ddu Quarry cannot be traced, but it is believed to have been carried out at the same time as the construction of the Mawddwy Railway (1867) or very shortly afterwards. Sir Edmund Buckley, Bt, was responsible for the tramway being built. Construction on the standard gauge 4 ft 8½ in. was envisaged and the formation allowed for this width, but the narrow gauge of 1 ft 11 in. was adopted. In order to prevent the establishment of a public right-of-way the tramway was closed on one day each year at its lower reaches (Aberangell), when everyone passing over it had to pay one penny. The tramway was lifted in 1939, shortly after the outbreak of World War II.

The 'main line' was single, though there were several sidings. Bridge rails spiked to wooden sleepers, 3 ft in length, and at the same interval distance formed the track, except for a short distance laid in bull-headed rails near Esgairangell in 1921. Stub points were in operation.

The terminus at Aberangell was on the trans-shipment platform adjoining the southern end of the Mawddwy Railway's siding and emergency loop immediately to the north of Aberangell station latterly. On leaving the platform the tramway at once turned in a north-westerly direction and crossed the village main road on the level. There was a different route in use until about 1892 (*see map*): on entering the road the tramway turned in a northerly direction and, climbed steeply to a point just short of the school. Here a sharp curve enabled the tramway to pass through the upper part of the village, for the most part following the course of the road and running on a comparatively level course, before descending steeply to Abermynach. This route must have been heavy work for the horses then used. A more easily graded route was substituted through the village. Onwards from the road level crossing immediately beyond the platform, the tramway climbed between walls before entering meadows flanking the Angell stream. On the left-hand side and terminating against the boundaries of the grounds of a large house, Brynderwen, occurred a short siding serving a shed; access was gained by trailing points. The tramway crossed the Mynach stream just above its confluence with the Angell. (Here occurred Branch 1.)

Shortly beyond the formation of the original route a junction was effected (41 chains from Aberangell). (Here occurred Branch 2.) Within the junction formed by the early and later routes was a building known as the White Shed, used for locomotive and storage purposes. The remaining mileage of the tramway lay alongside the northern bank of the Angell, except for a short distance where it crossed to the southern bank beyond Nanthir. At 56 chains there was a small shed alongside the tramway and on its northern side. Built of wood and known as the Black Shed this building was served by a loop. The general direction was south-westerly.

Shortly beyond occurred Branch 3. At 70 chains the tramway curved north-westerly and at 1 mile 9 chains occurred Branch 4 to the right, and Branch 5 to the left.

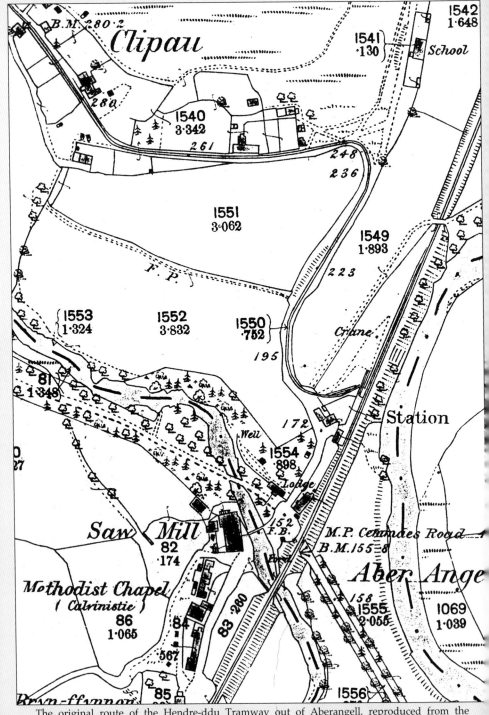

The original route of the Hendre-ddu Tramway out of Aberangell, reproduced from the Ordnance Survey. Note the very tight curve required south of the school.

Between the wooded slopes of Mynedd-y-Cefn-Gwyn and Coed-y-Gesail the tramway made for Gartheiniog. This section contained bull-headed track.

At 2 miles 1 chain occurred Branch 6, serving Maes-y-gamfa Quarry and an off-shoot, Branch 7, serving a further quarry. At 2 miles 8 chains occurred Branch 8, serving the Gartheiniog Slate and Slab Works and Quarry. At 2 miles 33 chains occurred Branch 9 - the last (Nanthir).

Shortly beyond at 413 feet above sea level and having climbed 250 feet from Aberangell, the tramway crossed to the southern bank of the Angell before regaining the northern bank at 2 miles 52 chains. The tramway now ran in a northerly direction through a more open countryside with the derelict Capel Soar across the stream and passing Gartheiniog (3 miles 9 chains) and Hendre-ddu Farms - the latter across the valley - came into sight of Hendre-ddu Quarry.

At about 3¼ miles occurred a siding to a 'locomotive' shed to the right of the main tramway. Immediately beyond, and on the same flank, was a siding serving a storage platform. Access to the main tramway was by means of trailing points (3 miles 35 chains).

The tramway now turned due west and by means of an incline ascended through approximately 225 feet to a height of 800 feet, by a gradient of 1 in 3. Just beyond the customary winding drum was a small siding, used for holding wagons. The tramway ran alongside a ledge and passing the quarry sheds threw off several short branches, some of a temporary nature, before terminating at 3 miles 70 chains and 830 feet above sea level, amid the solitude of the bare mountains.

The Branches

Branch 1. This branch was thrown off left-handed at Abermynach, a few yards before the White Shed. Crossing the Angell it ran below the slopes of Cefn Llandybo, passed Allt-ddu and on reaching Coed Ceunant turned southwards as it climbed Cwm Llecoediog. Running alongside a large fishpond it served the quarry at Coed-y-Charwel, 1¼ miles from Abermynach and 430 feet above sea level. By means of a reversing junction the branch climbed the hillside to reach the outbuildings of Cwmllecoediog Hall.

Branch 2. To serve a brick-works near Abermynach; physically connected to the main tramway by a junction with the siding to the White Shed.

Branch 3. On the northern side and shortly beyond the Black Shed. This branch was connected by a trailing junction and ran 9 chains up a valley to serve a sawmill.

Branch 4. At 1 mile 9 chains, also on the northern side and connected by a trailing junction, this branch climbed initially very steeply (about 1 in 5) before levelling out. The terminus was at Cefn-Gwyn farm (12 chains).

Branch 5. This 1 mile branch occurred immediately beyond Branch 4. Leaving the main tramway by facing points the branch crossed the Angell by a bridge and ascended Cwm Caws, running alongside the Afon Caws throughout. This well-timbered valley is particularly beautiful, and the Caws was crossed no fewer than seven times.

The tramway left the exchange sidings at Aberangell station, crossed the road and then entered a cutting between walls of slate before opening out into meadow land. The cutting, seen here in 2002, was also used for penning the 'away wintering' sheep awaiting loading to their journey to Criccieth.   *B. Poole*

The second and easier approach of the tramway to Aberangell, as it was in 1971. The formation can easily be seen within pasture land. There are slight embankments and cuttings to keep the gradient to a mean of 1 in 40. It was designed for loaded trucks to descend by gravity and empties to return horse-drawn.   *R.W. Kidner*

The so-called 'White Shed' with the site of the main tramway on the right in 2002. Meirion Edwards thinks that this was used for storing and servicing trucks. The original high route to Aberangell would have started just beyond this shed. *B. Poole*

In the late 1930s lorries worked to the quarries straddling the tramway line. The route has either become part of the forest roads or has been metalled for access to the few hill farms in the valley. This view was taken near Gartheiniog Farm in 2002. The road is still gated so opening and shutting is a necessary skill, just as it was for the brakemen many years previously. The commonest accident was crashing through the gates. Note the vertical slabs used as a boundary to funnel driven sheep. *B. Poole*

The tramway route within the forest leading to the open quarry in 2002. It is carefully graded, following the contours.   *B. Poole*

Hendre-ddu quarry is now sited within the Dyfi Forest. The total area of quarry cannot be seen. This level is above the incline and above the office and house now being restored. It almost certainly shows one of the tramways feeding to the incline and then the line down to Aberangell.

B. Poole

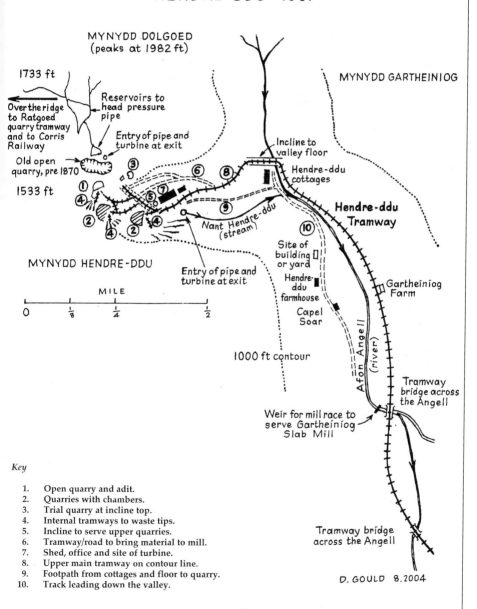

HENDRE-DDU 1901

MYNYDD DOLGOED
(peaks at 1982 ft)

MYNYDD GARTHEINIOG

1733 ft

Reservoirs to head pressure pipe

Over the ridge to Ratgoed quarry tramway and to Corris Railway

Entry of pipe and turbine at exit

Incline to valley floor

Old open quarry, pre 1870

Hendre-ddu cottages

1533 ft

Hendre-ddu Tramway

Nant Hendre-ddu (stream)

MYNYDD HENDRE-DDU

Entry of pipe and turbine at exit

Site of building or yard

Hendre-ddu farmhouse

Gartheiniog Farm

MILE

0   ⅛   ¼   ½

Capel Soar

1000 ft contour

Afon Angell (river)

Tramway bridge across the Angell

Weir for mill race to serve Gartheiniog Slab Mill

Tramway bridge across the Angell

D. GOULD 8.2004

Key

1. Open quarry and adit.
2. Quarries with chambers.
3. Trial quarry at incline top.
4. Internal tramways to waste tips.
5. Incline to serve upper quarries.
6. Tramway/road to bring material to mill.
7. Shed, office and site of turbine.
8. Upper main tramway on contour line.
9. Footpath from cottages and floor to quarry.
10. Track leading down the valley.

The site of the demolished mill and restored office/manager's house in 2002. The hidden incline is to the left of the picture. The main tramway terminus would have been in front of the house and the mill.   *B. Poole*

A 2002 view of the adit or tunnel entrance which leads to the quarried area. Over the years, sediment deposit gradually fills in the entrance floor. There would have been an internal tramway through this entrance.   *B. Poole*

Left: An advertisement for the Hendre-ddu Slate & Slab Co., note arrangements for tourist parties.

Below: A view in 2002 of the derelict Hendre-ddu tied cottages for six quarry families. The main incline is to the left of the picture. The main footpath both for the cottagers and quarry workers coming up on the train is on the right.   *B. Poole*

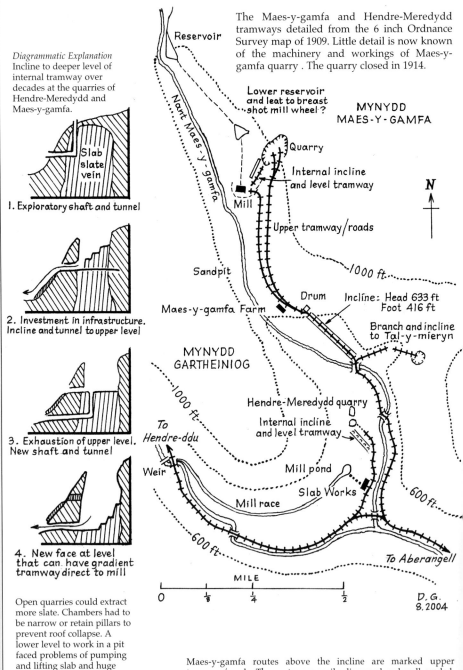

The Maes-y-gamfa and Hendre-Meredydd tramways detailed from the 6 inch Ordnance Survey map of 1909. Little detail is now known of the machinery and workings of Maes-y-gamfa quarry. The quarry closed in 1914.

Diagrammatic Explanation
Incline to deeper level of internal tramway over decades at the quarries of Hendre-Meredydd and Maes-y-gamfa.

Slab slate vein

1. Exploratory shaft and tunnel

2. Investment in infrastructure. Incline and tunnel to upper level

3. Exhaustion of upper level. New shaft and tunnel

4. New face at level that can have gradient tramway direct to mill

Open quarries could extract more slate. Chambers had to be narrow or retain pillars to prevent roof collapse. A lower level to work in a pit faced problems of pumping and lifting slab and huge waste quantities against the gradient.

Reservoir

Nant Maes-y-gamfa

Lower reservoir and leat to breast shot mill wheel ?

MYNYDD MAES-Y-GAMFA

Quarry

Internal incline and level tramway

Mill

Upper tramway/roads

Sandpit

1000 ft.

Drum

Incline: Head 633 ft Foot 416 ft

Maes-y-gamfa Farm

Branch and incline to Tal-y-mieryn

MYNYDD GARTHEINIOG

1000 ft.

To Hendre-ddu

Hendre-Meredydd quarry

Internal incline and level tramway

Weir

Mill pond

Slab Works

600 ft.

Mill race

600 ft.

To Aberangell

N

MILE

0   ⅛   ¼   ½

D.G. 8.2004

Maes-y-gamfa routes above the incline are marked upper tramway/roads. The routes are easily discerned and well graded. Maps are not clear, so the routes could have been either, or have changed from one system to another during the life of the quarry.

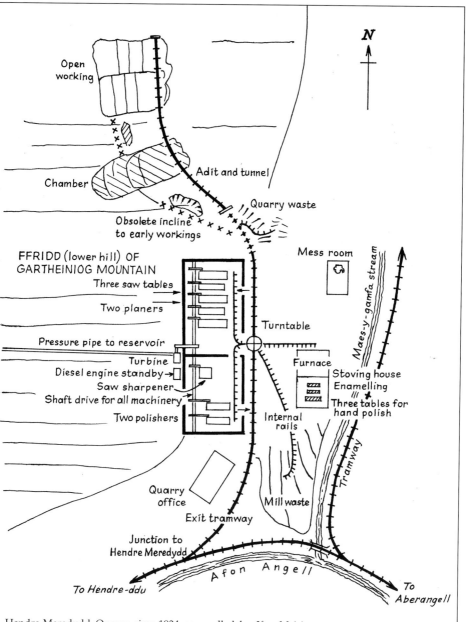

Hendre-Meredydd Quarry *circa* 1934 as recalled by Ifan Meirion   D. G. 8. 2004
Edwards (not to scale). The mill area is exaggerated for clarity and
both the quarry sites and tramway lengths have been curtailed.

The line from Gartheiniog quarry at Hendre Meredydd joins the now farm road on the main Hendre-ddu Tramway. The wagons had to come down with enough velocity to move up the gradient and clear the points prior to descending to Aberangell. *B. Poole*

The large slab works tip of Gartheiniog is close to the confluence of the streams of Maes-y-gamfa and Angell. Cut slab waste, raw slab and the smaller pieces from processing can be seen. Many quarries sold raw slab to other finishing shops as well as their own finished products. *B. Poole*

Left: Gartheiniog slab mill can be seen far left in this 1971 view. In 1934, the mill contained three saws with moving tables, two planers, two polishers and a saw sharpener all driven by water turbine or standby diesel engine. In the foreground is an interesting front-tipper wagon at the primitive turntable. *R.W. Kidner*

Below: The office of Gartheiniog quarry is hidden within the trees. The photograph was taken on the tramway between the quarry and the junction in 2002. The stoving house (enamelling) and the mess room have been demolished. *B. Poole*

The Maes-y-gamfa quarry ceased to work on an economic scale at the start of World War I. However, the Maes-y-gamfa Tramway remains the best preserved as it is just outside the Dyfi Forest. There was some recovery of slate after main closure. The line climbs on the right-hand side of the Maes-y-gamfa stream. This gradient/horse tramway is evenly graded with slight cuttings and embankments as it curves up the valley.   *B. Poole*

The tramway crosses to the left-hand side of the stream. This is the first bridge crossing to a stile. Maes-y-gamfa could translate as a meadow with a stile.   *B. Poole*

The Maes-y-gamfa incline viewed from the head looking down in 2002. A rope (spliced steel cable) would run the length of the incline. The weight of the loaded trucks coming down pulled the empties up. This is known as a self-acting gravity incline. The incline had two sets of tracks set close together on the same sleepers but with a passing place bulge halfway down. The grade is even with cuttings and slate wall banks and is over 300 yards in length. This system would have been very common in the slate districts. If the incline exceeded around 600 yards, both the friction and weight of the cable would be too great to make the system function. Longer inclines would have a single track with a steam driven winder.   *B. Poole*

The remains of the drum house at the head of the incline in 2002. The cable was wound around a horizontal drum several times to achieve purchase. One end of the cable was attached to the empty trucks, the other to the loaded trucks. There was a band brake at one end of the drum to control speed operated by a long arm. The trucks passed to the left, many drum houses were set higher still allowing trucks to pass under the drum which was an easier system.   *B. Poole*

THE MAESYGAMFA
SLATE AND SLAB QUARRY CO.,
ABERANGELL, MERIONETHSHIRE.

THE SLATE and SLAB supplied from the Maesygamfa Quarries are unsurpassed for **Quality, Strength,** and **Durability.** Acknowledged the best in the district.

Makers of
Brewers' Tanks, Cisterns,
URINALS.

ALL KIND OF SLATE WORK EXECUTED.

Prices on application to the Manager, Mr. E. H. DAVIES.

Right: Maes-y-gamfa quarry was the first to close - during World War I. It is the only quarry out on sheep walks so the whole site can be seen. This 2002 picture shows a vertical wall where the slab would be taken out. It gives some idea of scale, the trees are not saplings but the canopy of mature trees that established on ledges away from grazing sheep.   *B. Poole*

Branch 6. At 2 miles 1 chain this branch, by means of facing points, struck northward up the valley down which flows the Maes-y-gamfa stream, which it crossed at 18 chains. At 30 chains occurred Branch 7. Branch 6 re-crossed the Maes-y-gamfa and by a lengthy incline was lifted to 669 feet above sea level alongside Maes-y-gamfa House. The incline was of an early form, with two separate lines. The branch, again single, continued along the flank of Ffridd Maes-y-gamfa to a terminus at Maes-y-gamfa Slate and Slab Quarry (1 mile 14 chains). As is usual in such quarries the tramway was connected to the sheds by several turntables and local branches, some of a temporary nature, were in evidence.

Branch 7. This branch was entered by facing points off Branch 6, at the confluence of the Mes-y-gamfa and Tal-y-Miern streams. It served a slate quarry by means of a short 3-rail incline; length of branch 12 chains.

Branch 8. This branch made trailing connection with the main tramway at 2 miles 8 chains. Rising on a considerable gradient it passed the Gartheiniog Slab Works *en route* to its terminus at Hendre-Meredydd Quarry (27 chains). Across the valley the Maes-y-gamfa branch (No. 6) was clearly visible.

Branch 9. The last, and the shortest of all. Only 2 chains in length, access to Nanthir Farm was by facing points at 2 miles 33 chains.

Operating

As already indicated the first quarry served by the tramway in its course to Hendre-ddu was that supplying Gartheiniog Slab Works - the quarry itself was about ¼ mile to the north at Hendre-Meredydd on the slopes of Coed Mawr. This quarry was in operation before the close of the 19th century (Messrs Owens & Mallory were the proprietors in 1893) and continued to function until about 1937. The number of men employed varied between 3 and 20 - a range typical of the varying fortunes of the slate trade.

The quarry in Coed Tal-y-Mieryn was worked in the mid-19th century, but was derelict by 1900. Activity in the vicinity during World War I was connected with the quest for pit props.

Maes-y-gamfa Slate and Slab Quarry was opened about 1892, with Major Walton as Proprietor and Mr E.H. Davies as Manager, and continued in operation until 1914. It was Major Walton's interest in this quarry together with the fact that the Angell meadows were in his ownership that route A through the village was abandoned in favour of route B (*see map on page 78*). Upwards of 20 men normally found employment, but there were only six at the finish.

The final and most important quarry was the Hendre-ddu. This quarry is believed to have been working in the 1850s. The Hendre-ddu Slate and Slab Co. was established by Sir Edmund Buckley, Bart, in 1864 and gave much local employment.

An 1893 advertisement for the quarry contains the following:

There is a Narrow Gauge Tramway running from Aberangell Station of the Mawddwy Railway up to Quarry, through splendid scenery. Arrangements can be made for conveying tourist parties to and from the Quarry at low prices on previous application being made to the Manager.

The first of two views at Aberangell trans-shipment platform *circa* 1925. A standard gauge
wagon can be seen on the extreme left.   *R.T. Pugh*

A Simplex locomotive waits to depart Aberangell with a train for the quarries. The slate wagons
in this view are empty, the larger slabs were carried against the trestle and wood sheet in a
similar manner to that for plate glass on a lorry.   *R.T. Pugh*

One presumes that the quarrymen's gravity cars, horse drawn, were pressed into service!

In common with many another slate quarry ownership frequently changed hands. Subsequent proprietors included: *circa* 1925-1933, Hendre-ddu Slate Quarries Ltd (of which Mr J.H. Harris was Governing Director and Mr W. Bowley a further Director);1933-1939, a Mr Williams. Managers during the period 1920-1936 included Messrs Richard Lewis and John W. Disley. The number of men employed varied between 12 and 100 and final closure was applied late in 1939.

Crude electrical systems were installed in both Hendre-Meredydd and Hendre-ddu Quarries about 1925; improved installations were at work two years later. Hendre-ddu Quarry was utilised for the storing of explosives in World War II. The Forestry Commission has considerable interests in the countryside west of Abermynach and occupies buildings both at Hendre-ddu and Gartheiniog.

Branch 1 was in use during World War I only, in connection with pit props; Branch 2 was out of use and lifted before World War II; Branch 3 was in use during World War I only and served a sawmill; Branch 4 was lifted about 1925, Branch 5 was in use for total length during World War I only and truncated to a siding which was lifted when the main tramway was removed. Later the Forestry Commission relaid and worked part on 2 ft 0 in. gauge. A 'Simplex' tractor and horses were used in connection with trucks mounted on Hudson chassis.

On Branch 6 the rails from the main tramway junction to the foot of Maes-y-gamfa incline were removed at the same time as the main tramway; from the foot of the incline to the quarry the rails were lifted in World War I. Branches 7 to 9 were lifted with the main line of the tramway.

Although most of the tramway was lifted in 1939, some minor use was made of it for many years and much material was left, especially in the triangle adjacent to the Gartheiniog slab mill, which was used for forestry. Almost all the track bed was over-laid for forestry road transport, except for the portion close to quarry, and the incline. The first few hundred yards of the later route up to Clippau, however, were not converted, and approach to the area is now along the old route.

Motive Power and Rolling Stock

The Hendre-ddu Tramway proper was owned by the successive proprietors of the quarry of the same name, whilst the quarry branches were in the ownership of the respective quarry owners, passing with the closing of the quarries to the local farmers. It is natural, therefore, that the Hendre-ddu Quarry proprietors should have been provided at all times the lion's share of the motive power and rolling stock.

In addition to the horses already at work, the quarry introduced in 1920 a 'Simplex' petrol tractor supplied by the Motor Rail & Tram Co. Ltd, of Simplex Works, Bedford (Works No. 2059). This vehicle was of the following principal dimensions:

Timber stored along the Maes-y-gamfa branch in 1971 with a bolster wagon in the foreground.
R.W. Kidner

Hendre-ddu Tramway: a private owner's vehicle photographed on the site of the tramway in 1953.
Lewis Cozens

Length over 'buffers':	9 ft 3¼ in.
Length over headstocks:	7 ft 11 in.
Wheelbase:	3 ft 4⅛ in.
Maximum width:	4 ft 10 in.
Height (rail to radiator cap):	4 ft 9 in.

About 1930 the quarry built a 'locomotive' of light construction embodying an Overland lorry engine. To give ballast because of the lightness of this unit a block of slate was built into the frame. A brake failure brought this vehicle to an untimely end, and the 'Simplex' alone did haulage daily until the outbreak of World War II.

During the final months a lorry straddling the rails was used to draw the wagons on the tramway.

In the mid-1920s Mr David Roberts (Aberangell) drove the 'Simplex', and was succeeded by Mr John Breese. The latter, together with his mate, Mr David Jones, also maintained the track during the years 1925-1933, by no means a sinecure, and particularly so when winter snows blanketed the valley.

The tramway's slate trains were operated by two men, one acting as driver and the further man as brakeman and opener of the gates, of which there were about six. The 'locomotive' hauled six to eight full wagons, whilst it would return to Hendre-ddu quarry with all empty wagons offered.

There was at least one petrol 'scooter'.

For their journeys from and to Aberangell the quarrymen were carried in two types of vehicles. They were two large gravity cars built on Hudson chassis with timber top and brake handle in centre of top. These cars, in common with all other rolling stock, were springless. For the quarrymen's convenience footboards encircled these cars, the seating capacity of which was 16 each. Principal dimensions were overall length: 10 ft 6 in.; width of seat 3 ft 3 in.; wheelbase: 3 ft 10 in.

There were at least three small gravity cars. The footboards were on the sides only. Seating capacity was about 10 each. Principal dimensions were, overall length: 5 ft 8 in.; width of seat: 2 ft 8 in.; diameter of wheels: 1 ft 6 in.; wheelbase: 3 ft 0 in.

Before the closing of the tramway one of these cars had been given to a local farmer who proceeded to equip it with a Morgan petrol engine.

The quarry possessed about 30 wagons and trucks of various types, slab cars and crude narrow gauge wagons with 4-spoke large wheels (2 ft 0 in. diameter) and wheelbase of 3 ft 0 in. Also wagons with one side and one end removable; buffers (dumb) at one end only. Livery: Bodies grey, solebars red oxide. Bend brakes and spoked wheels were fitted. Principal dimensions:

Overall length:	7 ft 0 in.
Length over body:	6 ft 6 in.
Width over body:	3 ft 4 in.
Height of sides:	2 ft 5 in.
Diameter of wheels:	1 ft 3 in.
Wheelbase:	3 ft 0 in.

Finally there were flat cars provided with removable sides and ends. Principal dimensions:

Overall length:	6 ft 11 in.
Width over body:	3 ft 2 in.
Diameter of wheels:	1 ft 4 in.
Wheelbase:	2 ft 9 in.
Brakes on all wheels	

All vehicles were branded 'HSQ' but were not numbered. Messrs Turner Bros, of Newtown, Montgomeryshire, were responsible for the castings, axles and wheels of the early vehicles and also for their oak frames.

It is understood that the quarry at Gartheiniog boasted about 12 wagons at its closing; the figures for Maes-y-gamfa are not available.

The farms served by the tramway and its branches each operated at least one vehicle over the metals. Tolls were paid to the successive proprietors of the Hendre-ddu Quarry to secure running rights. One farmer in respect of a farm bought many years ago paid the low rate of 1*d*. per ton goods carried, though for a property more recently acquired the rate had been raised to 6*d*. per ton. In addition to the carriage of their goods these vehicles were used by the farmers and their families for visiting church and chapel. The journeys to Aberangell were made by gravity, whilst the return was made with the assistance of, first, horses and latterly by the Hendre-ddu Quarry 'locomotive' in which quarry's train the farmers' vehicles were incorporated as required.

The Aberangell Quarries

The tramline following Cwm Angell to the quarries operated until 1939. So there are still people in the Dyfi Valley who can remember the operation and traces of the lower line can easily be seen.

Ifan Meirion Edwards of Dinas Mawddwy was one of about 25 workers at Hendre-Meredydd (Branch 8). It was his first job on leaving school and he worked there for about four years in the mid-1930s. His job was saw sharpening and clearing waste. He would cycle every day by himself except Sunday from Dinas Mawddwy leaving about 7.00 am to start work at 8.00 am. The older men left earlier but Meirion was 14 so there was a restriction of hours for him. However he would cycle back in the evening with the other Dinas men.

Other quarries were served by the petrol-engined locomotive and the men had a lift up from Aberangell in the morning. Meirion and the others at Hendre-Medydd had to make their own way up as horses were used to pull empty wagon up to their quarry. The loaded wagons would come down in a group with several men riding as brakemen. The Hendre-ddu wagons came down with the locomotive but also a number of brakemen riding on the wagons. Meirion thought that a dispute had arisen on the cost of locomotive hauling which is why their quarry used horses. Maybe every quarry had rights to use the tramway. Ifan never rode down on the tramway.

Will Breese worked with Meirion; Will has written many articles about the quarries. Each saw was sharpened twice per day with a carborundum. Waste was loaded into a handpushed wagon and pushed along the rails to the waste tip. It was very hard work. The line fed into the quarry on the level; there were no inclines. There was a crane to lift the slabs on to the wagons, there were not many wagons, maybe eight to ten, in use. There was no run round or turntable at Meredydd. All three quarries produced slab slate, they were cut to the size required. Examples were mantelpieces, bar counters, urinals, gravestones, brewery vats and paving or flagstones. The slate from Meredydd had a bluish tinge to it. The other quarries had inclines; Meirion thinks they had a balance drum and the full wagon coming down pulled the empty wagon up. Only Hendre-ddu was also operating; Maes-y-gamfa had already closed.

It was a hard day but at least they cycled from Dinas. Their parents had to walk in earlier decades. Quarry work was not easy and there were casualties. The tramline also had mishaps of brake failure and derailment. The problem on the use of the line finally led to the owners of Hendre-Meredydd buying a lorry or a van for transport directly from the quarry to customers in England. It could only just clear under the Aberangell rail bridge. Ernie Davies was the local driver. The two remaining quarries only had a short while before closing. Meirion was himself a casualty with a neck injury so he left and worked with a contractor for a year collecting moss and rhododendron shoots which were sold to florists. By 2002, the rhododendrons are now considered a rampant weed in Snowdonia. They originate from Nepal and have no pests or diseases in Wales so they shade and kill native flora. Meirion then worked in one of the forests before being called up for World War II service.

Gwyndaf Breese confirms much of Meirion's story in his essay *Gweithio'r Garreg Lâs* (Working the Blue Rock) and he used Will Breese, Meirion's old quarry colleague, for much of the source material. He confirms the problems of the gradients of the tramway. In 1877, a wagon full of quarrymen had a smash and some were badly injured but there was a doctor in the village. Wagons went through gates; brake handles were pulled so hard that they could snap. Maybe this was the reason that single wagons coming down had to cease in 1920 when the petrol-engined locomotive came into use. Groups of wagons with several brakemen should have been an insurance. However, control was lost on one load in 1926 and it ran into Aberangell yard and hit the passenger train. No one was hurt but many were frightened.

Meirion left the quarry work as it was coming to an end. Some of these quarries were used for storing munitions during the war. Hendre-Meredydd was taken over by the Forestry Commission so now most is hidden under a green mantle. One wag said 'Aberangell station, famous for loading ewe lambs and urinals'. All history now.

A further concerted effort was made in late 2002 to find anyone else who may have worked in the quarry prior to closure in 1939. The consensus of opinion is that there is now no one. The research should have been pursued a decade earlier.

Much of the following is drawn from articles written in the early 1970s by the late Will Breese summarised by Gwyndaf Breese's *Gweithio'r Garreg Lâs* in a

A quarry scene at Aberangell, although which quarry is not known. The dress indicates pre-World War I. The truck is likely to be loaded with waste, ready for the tip. The vertical slabs to be prised out can be easily seen. The system for payments would not be known for this quarry but they could be complex.

Gwynedd Archives, Dolgellau

local book about the village of Aberangell. Gwyndaf has given permission to use both his own essays as source material.

A vein of slate runs along the border of Montgomeryshire and Merionethshire. The most eastern extreme was at Llangynog. The Ratgoed Quarry feeding to the Corris Railway is just over the western brow of the mountain from Hendre-ddu. It is thought that Hendre-ddu may have been the more efficient of the two with a better layout for both internal and external transport. No one really knows how quarrying started in the Aberangell area as slate was used for local building material long before the industrial revolution. The old level above the main quarry would have been used before the capital injection which started in the late 1860s.

There are many slate quarry sites in Mid and North Wales. Most were only very small where a few men supplied a local need only. Only a few became very large enterprises and these were further north at Ffestiniog, Llanberis and Bethesda. Hendre-ddu would have been an intermediate enterprise employing up to 160 men at the peak boom of the 1870s but only a small team of around 20 after World War I. The tramway was not unique. There are up to 40 tramways but most were relatively short to either road or rail exchange. It is the length of the Hendre-ddu tramway of nearly four miles serving relatively low volume output which makes it so unusual.

Sir Edmund Buckley expanded the quarries both at Hendre-ddu and Minllyn (Dinas Mawddwy) just after the standard gauge branch was built. Demand for slate boomed and share prices boomed. The bubble and burst story followed when supply caught up with demand. Prices fell and the marginal quarries, especially those that could not split thin slate for roofs, started to struggle. The Aberangell quarries survived on a niche market of slab slate. The early quarries were worked on open level into the slope. Buckley started to use adits (tunnels) to move into chambers to reach the highest quality slabs. Once he was certain that the initial exploration was good, the investment on an industrial scale followed.

Buildings for the quarry and the fitting of machinery took place. The skills of quarrying were acquired by the expanding labour force. The tramway of 3 miles 70 chains was completed to connect with the standard gauge exchange at Aberangell by the early 1870s or before. Workers came from a distance as well as a three mile walk from the nearest village. The common solution for the isolated quarries and mines then took place. A barracks was built where 22 men could stay during the week under the care of Catrin Pugh. For a period, shift work took place and as men went to work, those coming off the previous shift fell into the same bed space. The six Hendre-ddu cottages housed key workers at the foot of the main incline. A large mill shed was built with adjoining offices and a manager's house. When the company changed hands, the valuations showed 16 saws, 8 planers, saw sharpeners and a polisher all designed for slab working.

There could have been various types of saw, the word 'byrddau llifio' indicates a set circular tooth saw protruding from underneath with a moving table where the slab was secured by wedges. Planers smoothed the cut slab with blades to both remove the saw marks from the surface and to contour the edges. The polisher was a mill type stone fed with water and sand to polish the slate. The real ingenuity was the power source. Two reservoirs were built above the old level. A 500 yard length of 8 to 9 inch pipe brought pressurised water to a turbine which could develop up to 50 hp and powered the machinery. A pressurised turbine would develop far more power than a pelton wheel or a large water wheel. Later some discussion took place as whether to purchase a stationary steam engine but this never took place. A steam crane was on site.

The ownership of the tramway remained with the company who owned Hendre-ddu Quarry. Other quarry companies, the forestry, the brick works and farmers paid for use as if it was a turnpike tramway. This would cause some dispute later. The Hendre-ddu Quarry would hold back water for its own use and this would again lead to dispute with other users further down the valley during a dry summer or prolonged winter freeze.

The tramway was designed for loaded wagons down by gravity and the empty wagons to be horse-hauled back. However, most of the materials for the quarry would have been horse-hauled back. Examples would be lubricating oils, grease, coal for the crane, ropes, candles, machinery parts, etc., flour, sugar, tea, etc.

The success of the investment around 1870 was short lived because Buckley became bankrupt in 1876. The quarry had not failed, the problem was with stock investment especially Turkish Bonds. The Hendre-ddu Quarry was purchased by Bradwells, Silk Merchants, from Cheshire. The quarry was successful, shipping out over 200 tons of shaped slate every month. Joseph was the Bradwell brother on site. There was a problem of industrial relations between the workers and owners. This became common in many quarries. Some of this could be justified, as safety procedure was poor. The quarry face work was dangerous requiring a high degree of team work but there was also a dust problem within the mill. Whether right or wrong, men felt that donkeys may have received better treatment and that the command to open the doors wider when dust was bad did not solve the problem. There was also much misunderstanding with language and the owners would have made little effort to understand Welsh.

The profitability of the quarry would not have been good after 1900 as other materials started to replace slate. A Henry Davies purchased the quarry during 1912. All three quarries closed during World War I but the machinery was kept in good condition. Only Hendre-ddu and Hendre-Meredydd re-opened and resumed volume production. Some investment took place including a primitive electrical generating system. The tramway was used during the war for forestry extraction and the Board of Trade became the first to use a locomotive although little is known about its success or failure.

Ownership changed to the National Welsh Slate Quarries in 1920 and this company soon ordered the 'Simplex' engine. The Bradwells had given generous terms to other users of the tramways and several farms even had their own painted wagons. Users just let their own wagon go down with a brakeman and would haul back with a horse at their own convenience. Maybe up traffic was done in the morning but whatever arrangement existed, minor accidents were common. There were a number of gates on the line and the problem of gravity speed plus poor braking or misjudgment plus ice, dampness or leaves on the line meant that the wagon would skid into the gate causing damage. It must be assumed that the brakeman jumped just before the impact. If control of the wagon were lost, the gathering speed would cause it to come off the rails on one of the numerous curves.

Once the engine had been purchased, the old system had to cease. Wagons had to descend and return in blocks. The single engine ensured that the line was safe as only the engine would haul up and down. A brakeman had to ride on the train. It was thought that it was one brakeman to every six wagons. However, problems of failure still continued and gates were still smashed. The little 'Simplex' engine was filled up with petrol once a week, every Friday evening, at the petrol pump near Felinfoel.

By now, a dispute had occurred between the owners of the tramway and Hendre-Meredydd who reverted to using horse and gravity, maybe having failed to pay their dues, so a lorry was purchased and used for the final two or three years of the quarry use.

By 1930, the recession was severe and the skilled young men commenced to leave Aberangell to seek their fortunes elsewhere. Hendre-ddu Quarry was virtually mothballed in 1934 but re-opened again in 1938 but within the year had closed again. At this point, most of the line was scrapped and the 'Simplex' engine disappeared overnight. Already lorries had been travelling for several years along the tramway, straddling the track and causing damage. The mill shed at Hendre-ddu was used to store explosives during World War II and was dismantled in 1946. The house and office became a hostel for walkers for several years, then became derelict but is now being restored. The Forestry Commission took over the site; they shut off levels and now much is buried under a sea of green conifers.

A home-made locomotive using a six-cylinder Overland engine was also built, but was involved in an accident and the gear box and engine were used as winch power within the quarry somewhere around 1935. During World War II a section of tramway was installed to Coed-Cwm-Caws (Branch 5). Both the tramway engine and wagons were drawn from the Chirk Forestry Depot. There was only limited slate production after 1945 with only the internal quarry traffic of hand-propelled tip wagons to the waste tip.

Now the quarries, which gave work to the village for over 60 years, are as quiet as the blue-black Aberangell gravestones that are in so many cemeteries of Mid Wales and further afield.

Machinery and systems at a slab quarry

Ifan Meirion Edwards of Dinas Mawddwy is now the last survivor to have worked at an Aberangell quarry. He started at the age of 14 at Hendre-Meredydd Quarry in 1934. Meirion's father worked at Hendre-ddu after World War I and was a close friend of John Breese, who was one of the drivers of the 'Simplex' locomotive. The quarry struggled to survive throughout the 1920s and once dad went six weeks without any pay until one of the purchasers of slate paid the quarry and then they could pay the men.

Hendre-Meredydd produced a very high quality slab with a blue/green/black colour. The quarry was a very small operation in World War I. There was both a chamber and an open quarry and the incline to the higher level could still be seen in 1934. A second tunnel was driven through just above mill level so the

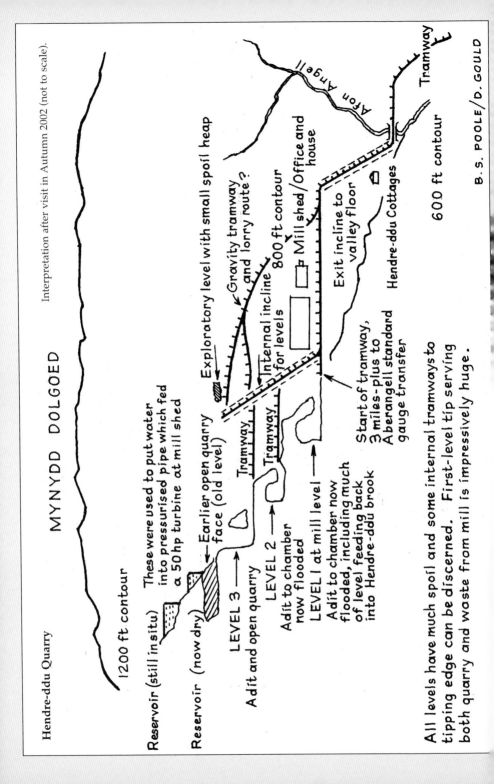

Hendre-ddu Quarry

MYNYDD DOLGOED

Interpretation after visit in Autumn 2002 (not to scale).

1200 ft contour

These were used to put water into pressurised pipe which fed a 50 hp turbine at mill shed

Reservoir (still in situ)

Reservoir (now dry)

Earlier open quarry face (old level)

LEVEL 3
Adit and open quarry

Tramway

LEVEL 2
Adit to chamber now flooded

Tramway

LEVEL 1 at mill level

Adit to chamber now flooded, including much of level feeding back into Hendre-ddu brook

Exploratory level with small spoil heap

Gravity tramway and lorry route?

800 ft contour

Internal incline for levels

Mill shed/Office and house

Exit incline to valley floor

Start of tramway, 3 miles-plus to Aberangell standard gauge transfer

Afon Angell

Tramway

Hendre-ddu Cottages

600 ft contour

B. S. POOLE/D. GOULD

All levels have much spoil and some internal tramways to tipping edge can be discerned. First-level tip serving both quarry and waste from mill is impressively huge.

same two quarries continued to be used but at a deeper level. The open quarry by 1934 had a huge cliff overhang and the chamber was cavernous.

Meirion's work was to sharpen saws, take waste from the mill to the tip and look after the mess room. He would not have gone to the quarry faces very often. Light in the chamber came from candles. The men were issued with candles and a ball of clay. They would shape the clay to hold the candle and stick the result to the rock face. Explosives were used to drive the face forward and weaken the vertical seam. Holes were driven into the face in a line. This would weaken the slabs above almost like a perforation of stamps. The drilling had been done by brace and bit by hand, but by the 1920s, a compressor was used. Chisel/crowbar and hammers were then used to prise the slab off the face. There was a crane which was hand-cranked with gears to load the slab to the truck. The truck would be hand-pushed to the mill on a very slight gradient. The empty trucks were hand-pushed back. However, horses were used at Hendre-ddu where the tramway was far longer to the higher levels.

The power source at the mill was a water driven turbine. The reservoir was far smaller than that at Hendre-ddu and Maes-y-gamfa and the water pressure would soon run out if there was a dry spell. There was a diesel engine on standby; earlier there had been a portable steam engine. A pulley from either drove to a shaft set high through the length of the mill. Belts and pulleys could then drive any machine within the mill.

The slab arrived at the turntable outside the mill and moved to one of three fixed circular saws set on a slowly moving table. The slab was lifted from the truck by hand chain/hoist. There was a gantry rail suspended from the rafters so that the slate could be positioned to the table. The table would crawl forward by worm drive and rack. The table had holes and the slab was held by wedges. The sawn slab now moved to one of two planers. Again this was a moving table driving on to a wide flat blade which would make the slab even along the face; for example a constant depth of 4 inches. Both sawing and planing left minute pockmarks and blade marks. There was plenty of space in the shed indicating there may have been more machines in an earlier period. Meirion believes there had been some machinery modernisation on re-opening around 1920.

The cut slab now moved to the other main room of the mill shed for polishing. The slate was fed through a reciprocating flat carborundum plate and this was constantly lubricated by a mixture of sand and water to smooth the slab. There were two polishers. The saw sharpener was also in the corner of this section.

The polished slate now moved out to the turntable. It could now be ready for shipping out. However, fireplace slate and some gravestones moved to a further process of enamelling. A stove or oven heated the slate to add an extra finish and there were three boards and three men where the final hand polishing took place. In 1934, the finished slate for shipping out was now placed on a tram and went by gravity and brake to Aberangell station and the empty trucks were hauled back by horse. The quarry did not use the locomotive. A lorry replaced this system by 1936, by-passing both the tramway and the Dinas branch with direct delivery to customers. All machinery processes at

Hendre-ddu would have been similar except that it was on a larger scale with more saws, planers and polishers but no enamelling process.

There were numerous names for the quarry wagons, both in English and Welsh. Tram is used in North Wales, dram in South Wales and there is wagon, tryc and twb. Meirion used 'tryc' for the wagon with sides that could hinge down and was used for taking waste to the tip while 'tram' was used for a flat wagon that brought the slab from the quarry to the mill.

Meirion confirmed that both inclines at Hendre-ddu worked on a balance where the weight of the loading wagons going down also raised the empty wagons back. There was a drum house at the top where a cable wound round a horizontal drum. The speed had to be controlled as the inclines had the four rails close together both at the top and the bottom with a passing place. The brake was a metal band (brake shoes were fitted either to the band or the winding drum?) and a long handle gave leverage to control the speed of the drum. It could also be pinned down to hold the loads on the incline. This was necessary on the internal incline at Hendre-ddu where wagons moved to the lateral tramway.

Meirion worked at Hendre-ddu for a few months in 1939 after the quarry had briefly re-opened, while he was waiting to join the army. The quarry had changed ownership; the main tramways were no longer used and had been replaced by a lorry. The rails were ripped up and sold for scrap. If there had been less haste, the tramway may have earned revenue from the forestry and transport of explosives during the war and the scrap price would have been far higher in 1942.

Meirion worked the last truck to the tip on the last day of operation. He regrets that the extra effort was not made to take a photograph with flags and a notice saying 'Last Hendre-ddu truck from mill to tip'. The quarry was not to re-open after the war. The noise and dust on a working day at Hendre-Meredydd could be a problem. Various quarry and mining acts had improved safety within the technology of the 1930s.

The mill shed and the office with outside toilet still stand, and were used by the Forestry Commission. The mess shed and the stove house have long been demolished. The whole area is now covered with mature conifers; even the spoil heaps are covered with lichen and moss and have merged into the green. Only some of the internal tramway can now be traced. Extreme caution must be taken when exploring such sites.

Meirion was asked if he could remember the stables. He could not. Maybe the quarries used local farmers' horses on a contract basis that was a common system. The horses could have hauled the wagons up (including the quarrymen) early in the morning, then returned with the farm staff to carry on with the farm work. Maybe a horse was kept at Hendre-ddu during the day. The common quarry gauge around two feet may have been a compromise between that for men pushing trucks in the quarry and the space between the rails for horses to haul which was almost too narrow.

In mid-November 2002, the last trudge was completed along the tramroad by the side of Nant Maes-y-gamfa to the quarry of the same name. During less than eight months, Brian Poole had walked all three railway branch lines, most of the tramways and numerous inclines in some of the most beautiful upland country of Montgomeryshire and the very tip of South Merioneth.

Chapter Six

The Van Railway

Introduction

The Van Railway at the time of its closing formed part of the Great Western Railway and from its terminus adjoining the GWR's Caersws (Montgomeryshire) station carried its standard gauge single line in a south-westerly direction to reach the formerly celebrated Van lead mines in a distance of 6 miles 46½ chains.

The principal dates in the railway's history may be given thus:

1870	9th June. The Van Railway Company Limited registered.
1871	14th August. Opened for freight traffic.
1873	22nd May. Board of Trade Certificate issued under the Railway Construction Facilities Act of 1864 (the certificate became binding on 3rd June, 1873).
1873	1st December. Opened for passenger traffic.
1879	Passenger traffic discontinued
1893	Railway closed entirely
1896	1st August. Re-opened for freight traffic, being maintained and worked by the Cambrian Railways Company.
1923	1st January. Railway absorbed by the GWR.
1940	4th November. Last day of freight traffic.*

Traffic was dealt with by a single main running line. Run-round loops were furnished at Caersws and Garth & Van Road stations - though that at the latter had been removed prior to 1939. The majority of stations and halts were provided with siding accommodation. Heavy rails and chairs were used on the main line for the first half-mile from Caersws, with flat-bottomed rails keyed to the sleepers thereafter and in the sidings. Several of the level crossings were protected by signals of an early pattern.

The railway was operated on the principle of one locomotive in steam and worked by 'pilot guard'. Turntables were not provided. The locomotives ran bunker first to the mines.

Until 1893 the line was in charge of the station master of its own Caersws station: as from 1896 control passed to the Cambrian main line station master. In the closing years, trains were subjected to a speed limit of five miles per hour. Mileposts were provided but not gradient posts.

1850-1870

The story of the Van Railway is bound up with the rise and fall of the Van lead mines. In the years between 1850 and 1868 £2,000 was spent in search for lead in the neighbourhood of Van, in the Plynlymon foothills. At this period no less than 16 mining companies were operating in the district.

* It has been suggested that there was a 'last train' on this date, but as the only loop other than Caersws was taken out more than a year earlier, it seems this was only the day on which the GWR announced closure.

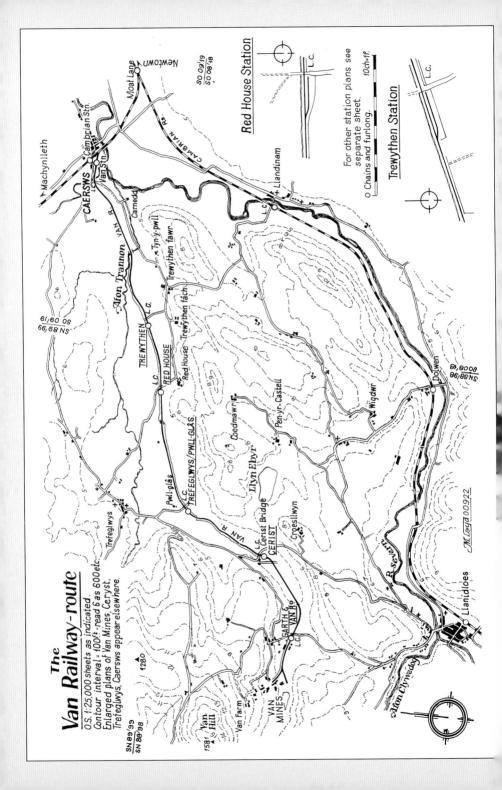

The
Van Railway-route

O.S. 1:25 000 sheets as indicated.
Contour interval = 100ft: read 6 as 600etc.
Enlarged plans of Van Mines, Ceryst,
Trefeglwys, Caersws appear elsewhere.

SN 89/99
SN 88/98

Red House Station

SO 09/19
SO 08/18

Trewythen Station

For other station plans see
separate sheet.
10ch=1f.
o Chains and furlong.

← Machynlleth

CAERSWS

← Cambrian Stn.
Van Stn.
L.C.

Moat Lane
Newtown →

Cambrian R.

Carnedd

Tyn-y-pwll

Trewythen fawr

Trewythen fach

Red House

+ Llandinam

L.C.

Afon Trannon

Van R.

TREWYTHEN

L.C.

L.C.

RED HOUSE

L.C.

Coedmawr

Llyn Ebyr

Pen-yr-Castell

Wigdwr

Dolwen

SN 88/08
SN 89/18

Pwll-glâs

TREFEGLWYS/PWLL-GLÂS

Van R.

Cerist Bridge
CERIST
L.C.

Croesllwyn

Trefeglwys

1280

Van
Hill
1581

Van Farm

VAN
MINES

GARTH &
VAN R.
L.C.

R. Severn

Afon Clywedog

JM Lloyd 00922

Llanidloes

Prior to the opening of the railway the Van mines had successively belonged to Messrs William Lefaux & Jackson, then a Mr Edward Morris, whose executors sold it for £46,000 to the Van Mining Company Ltd. This company, largely financed by London capital, was incorporated on 1st February, 1869. A tablet at the mines quoted the original Directors and Officers as follows:

T.C. Mundey, Esquire	Chairman
Robert Oldrey, Esquire	Director
William Page, Esquire	Director
Julius Alington, Esquire	Director
F.L. Slous, Esquire	Director
W.J. Lavington, Esquire	Secretary
Capt. William Williams	Manager

No fewer than 700 men found employment at the mines and increasing traffic brought the question of railway communications into the limelight. Only 2½ miles away lay Llanidloes, the terminus of the Llanidloes & Newtown Railway (opened in 1859). Caersws on the Newtown & Machynlleth Railway, though a greater distance - approximately 6½ miles - was in favour, as the valley followed by the rivers Cerist and Trannon presented an easier route than any that could be envisaged over the hills between Van and Llanidloes.

The Newtown & Machynlleth Railway was opened in 1863 and it was natural therefore that two of its leading figures, the Chairman, Earl Vane (later to become the Marquis of Londonderry) and Mr David Davies, contractor, of Llandinam, should join forces in promoting the Van Railway.

The Van Railway Company Ltd was registered on 9th June, 1870, under the Companies Act, 1862, and Messrs Powell & Swetenham were appointed contractors and the construction of the railway proceeded apace. From a junction just to the south of the Cambrian Railways Company's Caersws station in the parish of Llangwog, it was laid over land for the greater part in the possession of the following: In the neighbourhood of Caersws and Llandinam: Capt. Offley Malcolm Crewe-Read, RN; Mrs General Wemyss, The Master and Fellows of University College, Oxford; the Rt Hon. Lord Sudeley and; Mr David Davies (Llandinam). In the upper reaches the principal landowners concerned were the Marquis of Londonderry, Mr David Davies, Mr Evan Woosnam. The building of the railway did much to improve the drainage of the valley and by August 1871 the rails had reached the mines.

Physical Description

This description of the railway covers the system when operating in its fullest form. Shortly after leaving Moat Lane Junction on the main line from Oswestry to Aberystwyth the River Severn is crossed and Caersws station comes into view. On approaching the station a line is thrown off to the left at 53 miles 18½ chains (distance from Whitchurch, Salop) - this is the commencement of the Van Railway. Immediately a siding goes off right-handed to serve a freight shed.

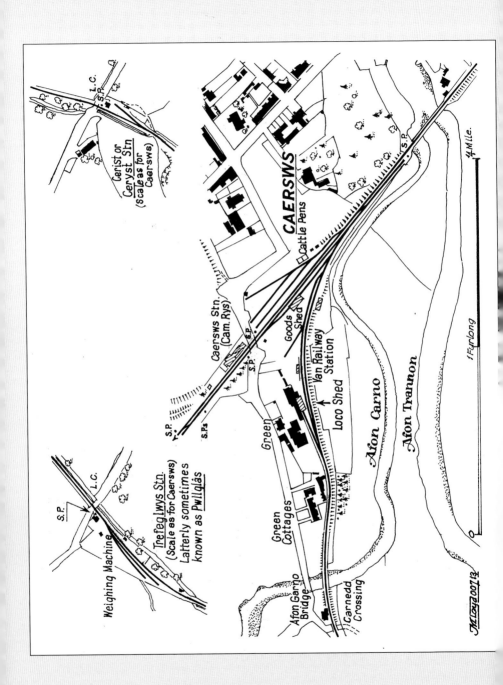

Cerist or Ceryst Stn (scales for Caersws)

L.C.
S.P.

CAERSWS

Cattle Pens

Caersws Stn. (Cam. Rys)

S.P.

Goods Shed

Van Railway Station

Loco Shed

Green

S.P.s

Green Cottages

Afon Carno

Afon Trannon

Afon Garno Bridge

Carnedd Crossing

Weighing Machine

Trefeglwys Stn. (Scale as for Caersws) Latterly sometimes known as Pwllglâs

S.P.

L.C.

S.P.

¼ Mile.

1 Furlong

0

J.M.Lloyd 007½

The single line splits to form a run-round loop with the platform (12½ chains from the junction with the main line) (the station buildings adjacent to the loop nearer the main line were modernised to form offices for the Bridge Department, Central Wales Division, British Railways (Western Region); a short siding is carried to the rear of these buildings). The large brick-built locomotive shed lies shortly beyond the further platform ramp and on the same side: the siding points are at 18 chains.

The River Carno, a tributary of the Severn, was crossed by a wooden trestle bridge (at 25 chains) with Carnedd Villa (the home of John 'Ceiriog' Hughes, the General Manager from 1872 to 1887) at the right hand on the further bank: here occurred a gated level crossing (26½ chains) protected by signals. The signal posts were of lattice work type and boasted wooden semaphores, an arm for each direction pivoted at the top.

At this point the nearby Severn flows through low-lying country, but soon the railway turned south-westerly towards the wooded heights of Cefn Carnedd (908 feet) lying across the valley beyond the River Trannon.

Crossing two further wooden trestle bridges (at 45 chains and 1 mile 18 chains) the railway made for Trewythen Siding (2 miles 2 chains), where a single siding only was provided. No platforms or buildings were in evidence and the nearby farm of the same name furnished the normally scanty traffic.

Beyond Trewythen came Red House (2 miles 61 chains), a similar siding, with a further stream, the Cerist, keeping company on either side alternatively. A level crossing immediately preceded the siding. This halt was out of use at an early date.

In the early days the next stop was known as Trefeglwys, though for many years before the closure it was designated Pwll-glas (4 miles 7½ chains). The station house still stands guard over the vanished level crossing, which was protected by signals. Remains of a coal wharf and a weighbridge and the traces of two sidings persist.

The railway turned southward as the valley narrowed and crossed the Trefeglwys-Llanidloes road at Cerist (5 miles 10 chains); the crossing was protected by signals. The station house is still in evidence together with the formation of the former single siding. Revenue was secured from timber felling.

Leaving Cerist the line climbed south-westerly past Herverth level crossing (5 miles 19¼ chains) and forsaking the Cerist ran almost due west as it crossed the Llanidloes-Van road by a level crossing (6 miles 13½ chains) protected by signals. Where the line met the road from Garth, the River Cerist, which had now been close alongside the track, was slightly diverted to allow space for a station house (Garth & Van Road) and a siding, which may have been a loop in passenger days.

This station represented the official terminus of passenger trains during the years 1873 to 1879. The railway ran below Van Terrace and on to the terminus at the Van Mines (6 miles 46½ chains). This mineral terminus was equipped with a ballast siding and a short length of double track (the points at 6 miles 40½ chains and 6 miles 43 chains respectively). The approach was protected by signal: the rise from Caersws was 120 feet. The scenery here is of a wild nature with the Van pool and spoil heaps providing a sombre picture in the valley between the hills of Van (1,580 feet) and Garth (813 feet).

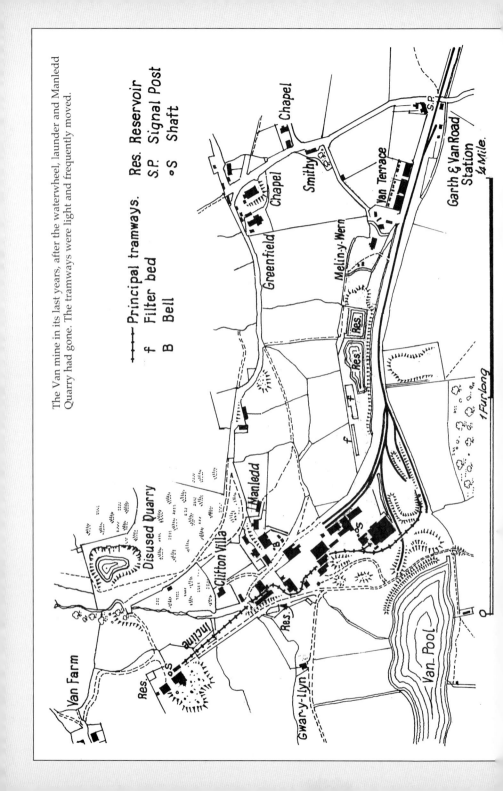

The Van mine in its last years, after the waterwheel, launder and Manledd Quarry had gone. The tramways were light and frequently moved.

—— Principal tramways.   Res. Reservoir
f   Filter bed   S.P. Signal Post
B   Bell   ∘S   Shaft

Van Farm

Disused Quarry

Incline

Clifton Villa

Manledd

Res.

Res.

S

Gwar-y-llyn

Van Pool

Greenfield

Chapel

Chapel

Smithy

Melin-y-Wern

Van Terrace

Res.

Res.

f

S.P.

Garth & Van Road Station

¼ Mile.

1 Furlong

1871-1893

The opening of the railway for freight traffic on 14th August, 1871, came at a time when the mines were at their zenith. Coal, machinery and timber were brought by rail from Caersws and lead and blend ore (zinc sulphide) taken away. From a purely local venture the mines had expanded until the capital value reached just over £1,000,000, shares initially quoted at £4 5s. 0d. in 1869 having risen to £85 on 13th March, 1870. It was all good to be true and Spanish competition was soon to prick the bubble. Capt. Wm Williams, who was Mines Manager at this period, was born at Golch, near Holywell, Flintshire, in 1825. He was Mayor of Llanidloes in 1871/1872, and died at Van in 1879.

The railway is believed to have hired locomotives from the Cambrian before their first was delivered, one such being *Merion*, a Manning, Wardle 0-6-0ST which was built in 1862, No. 17 in the early CR list.

Their first engine a 'K' type 0-6-0ST built by Manning, Wardle in December 1871 arrived in early 1872 (it was later CR No. 25 and withdrawn in 1899).

The arrival of John 'Ceiriog' Hughes, the well-known Bard, in 1872 brought added interest to the railway and passenger traffic commenced operation on 1st December, 1873, the Board of Trade Certificate, under the Railway Construction Facilities Act of 1864, having been granted on 22nd May, 1873.

John Hughes was born on 25th September, 1832, at Llanarmon-Dyffryn-Ceiriog, Denbighshire. He started his business career in Manchester, but returned to Wales to assume the position of station master at Llanidloes before coming to the Van Railway as Manager. He was a man of eccentric habits and his admirers on visiting the railway would one day find him dressed in his best frock coat, cravat and top hat, whilst on the next day he would appear in an old coat and rough cap. He dubbed the two store rooms at Caersws 'Machynlleth' and 'Llanwrst' for no apparent reason. He lived at Carnedd Villa for the 15 years preceding his death in 1887.

It will be recalled that the original company was registered as 'The Van Railway Company Limited'. Following the issue of the Board of Trade Certificate in May 1873, this company went into voluntary liquidation, with Messrs William Page and William John Lavington as liquidators and the assets were taken over by a company incorporated under the title 'The Van Railway Company'.

Amongst the agreements entered into by the company were two dated 24th December, 1874, and 10th February, 1876, respectively, both relating to Mr David Davies, MP, of Broneirion, Llandinam, Montgomeryshire. That of 1874 was in respect of an agreement between Mr Davies and the original company under which he assigned for railway use lands totalling 2 acres 2 roods 14¾ perches situated in the parish of Llandinam, from the crossing of the Trannon River to a point shortly before Trewythen siding and a small parcel of land (18½ perches only) just beyond the siding (the short distance intervening was in the possession of Capt. O.M. Crewe-Read, RN). The perpetual rent charge was £9 per annum, payable by half-yearly instalments on 25th March and 29th September; the company convenanting to maintain certain works, viz: two level crossings, a bridge, and two cattle creeps.

VAN RAILWAY,

TIME TABLE
From APRIL 3rd, 1876, until further Notice.

DOWN.	a.m.	p.m.	a.m.
OSWESTRY (Cambrian) ...	...	...	10 33
NEWTOWN	5 22	3 59	12 10
CAERSWS	5 43	4 37	12 28

Van Railway.	Daily.	Daily except on Sundays.	On Saturdays only.
	a.m.	p.m.	
CAERSWS ... ... dep.	6 15	5 5	12 45
TREFEGLWYS...	6 30	5 20	1 0
CERIST	C	C	C
GARTH & VAN ROAD arr.	6 50	5 35	1 15

UP.

Van Railway.	Daily.	Daily except on Saturdays.	On Saturdays only.
			A.
	a.m.	p.m.	p.m.
GARTH & VAN ROAD dep.	8 0	6 10	2 15
CERIST	C	C	C
TREFEGLWYS	8 15	6 25	2 30
CAERSWS ... ... arr.	8 40	6 40	2 45
	B		Meeting at Caersws on Saturdays the Cambrian 3 35 up & 4 47 down trains.
CAERSWS (Cambrian) dep.	10 12	7 57	
NEWTOWN arr.	10 29	8 15	
OSWESTRY	11 55	9 45	

A. For the accommodation of Workmen this Train will depart at 3·0 p.m. on Van Pay-Days, leaving all Stations correspondingly later.

B. Meeting the Cambrian 9-10 Train on Tuesdays.

C. Stopping at Cerist with or for goods only.

MARKET TRAINS.—On Tuesdays through "MARKET TICKETS" to Newtown are issued at Trefeglwys and Garth and Van Road, and will be available only by the Cambrian Market Trains arriving at Caersws. The evening Market Train will stop at Cerist and Red House Siding when required.

For the convenience of Workpeople at the Mines. "WORKMEN'S TICKETS" are issued at Two Shillings per week, available from any Station to any Station. Holders of these Tickets will have special compartments apportioned to them, and in no other class will they be permitted to travel. "Workmen's Tickets" expire on Saturdays without regard to date of issue.

Second and Third Classes on all Trains. No Sunday Trains.

Caersws, March 31st, 1876. BY ORDER.

Timetable for the Van Railway, 3rd April, 1876.

The common seal of the company was attested by Messrs Robert Oldrey and William Page (Directors) and W.J. Lavington (Secretary). The seal of the second company was 1⅜ in. in diameter with the title 'The Van Railway Company' in full occupying the perimeter, with the exception of the base which was decorated with filigree. Two shields filled the centre, that on the left bearing two crossed keys whilst the Welsh Dragon was the subject of that on the right (which partly covered the further shield): a knot was place centrally above the shields. Those previously interested in these lands included Sir James Allan Park, Sir Francis Molyneux Ommaney Alexander Stewart and Sir John Kirkland.

The Agreement of 1876 was in consideration of the Agreement dated 4th July, 1871, for the sale by Mr Davies of certain lands to the original company in lieu of which he received two small pieces of land (each of 26 perches) adjoining the Trannon river crossing, the mining rights being reserved to the Master and Fellows of University College, Oxford.

The passenger traffic, which operated on weekdays only, comprised two mixed trains in each direction except on Tuesdays, when a further return journey was made. Two four-wheeled carriages fitted with handbrakes and built by the Midland Carriage & Wagon Co. Ltd, Birmingham, were provided. The first arrived in 1873 and the second in 1876, the carriages, which were composite second and third class, each comprised four passenger compartments with a separate guard's compartment; one carriage and a van were normally attached to each train. Passengers were certainly conveyed in open wagons on occasions. Second class passenger receipts averaged £1 annually, with third class returns ranging between £70 and £80 for the same period. In 1876 season tickets were introduced and produced £283 in that year.

A further 0-6-0 Manning, Wardle saddle tank locomotive arrived in 1877 another 'K' type, later CR No. 24.

By this date traffic, both passenger and freight, was falling away despite the facility of through bookings to Cambrian Railways stations and the inducement of excursion fares to Aberystwyth and Barmouth. Regular passenger services ceased in 1879, when third class receipts had fallen to £31 annually and season tickets were no longer issued. Special excursion trains were run once or twice a year in the 1880s. Ceiriog Hughes, who was particularly fond of children, continued to carry them in his van as they made their way to and from Manlledd school beyond the Van mines. Other passengers, too, no doubt found themselves carried in that friendly van.

The net profits of the railway in the half-year ended 30th June, 1882, were £114 14s. 0d.

The wedding of Ceiriog Hughes' eldest daughter, Delilah, was associated with the railway in a peculiar manner, for we read:

Sixty-seven years ago a wedding a special interest took place at Caersws . . .
The wedding ceremony took place in the old Parish Church at Llanwnog . . .
The wedding rejoicings were kept up in a typically Welsh rural fashion, and culminated in an all-night dance in what was then the locomotive shed of the Van Railway Station. A locomotive shed may not coincide with the modern idea of a dance hall; the sooty walls and oily environment at once spell disaster to the dresses of the

Driver John Aldridge leans out of the cab of one of the Manning, Wardle engines in this view at Caersws *circa* 1877.

A ballast train at Van about 1900; the engine is No. 25. The material was too dusty for much use, except for weed-killing.   *L. Bradley*

ladies, to say nothing of the boiled shirts and cuffs of the men of those days. But the ingenuity of Mr John Evans (the village builder and contractor of those days) solved the problem, for he and his workmen completely transformed the engine shed into a real Palais-de-Danse.

Walls and ceilings were cleaned down and whitewashed and a splendid temporary new flooring fixed. Chinese lanterns, flags, bunting and flowers helped to complete the metamorphis.

When the guests arrived they found everything spic and span. They included a number of ordnance surveyors from London, then conducting a survey of the country, and what they didn't know about 'keeping up' a wedding wasn't worth knowing. The band consisted of a famous Newtown family of musicians, Messrs Roberts the harpists, later to become the Royal Welsh Harpists after a Command Performance before Queen Victoria. The rejoicings went on into the small hours and Ceiriog's ready wit and amusing stories added to the fun.

Ceiriog Hughes died on on 23rd April, 1887, and was buried in Llanwnog cemetery. The passing of this patriarchal figure was a double loss to Wales, for it is related that he was acclaimed by no less an authority than the Revd H. Elvet Lewis to be 'one of the best lyrical poets in Wales' who had rendered excellent service to the National melodies of 'Cymru Fu' by writing words congenial to their spirit - a work which Robert Burns did for Scottish Melodies. To the World at large he is probably best known for his words to the great traditional air, 'Men of Harlech'. His years at Carnedd Villa are commemorated by a mural tablet placed there in August 1912.

In November 1887, it was proposed that the Van Railway be let to the Van Mining Co. Ltd on an annual tenancy, the mining company to afford all reasonable facilities for conveying public traffic. At that date the office of Secretary of both the railway and the Mining Company was held by Mr W.J. Lavington. The declining fortunes of the mines, and with them the railway, would appear to have brought the proposal to naught.

The mines spoil heaps had by now attracted attention as the ballast they provided was renowned for its weed killing properties and was in much demand by the Cambrian Railways Company. Ballast was removed in wagons of seven tons capacity at the rate of 12 wagons per day in June 1889. A further ballast siding at the mines was suggested in a letter of 11th August, 1889 from Mr David Davies (of Llandinam) to Mr Charles Clark, of 20, Great St Helens, London, EC. the siding, 350 yards in length, was in operation within three weeks; construction costs amounted to rather more than £100.

The Van Railway apparently felt that they could raise substantially the rates for this traffic, a course which led to much correspondence between the railway company, whose registered address was Dashwood House, New Broad Street, London EC, and Mr George Owen, Cambrian Railways Company, Oswestry.

On 20th July, 1890 Mr David Davies died at the age of 71 and the railway had thus suffered two grievous losses in no more than three years and three months. Mr Davies' extensive interests in the railway, mining and philanthropic fields are well known to all students of Welsh social history: suffice to state here that he was responsible for the building of the following railways; Vale of Clwyd (1858), Llanidloes & Newtown (1859), Newtown & Machynlleth (1863),

Right: The grave of Ceiriog Hughes, poet and manager of the Van Railway, in Llanwnog churchyard.

Below: This photograph was almost certainly taken at the unveiling of the plaque at the station master's house on the Van Railway at Caersws. The dignitaries are below the plaque with the surrounding guests. The Van train can be seen by the level crossing to the Carnedd Pastures. The plaque reads: 'John Ceiriog Hughes 1872-1887, Paid byth angohofio'th gartref, Na'th wlad, na'th iaith, na'th Dduw, Erected by the Cedewain Field Society August 1912'. The Welsh text translates as 'Don't ever forget your home, your country, your language, your God'. *Mrs Violet Rees' Collection*

Pembroke & Tenby (1863), Tenby & Whitland (1866), Manchester & Milford (Pencader to Aberystwyth) (1867), and the Van Railway (1871), a total of 144 miles.

It is not without interest that the village of Trefeglwys should have been the birthplace of the noted engineers, Robert Piercy (1825-1894) and his brother Benjamin (1827-1888). From their plans many of the railways in Mid Wales, including the Bishops Castle, were built, whilst the construction of systems in France, Italy and India came under their supervision.

About 1890 the mines suffered one of their periodical closures, whereupon the miners made for the coal mines which in those days absorbed all comers. The scanty traffic remaining to the railway was insufficient to enable profitable operation to continue and total closure was effected in 1893.

1894-1922

Years of dereliction followed until, by virtue of Section 24 of the original Board of Trade Certificate, an Agreement dated 29th July, 1896 was entered into with the Cambrian Railways Company under which the latter undertook to maintain and work the line for freight only. Thus the Cambrian reopened the line on 1st August, 1896, working it with the two Van locomotives of 1872 and 1877 vintage, which they renumbered 25 and 24 respectively. An additional locomotive was soon provided, No. 22, an 0-4-0 Manning, Wardle saddle tank built in 1901. Trains were run on Tuesdays, Thursdays and Saturdays only: the working of the two Caersws stations became the responsibility of the main line station master.

In 1905 a diamond drill was engaged to prove the rock below the then mines working area: a hole 1,150 feet in depth was bored, but failed to give encouraging results.

HRH Prince Francis of Teck visited the mines by rail in 1909. Included in the party accompanying the Royal visitor were Lord Herbert Vane Tempest (who was killed in the Abermule railway disaster of 26th January, 1921), Mr David Davies (grandson of the David Davies previously mentioned and later to become 1st Baron Davies of Llandinam), and Mr H. Lloyd, Mine Manager. The party travelled in a Cambrian Railways saloon hauled by No. 22, which ran bunker first to the mines. The four-wheeled, first-class saloon in question was numbered 9 in the Cambrian lists. Built in 1889, it was gas lit and of the following dimensions: length 23 ft 3 in., width 8 ft 0 in., seating capacity 12. The saloon was taken over by the GWR by whom it was converted and numbered 9218.

During the period 1899-1920 six different managers held sway at the mines, the largest number of men employed being about 200 in 1907. By 1912 the number had dropped to 150 plus a pit pony, which was brought to the surface each evening.

The two former passenger carriages lay derelict in 1912 at Pwll-glas and Caersws; the latter was still in evidence just beyond Carnedd Villa level crossing for a short period after World War I.

This posed picture *may be* of the Royal visit to the Van mines by Prince Francis of Teck on 3rd September, 1909. The locomotive is 0-4-0T No. 22, formerly Van Railway No. 2. The location is not Caersws because the engine shed is brick. There were sheds to the left of the terminus at Van just before the loading tunnel and this is likely to be the place the photograph was taken. The *County Express* reported that the Prince wore an alpine hat so he may be the man with the stick by the corner of the coach.

This view of No. 25 was taken *circa* 1910. The man with the moustache standing at the centre on the locomotive's footplate is driver Pryce Trow. *R.W. Miller Collection*

World War I saw the Government in control of the mines. It was rumoured the the pitch blends, mined about 1915, contained radium, but it failed to prove a commercial proposition. The mines were 900 feet deep, with the lead vein varying in width from four feet to a few inches. Mr T. Jones (of Llawryglyn) was in charge of the crushing and washing plants, which yielded about 20-30 tons of lead per week - blende was a secondary product.

Mr W.T. Fryer was station master, Caersws, 1910-1922, and during World War I heavy timber removals by rail were made from Trewythen.

The war over, lead mining was again in the doldrums and the mines closed in October 1920. The mines remained closed, though a new company, registered in June 1951, the Van Lead Mining & Smelting Co. Ltd, of Old Bond Street, London, W1, hoped to restart operations.

Another blow had been struck at the railway, but it survived to be absorbed into the Great Western Railway as from 1st January, 1923. It will be appreciated that although the Cambrian Railways Company was acquired by the GWR in 1922, the Van Railway was only 'worked and maintained' by the Cambrian and was therefore the subject of special legislation.

1923-1953

The GWR operated freight trains on Tuesdays and Fridays only, if required by Caersws station master. Everyday running was resorted to under the 'pilot guard' principle when ballast was being loaded at the Van mines.

Locomotive No. 824 - an 0-6-0 Manning, Wardle tank of 1864 vintage - was introduced to the railway by the GWR and was in regular use until the closure in 1940.

Cerist was the scene of an accident on 20th December, 1923, relieved by the bravery of the crossing keeper, Mrs Margaret Hamer. A train was shunting into the siding when a small boy darted across the track and, in her successful efforts to throw the boy clear, she sustained serious injuries, but survived to live for many years. Her selfless action was recognised by an award from the Carnegie Hero Trust Fund.

Traffic continued to decline, but was temporarily augmented in 1936/7 when a Llandinam timber merchant dispatched much timber through Cerist. This, however, proved to be the last flourish and on 4th November, 1940, final closure took place.

Lifting of the track at the mine end had taken place by March 1939, the line then terminating at the points to ballast siding. At this time all the lower mineworks buildings remained, some ruined, and a further set of buildings up the slope of the hill and opposite the white houses, together with chimneys at the north top, with the slope of the rail incline.

Lifting of the remainder began in early 1941 and was complete by July [as shown below], including the removal of three timber bridges:

0 miles 25 chains removed on 14th June, 1941.
0 miles 45½ chains removed on 6th July, 1941.
1 miles 18 chains removed on 19th July, 1941.

The Van station at Caersws in 1934, showing the locomotive shed beyond the platform.
R.W. Kidner

A Bridge Engineering Dept van formed from a Cambrian Railways composite/brake in the loop
at Caersws Van station in 1934.   *R.W. Kidner*

The ex-Van Railway engine shed at Caersws on 20th May, 1937.   *R.W. Miller Collection*

The engine shed at Caersws viewed from the rear in 1948.   *R.W. Miller Collection*

View of the Van Railway looking to Garth Road. The small whitewashed shed with chimney was the communal bakehouse and oven for the miners' terrace.

Powys County Council, Llanidloes Museum

General view of Van. The railway line can be clearly seen in the centre climbing the last few hundred yards to the mine. The tree in the left foreground obscures the first edge of the slime heaps.

Powys County Council, Llanidloes Museum

Garth & Van Road station in 1939; station house to the left, with the remains of the platform and Van Terrace beyond on the right.   *R.W. Kidner*

By March 1939 track had been lifted in the mines area; almost all buildings, however, were still standing.   *R.W. Kidner*

The Cambrian's second No. 22, a Manning, Wardle 0-4-0ST, on a train at the Van terminus about 1904. Note the shafts at top right, the main plant below the incline, and further processing buildings at the lowest level.

Cambrian Railways 0-4-0ST No. 22 and goods train on the first bridge leaving Caersws to cross to the Carnedd Pastures. The bridge crosses the Afon Carno, and an arch of the road bridge to Trefeglwys can be seen in the background.

The portion between Carnedd road crossing and the main line junction was left in place and handed over to the bridge maintenance engineers, Central Wales Division, the station itself being converted to an office. Various service vehicles were kept in the loop.

The mine was allowed to decay and the slope became obscured by trees, while much of the lower complex was removed. Later the piles of spoil which remained had prominent notices placed to point out that the material was toxic. In the late 1990s it was realised that the mine was part of Wales's industrial history, and the western parts of the lower works were landscaped and turned into a tourist 'attraction'. However, it is a remote spot and not many people follow the signpost to Fan (its Welsh spelling).

Locomotives

The locomotives listed are those that were most commonly in use upon the railway. It was the practice of all locomotives to take water from the River Carno by means of a pump and flexible hose.

The two original locomotives of the railway were unnumbered until taken over by the Cambrian Railways Company in 1896. They were 0-6-0 Manning, Wardle saddle tanks, works numbers 374 and 668, built in 1872 and 1877 respectively with the following principal dimensions:

Cylinders:	12 in. diameter x 18 in. stroke
Driving wheels:	3 ft diameter
Boiler pressure:	120 lb. per sq. in.
Heating surface:	356 sq. ft
Tank capacity:	250 gallons
Coal:	18 cwt
Length over buffers:	21 ft 6 in.
Total wheelbase:	10 ft 9 in.
Tractive force:	6,480 lb.
Weight in working order:	15 tons

When taken over by the Cambrian Railways, these engines were numbered 22 and 24. The former was scrapped in 1899, and some confusion caused by the introduction of another Manning, Wardle also numbered 22, built for the CR in 1901. This was frequently absent, working on the Elan Valley waterworks railway, and was sold in 1916 for Government service.

When the GWR took over, they allocated No. 824, the former Mawddwy Railway engine, fully described in Chapter Three, to work what little traffic was left, from Moat Lane Junction shed, though 0-6-0T No. 819 (former Lambourn Valley Railway) was also noted. [In the 1930s, see Chapter Seven, No. 819 was used in preference to No. 824.]

View of the Van lead mine *circa* 1875, prior to the sinking of the top shaft and installing of the double incline and footpath. The tramway serving the above ground complex can be seen in the centre. The underground system worked at various levels brought tubs to the shafts for lifting to the surface. The aqueduct carried water from a leat to a big wheel which powered pumps. It is believed the gantry/pulley system connected to a drum and water ballast incline for lifting tubs with galena ore from the lower level workings.   *Powys County Council, Llanidloes Museum*

The Van lead mine, possibly photographed shortly after it re-opened in the early 1900s. The chimneys indicate smelting, it is thought that the lead ore was shipped out for smelting elsewhere in the final years of operation until 1920. The sidings of the Van Railway can be clearly seen.   *Mrs Violet Rees' Collection*

The Van Mines

The Van area was prospected in 1850, and a small mine operated at Pen-y-Clun, north-west of Van, but it was not until 1865 that a major lead vein was found, at 60 ft depth, and work began on it in 1866. The Van mine was on three levels. On the uppermost were shafts and ventilating chimneys, and at the middle a 50 ft waterwheel working a long flat-rod which was connected to a dewatering pump in the shaft. At the lowest level were various processing buildings. A rail incline beside the launder which brought water from above to the wheel lowered the ore, which was crushed by power from two smaller water wheels. When the railway arrived, it terminated at two sidings at the mouth of a tunnel down which rails from the incline were extended, all on the lower level, which soon also became a vast dump of spoil.

C. Le Neve Foster read a paper on the Van Mine before the Royal Geological Society in November 1879. A feature of the mine was that owing to weak natural structure, levels which had been denuded of ore had to be filled with rock, trammed in from Manlled Quarry. The lead ore fell into trams, which were sent to the shaft bottom, raised in a cage, and sent down a self-acting incline. The ore was tipped into a Blake stonebreaker, crushed by Cornish Rolls until it could pass through a sieve with 12 holes per square inch. It was then carried by water to a pyramidical separator and treated in 'spray buddles'.

At that time the monthly production was 500 tons of cleaned ore and 150 tons of zinc blende. The average content was 81 per cent lead, also 9 oz. per ton silver. Before the Van Railway was built it went to Llanidloes or Caersws stations.

It is worth noting that in 1871 there were 10 mine companies using the name 'Van': Van Consols 1½ m. west, Van East 1 m. north, and Van United, Van Central and Van Great West some way away. The Cornish mine 'captain' John Kitto sponsored Wheal, New, North and South which worked for a year or so at unremembered locations.

The working conditions at the mines in the period 1880-1895 were very hard. Surface workers commenced at 7 am and finished at 5 pm, whilst underground workers operated two shifts (6 am to 2 pm and 2 pm to 10 pm). On Saturdays surface workers finished at 2 pm except on the monthly pay day, when work ceased at 1 pm.

Boys of 14 were amongst those employed and received 5s. per week, whilst adult pay for the same period was 15s. with some earning £1 for their six days work by an incentive scheme. Miners came from considerable distances, from Cardiganshire (Ystumtuen and Ponterwyd), Minera in Flintshire and even distant Cornwall, lead having been mined in these places previously.

Three levels were then being worked, viz: 75, 90 and 105 fathoms; the 60 fathom level had already been abandoned. The lead-bearing stone was like a huge pocket in the rock. Most of the drilling was done by iron bar and sledge-hammer, though at a later stage a compressed air drill was introduced. The firing was done with a length of fuse with a candle attached. The light in the mine was by tallow candle. The men used clay to hold the candles - some on their helmets and others on the side of the rock, indeed anywhere to which the clay would adhere. The lead-bearing ore was worked forwards and upwards and when it would otherwise have passed out of reach stone was brought in to raise the flooring.

Sludge and lime from the washing of the lead and stone were run off into reservoirs near Melin-y-wern, Van, and were not allowed to run into the brook. The reservoirs were emptied in turn and the contents directed beneath the railway and road to a field of Garth Farm.

Employment at the mine varied: there were 335 men underground in 1877, with 308 on the surface, whereas in 1892 there were only 40 men below and 15 on the surface. The ore was unusually rich in silver content, often 8 oz. per ton, and zinc being also present, the total value of extraction was often in five figures (*see Appendix One*).

However, following the 1901 sale, there was a collapse. The Van Mining Co. took over from former owner Col Pryce Jones, and output rose again, before a take-over in 1908 by Llanidloes Mining & Metals Co. There was then a further decline, but 135 men were still at work as late as 1913.

Miners pose for a photograph on the incline at the Van mine at an unknown date. Note the double incline, the hawser wire on the right-hand track and central rollers above the miners. This incline worked on gravity where the loaded wagon coming down hauled the empties up.	*Powys County Council, Llanidloes Museum*

Chapter Seven

Van Memories

Note: There is no v in the Welsh alphabet, f is pronounced as v and ff is pronounced as f; hence Ffestiniog Railway. So the line should have been Y Fan as are the signposts to the area now. The word is Man meaning a place. This mutates after the definite article 'y' and softens to f, hence Y Fan. The area is also known as Manledd.

Clerical help at Moat Lane Junction

Olwen Williams neé Bound commenced work at Moat Lane for general clerical duties in February 1942 and left in August 1956. There were a number of ladies, porters, cleaners, etc. during the war but Olwen was the only one to be offered work in 1945 and became the sole lady on the site with around 70 men.

The Van line had closed when she started work but she can remember the train as a child and has travelled the length several times. Olwen and several others would open the gates at Carnedd during the summer holidays. They hoped the guard would be Ewart Thomas and with luck, he would say 'Dus tee want a lift'. Olwen cannot remember any shuntings at the sidings so the first stop would be Garth Road. Ewart would tell them to stay in the van and they would watch the engine push empties and bring back full loads of lead waste. She never thought that within less than 15 years she would be checking Ewart's time sheet (see also Chapter Nine).

The Kerry engine continued to be serviced at Moat Lane through the war. It was in steam each day but only went up to Kerry three times per week; it was used for shunting etc. as there was much extra freight traffic to sort at Moat Lane during the war. The engine was one of several pannier tanks but around 1948, they started to use 'Dean Goods' and then around 1950, the Kerry line was serviced from Oswestry. Like everyone else, Olwen was very fond of Ewart Thomas, he was a great character and he worked mainly on the Kerry and Van lines. The firemen/drivers were just drawn from the rota of about five regular crew. If others were drafted in from Oswestry etc. for some reason, the regulars were used for the Kerry because it was not the easiest with gradients.

Dad's childhood home was at Ty'n-y-Celyn, which was a smallholding close to Red House so Dad would buy coal off Red House as they could never have used a truck load. This was common practice up to 1930 that the farm close to the three sidings of Pwllglas, Red House and Trewythen would buy the full wagonloads and resell.

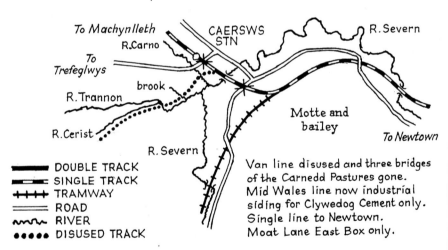

MINERAL LINES/SIDINGS/TRAMWAYS 1922

To Machynlleth

R. Carno

To Trefeglwys

CAERSWS STN

R. Severn

Carnedd Pastures

R. Trannon

Penstrowed

R. Cerist

MOAT LANE JUNCTION

Quarry Siding

Cambrian Line

Van Railway

Tumulus

To Newtown

R. Severn

Van line still in use.
Moat Lane Junction for
Mid Wales line.
Penstrowed Quarry Siding
Double line Newtown to Moat Lane

LLANDINAM STN

C.R. (Mid Wales Section)

To Llanidloes

0 ½ 1 ½ 2
MILES

MINERAL LINES/TRACKS OF DISUSED RAILWAYS 1966

To Machynlleth

R. Carno

CAERSWS STN

R. Severn

To Trefeglwys

brook

R. Trannon

R. Cerist

Motte and bailey

R. Severn

To Newtown

━━━━ DOUBLE TRACK
━▭━ SINGLE TRACK
++++ TRAMWAY
═══ ROAD
∿∿∿ RIVER
●●●●● DISUSED TRACK

Van line disused and three bridges
of the Carnedd Pastures gone.
Mid Wales line now industrial
siding for Clywedog Cement only.
Single line to Newtown.
Moat Lane East Box only.

By 2002 Moat Lane Junction was overgrown with only part of the platform and some smaller huts still *in situ*, the main road has been straightened which involved removing 100-yards-plus of Mid-Wales Railway trackbed.

Llandinam station was a private residence, the railway bridge over the River Severn at Llandinam had been removed.

Caersws had become an unmanned station, the passing loop and sidings had been removed.

In 2002 there were eight trains at two hour intervals operating between Aberystwyth and Birmingham (New Street) so 16 trains call at Caersws. On Sundays there were three trains in each direction.

The Coal Merchant and Caersws

Brian Poole did not really expect to find anyone with a direct connection to the line, which closed in 1940 but had been senescent for many years before. At the best he was hoping for someone from one of the family farms who could remember the train progressing through the broad valley or would find the son or daughter of one of the Moat Lane crew who took the train up the line.

Instead of finding weathered lead waste, the jewel now follows: Irene Morgan was born in Caersws in 1908. She was interviewed on 17th June, 2002. Her father was one of the local butchers. His wife was to inherit one of two coal merchants' businesses and so her father switched trades. Her parents moved to Cambrian Villa, which is close to the then coal wharf and very close to the Van junction. The 1916 school text from The *Story of Montgomeryshire* may help to understand the Van:

> The chief mineral in the county is lead. Between 1860 and 1880 there were 16 mining companies in the Pumlumon district and they employed over 4,000 men. At the Van mine alone 700 found employment. There are now less then 100 employed there. Output went from 100 tons per annum to over 4,400 tons and then the price of lead suddenly dropped and the mines were abandoned.

And that is the tragedy of the Van line built to exploit a Welsh Mountain bubble, share prices had little or no value.

Irene can remember the Van railway well and has travelled on it many times especially in the early 1920s. The line was only worked two days per week, certainly Tuesday and also Friday in the early 1920s. Three or four wagons would be a large load. Father would sell coal to farmers by the truck load (12 tons) and they in turn would share with neighbours. There was plenty of wood in the valley as well. Extra coal would go to the farm for the threshing contractor or a road roller if working in the area. Apart from Trefeglwys, there were really only isolated farms in the area. There were either no sidings or they were rarely used, such as Cerist, so procedure was as follows. Any coal truck would be placed behind the guard's van and would be unhooked and pinned on the track at farms such as Trewythen, Red House, Pwll Glâs and even anywhere between. The farmer who had ordered the coal had to unload it within about two hours before the train returned.*

Feedstuffs and fertilizer were also sent up the line by Montgomeryshire Farmers Co-op. Sometimes these goods had to be unloaded immediately by the trackside while the train waited. Irene can remember the farmers with their horses and wagons waiting. There was an experiment just after the GWR took over of using a horse to haul a coal truck along the very flat sections but it was too hard for the horse. Loads back were not common; there were wagons of lead waste, which were used as ballast because it had weed killing properties.

---

* Sidings existed at Trewythen, Red House, Pwllglas and Cerist Road and were operational until the late 1930s. The sons of farmers who used the sidings are quite clear that coal, slag and lime was usually unloaded at sidings with three days given to unload. Maybe Irene was confusing wagons being left at unstaffed sidings rather than not using the sidings. Her memory of the horse drawn experiment is correct. The bridges had a central plank put in for the horses. A horse was brought up from Newtown goods yard. The work was evidently too hard for the horse and the experiment was not continued.

An aerial view of Caersws *circa* 1958. The railway still shows the importance of the pick-up goods. Caersws station now has a single line and all the sidings have gone. The Van line can be seen curving away to the bottom right, it was used by the Bridge Department after branch closure and the line would have been lifted just beyond the right-hand corner of the picture. The ex-Van station and the engine shed can still be clearly seen.

Russel Bradley Collection

Maybe there was some traffic in wool in covered wagons, but the lorry or farmers' wagons delivery took any trade from the rail in the 1920s. The only other product carried was some timber. There was a run-round for the engine at Garth Road.

Irene's father would arrange that she could travel in the guard's van when their coal loads went up the line. It would not be fair for Irene to describe the journey from her memory except that it was really enjoyed. It really was a good outing. The guard's van was full of swap items such as pea sticks, rabbits, vegetables and eggs between Kerry, Caersws and the Van. The guard and the fireman sorted out the wagons because no railwaymen were employed on the Van.

The engine was more like a toy compared to the main line engines. The engine shed for the Van had closed before Irene's time so the engine was coaled, watered and serviced at Moat Lane. Edward Wilson (mother's brother) was the Moat Lane station master in the 1910s. The Caersws station master was a Mr Fryer and one of his sons, Reg, joined the railway and became the yardman at Kerry. Irene cannot remember the exact time of the train leaving and returning to Caersws but it took around four hours to do 14 miles so it was very slow. Towards the end, it would only operate if there was anything to take up or bring back and Irene believed that the Caersws station master had to authorise the journey.

Ewart Thomas was often the guard, certainly after passenger closure of Kerry. He did some days on the Van and the rest at Kerry. He was a character and a delightful man. The driver and the fireman were drawn from the Moat Lane rota and could be any of three to four crew. Ewart would often call in the coal yard to scrounge some milk. One autumn day, mother gave him some fat and the field mushrooms were fried on the fireman's shovel; the taste was delicious. She can also remember the train stopping and the driver, the fireman, the guard and herself gathering mushrooms where they grew in abundance in the late summer.

Irene had relatives, the Andrews, at the Goitre on the Kerry branch so she travelled many times to see them. She caught the Aberystwyth to Whitchurch train at Caersws and changed at Abermule. In the early 1920s, this journey could only be done on Tuesdays and Saturdays but she believed the GWR tried an improved timetable for a few years. Goitre Halt was a bleak place with no shelter to wait for a train in the winter. The Kerry guard's van was always attached to the coach; often several goods wagons would also be part of the train as well as the single coach. The tank engine was much larger and more powerful that the Van engine. The usual guard in the 1920s would be Ewart and he would collect and issue tickets at Goitre. His joke when asked for a single was 'I wish I was', which was a lie as he was happily married late in life to a lady from the boot department of the Newtown Co-op Store. They had no children.

Early in World War II , the line closed and was lifted except for the first 400 yards of curve from the junction, which became a siding. It died like it lived, hardly noticed at all. Irene cannot remember any livestock traffic; there were no loading facilities so farms from the Trannon valley would drive their sheep and cattle to Caersws market. Loading pens were close to the coal wharves and certainly Irene can remember the railway staff and the auctioneers' drovers loading stock when she was a child around World War I.

The line really had hardly any traffic. The company's main claim to fame was the Victorian manager and poet, John 'Ceiriog' Hughes. He must have had plenty of time to write. She is certain that many Caersws children must have got fed up learning his muse for eisteddfodau over the years. By the mid-1960s, the Moat Lane Junction had closed. The line to Newtown had been singled, pick-up goods ceased, Caersws coal siding closed and fewer coal merchants were now trading.

Irene Morgan qualified as a pharmacist but she returned to Caersws before commencing her profession due to her parents' poor health. She became an early example of equal opportunities because she became the village coalman! So she lived in the family home close to the Van Junction during the final few years of operation. Irene has a small book published detailing her memories of Caersws. It gives the names of many employed by the railway showing the importance of Moat Lane Junction. Harold Morgan was a signalman and he was transferred to Cemmes Road. He retired back to Caersws but has long since passed away.

Carnedd Pastures

Donald Hughes, born in 1932, was brought up at the family farm at Penstrowed, which is about 1½ miles east of Moat Lane. The main line was less that 100 yards from the house so Donald would often watch the trains with a child's fascination. During the war, long trains would struggle through with the extras of troop trains to Tonfannau and munitions trains including explosives from the ICI factory at Penrhyndeudraeth. Then early most mornings and late afternoon, a small pannier tank would pass through light engine, or with a few trucks and guard's van; it was the Kerry 'Jimmy'. Maybe when about six years of age, Donald saw two normal tanks and a little engine (the Van) all together early one morning clanging past and asked Dad why, and received the brief answer 'Kerry Sheep Fair today son'.

His wife Megan's father rented the Carnedd Farm house when Megan was a little girl. The Carnedd pastures are on the flat flood plain of Trannon on the first mile of the Van line from Caersws. Megan would cross the gated level crossing every day on the way to school. During the holidays, maybe the summer of 1939, the children would run along beside the train, the engine driver would toot and the guard would wave his flag. This would indicate how slowly the train travelled. Lewis Cozens' original volume mentions the date of the removal of three timber pile bridges between Caersws and Trewythen from 14th June to 19th July, 1941. Megan remembers the men dismantling the bridges and putting the piles beside the track and it was collected later by horse and cart and hauled away. The level crossing had warning signs of trespass but older people were annoyed that the bridges were removed for the rail track embankment became a walkway when this confluence of the Severn, the Carno and the Trannon broke the banks to flood several times most winters. The track bed remained weed free for many a year because of the lead in the ballast.

The Trewythen Siding

Roche Davies now lives at Trewythen Fach. He was born at Trewythen Fawr and the family now farms both lands. The line closed before Roche's childhood memory so he can only tell of the stories of his deceased father. The siding was used for both farms for coal, slag and lime until the early 1930s.

The bank edges by the Cerist are now as productive as the rest of the fields but Roche can remember lead toxicity would alter the flora for about three yards. This toxicity would show with barley that would struggle in competition with black grass.

The area of the siding is still intact; both the through line and the siding are a little drier than the flood plain and useful for feeding sheep. The Siding Lane leaves the road about halfway between Trewythen Fawr and Trewythen Fach. It is unusual in being almost straight so it would indicate that it had been built only 130 years ago for access. The siding length curves about 12 yards from the through track and there is about 30 yards length for the siding parallel to the track so maybe six wagons could be stored. The shunting would have been done on the way up to the Van.

Roche cannot really understand the generosity of the rail company putting in a siding for a land extensive operation such as farming especially as there were facilities at Caersws, Moat Lane and Llandinam around two miles from the farms. The low input, output of a pre-World War II farm would never generate such business; he could understand such a facility for a grouped resource such as a sawmill, a wool or feed merchant or a dairy factory, but a siding for a farm was generous beyond any reason.

Roche suggested that contact be made with a Dr Ithel Francis who was brought up at Trewythen Fach but is now retired and lives on the Wirral. Ithel was born in 1924. He attended the County School at Newtown and left for Liverpool University Medical School in 1941. Trewythen Fach was sold in 1942. Ithel confirms the goods and the use of the siding. The train would stop below the points and leave the guard's van and some wagons and then draw forward and complete the shunt. Often there was nothing to stop for; it would then continue to Red House and Pwllglas. The train would not stop on the return from the Van. There was a small hut. The field was known as Hut Field; this gangers' shelter was about 200 yards above the siding. Ithel and his friends would play and shelter in the hut as children.

In 1936, his father sold much timber, ash and oak, and Ithel helped extract the timber that summer. It was taken to the siding with a team of six horses and a timber carriage. The carriage posts acted as a bridge and the timber was rolled, levered and, if necessary, horse-pulled onto the truck. It was very hard work and many trucks left over the summer months.

The road to Red House and Trefeglwys was not metalled. It was potholed and either wet mud or dry dust. The side of the track was used for both walking and cycling. The River Cerist is dead straight and during flood the old course could still be seen. Ithel still enjoys returning to his home area and can still picture the Van 'donkey' working through the valley.

The site of Trewythen Siding in 2002. The through line is under the sheep racks, the single siding trailed back from the other side of the circular feeder.   *B. Poole*

Trefeglwys station in 1969; the level crossing to the right, and entrance to the goods yard at left.   *R.W. Kidner*

Mrs Mary Jones was born in 1914 and worked at Trewythen Fach on leaving school in 1928 until she married. Price Hamer, the linesman gave them a severe telling off for riding bikes along the line. In places, some of the side ballast had fallen away so they would cycle along the sleeper. Mr Hamer dug several holes between sleepers to try and stop this. Mary thought this was little unfair as one of the rides was on a Sunday to Gleiniant Chapel. Price was the husband of Margaret and they lived at Cerist. The lad injured by the train was the son of Price's brother Twm Pegleg (*see Chapter Six*). Margaret was helped by her two daughters after losing her arms at the crossing. Emily and Sally would take turns of staying at home or working on a local farm.

Mary's husband, Ieuan, was 11 years older and Mary recalled stories of Pwllglas. Ann Lewis from Top Ffalt would deliver coal, selling it in bucket loads from a donkey and cart. There was a weighbridge at Pwllglas. The husband's family home was at Y Ffatri (factory) which had been a tan house (local oak tannin was important) and then a wool factory. Hen taid (great grandad) had been evicted from the tied house for voting Liberal and they moved into the semi-derelict factory. The cottage further up the pant (valley) was bwthyn un nos, a shelter erected with 24 hours for squatters rights. This would be around 1860.

Both Newtown and Llanidloes were Chartist towns and the countryside was in turmoil with conflict between landowners and the established church against the tenants, farm workers and the non-conformist movement. A woodworking business was established and Mary's husband learnt the skill and was a carpenter at the Van mine from 1915 until closure around 1920. They were also undertakers and skilled carvers making both eisteddfod chairs and chapel carvings. The family lived in the area for the duration of the branch line and great grandad, born around 1840, may have travelled on it as a passenger in the 1870s.

It was a very hard life. Grazing geese were important for everyone in this tough upland environment. They were used for meat, goose grease as a food and a health ointment; the pin feathers made brushes and the down was used for duvet and mattress to try to keep warm on a winter's night. Mary can remember the preparation of 'teisen gwaed gwyddau'. The goose was bled, the blood collected and then heated in a bowl to coagulate and then mixed with oatmeal and dried currants. It was served either in a tart or as a dumpling. She found it revolting but there was little else to eat so she finally enjoyed it. It was considered a delicacy in the area and she helped to prepare goose blood tart in the late 1920s at Trewythen.

Red House Sidings

The story of Gwyneth Williams, her brother-in-law, Howell and a friend, Mona Lloyd, at Llwyn near Red House. Howell was born in 1933 and really cannot remember anything except the outline of a train. His older brother, Owen, died several years ago but Gwyneth can recall several of his stories. All the branch lines seemed to have very kind railway staff because Owen would be given a lift to Pwllglas and then either he would walk back or go on to school. This would be around 1935 and would indicate that the train then was going up to the Van around 9.00 am.

The family purchased about ½ mile of track bed from the railway around 1965 on the Red House farm. This trackbed was never ripped up; the higher linear ground above the flood plain is useful for feeding stock and a dry tractor route to adjoining fields. There is a wider section near Red House, which was a derelict siding. The River Cerist was straightened at the same time as the railway was built to help flood prevention. Howell thinks that some of the other lengths of the track bed may still be owned by the Rail Property Board or its successor, especially one or two large culverts.

The riverbed, maybe three miles from the mines, can still cause problems. If a JCB cuts into the silt too deeply, it will bring up dilute lead-based sediment, which will check plant growth on the stream edge for several years. There was one small area subject to flooding and it is only recently that the grass has started to look healthy; Howell's memory of it was virtually as a bare patch.

Mona Lloyd lived at the Van until six. Her grandfather was one of the foremen and died at the age of fifty-four. This early age is typical of those who worked with lead ore. Her memory is similar to that of Hywel Evans and Dai Cerist with stories of coal, lime and cattle feed in and lead waste out. She can remember Mr Hamer of the Cerist crossing coming up the line on the rail hand cart and thought that he was the line ganger and she can remember Margaret, his wife, who had no hands or lower arms because of the rail accident. Both Howell Williams and Mona recalled the German bomber of around 1940 which came down in the Trannon Valley towards Caersws dropping incendiary bombs. The joke was that they had bombed a strategic rail line that had just been lifted but the likely truth was that it was lost on the Liverpool route and was dropping the load to have enough petrol to get back home.

John Williams, Bronllan, Mochdre, older brother of Howell, Red House, Trefeglwys recalls his memory of the 1930s. The train time was Tuesday and Friday every week, sometimes there would be only two or three trucks, and it would be rare for more than six. No trains operated on three Fridays in late August/September as the little locomotive was taken to Kerry for sheep sale days. Although the engine usually hauled the train on both up and down journeys, there were days just before closure when the engine pushed wagons.

There was still a siding in use at Red House in the early 1930s, and at Pwllglas. Father would purchase one truck of coal each year from Morgans of Caersws and John can remember helping unload it into the horse wagons and thinking it was great fun. The wagon had to be emptied within a few days; if not there was a surcharge (demurrage charge).

Other goods in would still be slag and lime; it was not much sense to have a siding for about four to five trucks a year. The miller in Trefeglwys was already hiring a large lorry from Homer & Sons, which delivered either into his yard or direct to farms from Birkenhead Port. These lorries, sometimes with trailer, would pass the school and looked huge. Within a few yards of leaving Red House, John and his friends would cross the line, which had an ungated warning. There were gates to stop stock going on to the line, but they were set well back and did not act as a road barrier. Cattle and sheep were driven to Caersws; there was a market on the last Friday of every month. They could also be driven early on a Monday for loading onto the Welshpool livestock train. During the war, this changed to a grading system and usually stock would leave Caersws by lorry to abattoirs in Lancashire and the West Midlands. John still remembers the excitement of the little train passing the farm; it could be seen a long way both up and down the valley. It was sad to see the gangers lifting the track; it was all gone within a few months.

The Pwllglas Siding

Bert Owen, now 76 was brought up in Trefeglwys. He worked at Pwllglas first as a farm worker and then as bailiff for 45 years. The Van line had closed by then but he has childhood memories of the 'Donkey'. Pwllglas could have been the most important siding on the line for it served the village as well as the surrounding farms. Bert had been to the siding as there was a weighbridge there; this was with his dad. Also a load of planed wood of various lengths was delivered for the the school. Bert and several other boys went with the teacher; a farmer had provided a horse and cart. The wood was unloaded from a covered wagon and taken to the school.

The main agricultural merchant was J.R. Evans, Talgarth Mill, but in the 1930s the company started to use Homer Bros, a Liverpool haulage company so the railway lost that traffic. Another merchant, Edward Davies, had a depot at Pwllglas. The depot burnt down around 1931 and Bert can remember the flames. Unfortunately this company did not resume trading.

His father told Bert that Pwllglas was very busy around 1920 with trunk lengths when the Stokes Lone wood was cleared. Some of the wood was not replanted and is now the Cyll Farm. There is also a disused quarry in that area. Again around World War I, trains of 12 to 15 wagons would pass taking out lead ore. The other interesting point is that Bert would be wary of grazing heavily pregnant sheep by the Cerist after a flood because there would be an increase in lambs malformed at birth. The poisonous properties of lead were by now well known.

The gates were kept shut to stop sheep and cattle going on the line; the guard and fireman would open and shut the gates so Pwllglas Cottage had ceased to have a gate keeper within Bert's memory.

David Lewis, called Bert in his childhood, spent just over 12 months of his childhood in the Pwllglas Station House. Dad worked for the GWR at the Caersws Bridge Department. David would not have known the tenancy arrangement but assumes that there was some favourable arrangement between the railway company and one of their staff. The house was very small for a family with four children. David was born in 1919 and the family lived at Caersws; both before and after their short tenancy at Pwllglas during 1930/31.

The station yard was still being used for most of the goods coming into Trefeglwys and there would be wagons to shunt every visit. During the school holidays, the engine driver would always use the whistle both going up the valley and on return. This was with the hope that we would open the gates. One of us was always pleased to do this.

The lengthman was called Mr Hamer and he lived at the next crossing of Cerist. He had two vehicles for travelling the line. The first was a heavier four-wheel trolley with a see-saw pump. This could carry some stone etc. and would be seen with several lengthmen coming up or down the line when there was some work to do. The other vehicle was a light three-wheel unit almost like a motor bike and sidecar. This was used for inspection and was often kept at Pwllglas. In the centre, it had a seat, a pillion and a toolbox. The drive was pedal power. The boys knew where Mr Hamer hid the key and great fun was had along the line on a weekend. This contraption could really make a good speed. In retrospect, Mr Hamer must have known what they were doing.

Dad often worked in the engine shed of the Van Railway where bits and pieces for bridge repair were made. The children would often hide in the various sheds of the railway. In one there were barrels of cider waiting to go out to the farms. A railwayman came in without noticing the children. He had a bradawl and made a small hole, helped himself to cider and then hammered in a small plug.

David never travelled on the train. Mum would arrange to go down to Caersws to do her shopping. She would travel down in the guard's van and come back with Mr Hamer on one of his vehicles. Also Dad would give the guard some items in the morning at Caersws and the guard would give them to Mum a little later on. The children had learnt to swim in the pools of the River Carno and the Severn when living at Caersws. It was great fun to block the small bridge (now Van 16) just above the Pwllglas sidings until the pool was deep enough to have a swim. No one was really aware of the heavy lead pollution of the Cerist. The dam was then unblocked and the water surged away past the station.

The whole area of the Carnedd pastures could flood. The flood was observed because the children of the lower Trannon valley would be sent home early from Caersws School if the water were to rise rapidly. David and several of his friends saw a village tragedy. An older lady had taken her bucket to the Carno River to get water. The flood was strong and it whipped her bucket but she tried to hold on to the handle and slipped. The current was too strong and dragged the poor lady under the railway bridge of the Van. David rushed back to the station for help but it was too late and her body was recovered later further down the river (*see also next section*).

David spent a further year at Pwllglas after leaving school in 1935. He worked for Mr Edward Davies. The Davies buildings had been burnt down in 1931 so the store was now a new framed building. This small business of an Agricultural and Coal Merchant was economically fragile and was not to survive competition much longer. David was a big physical lad and he was paid a boy's wage for a man's work. There was a lorry delivering from the yard; the driver was a Tom Coates who lived at the Van. Most of the material for this business came in by rail. This may well have been the last general goods customer as others had switched to road transport. The covered wagons were parked by the depot. A small plank bridge was placed between the wagon door and the depot and a porter's trolley was used to wheel the goods in. Livestock feed was in 1 cwt hessian sacks. Grain was in 4 bushel railway sacks. Flaked maize and bran was easy to handle but wheat was very heavy. The worst item was bagged basic slag in small dense brick-like 1 cwt bags and always would leak an irritant dust down one's back when humping. The wagons would be moved, whether empty or full, a few yards along the track by using a crowbar in the spoke of one wheel. The siding was flat and it did not take much effort to get the wagon to roll the short distance for unloading. After all, there would not be another engine for three days. The coal wagons were parked closer to the weighbridge. The coal was weighed and bagged, loaded on to the lorry and sold around the village. Farmers did not buy coal from Mr Davies, but purchased a full wagon and collected themselves.

As soon as David was old enough, he took the opportunity to join the Welsh Guards in 1937, travelled away and gradually lost contact with the Caersws area. He now lives in Oswestry in a late Victorian or Edwardian house. There is a lovely fireplace with a magnificent mantle of polished black blue slate. Brian Poole wondered whether this was from one of the Aberangell quarries and had travelled down the Hendre-ddu tramway many years previously.

Left: All three of the gate crossing cottages have been attractively renovated as private houses. This view shows Pwllglas in 2002. The slate weather face has gone, the chimney was not safe and an extension added. The extension wall is plumb line vertical and the slight list of the original can be seen. The site of the sidings now form an attractive and extensive garden.

B. Poole

Below: The Pwllglas weighbridge cabin in 2002. It has been incorporated as a feature within the garden of Pwllglas Cottage. *B. Poole*

Cerist Crossing

David John Owen was interviewed at Bodlondeb, Llanidloes on 29th June, 2002. David John was born in 1919 near Machynlleth and his father moved to work at Lluestwen, Y Fan in 1930. The farm looked down on the Fan and had a sweeping view along the Cerist valley to the east. On leaving school around the age of 14, he worked on the local farms. One of the farms was Bwlch-y-Llyn just east of Cerist and in winter with tasks such as hedging or in summer the hay harvest. It was a break to watch the little train travel from Pwllglas to the Fan (Van). The only slight climb was between Cerist and Garth Road where the engine, always bunker first, made some smoke and noise as it laboured up.

David John moved to a house in Cerist close to the crossing on getting married in 1944. The line had closed by this time and he watched it slowly revert into the countryside over the years. He lived there for about 50 years until moving to a wardened flat at Bodlondeb.

Two trains a week, days uncertain, ran in the early 1930s; it would be four or five wagons for loads back of blende and lead sand and it was still taking up coal, lime, slag and covered wagons of feed and flour. By 1940, it would be two wagons return only of the lead sand ballast.

The line was gated at both Cerist and Garth Road. He had no idea of the arrangement; maybe a free cottage because a paid gatekeeper for two trains a week would have been expensive. The couple at the Garth was Tom Higgs and

A poor quality image of Cerist station cottage *circa* 1966.   *Elwyn Jones Collection*

his wife; they could have been semi-retired. The Hamers kept the gate at Cerist and since he worked as a permanent way man his wife opened the gates.

The Cerist was just a road crossing and the rail cottage. There was no platform but there was a little used siding. Both crossings were rough. The wagons behind the horse would really lurch and one could see lorries and cars almost bouncing. If coal or lime had been ordered, the trucks were shunted into the siding. Sometimes they had to be unloaded before the train came back. Usually they were there for three days until the next train. It was hard shovel work for 10 tons of lime and would need four horse-drawn wagons. David John has helped on this task. There was some timber loading both at Garth Road and Cerist. The timber was stacked near the Cerist crossing and the rail trucks were left in the siding to be loaded and collected three days later. Again in the mid-1930s, many of the lanes were metalled by a Newtown contractor (George, Jack and Sid Jones) and stone for the road and coal for the roller came up on the train. Then by 1940, traffic had almost ceased. The removal soon took place; nothing was left except the ballast; even the rails of the crossing were moved.

David John was involved in an accident with a threshing drum when feeding sheaves in. The damaged foot turned gangrenous so it was amputated. He took the chance to work with the then District Council as the rodent control officer; hence his nickname Dai Rats. Later on he worked for the roads section of the County Council until retirement. He thought it would not be easy to trace many other people who would have a direct memory of the Van Railway around the Cerist area. He could only suggest a Gwilym Davies who was born at Cerist and became a Moat Lane man working the Mid Wales line. He retired to Aberystwyth and would be around the same age.

Gwilym Davies has been found but it was his wife, Gwyneth neé Mills, who was the Cerist girl. Gwyneth only has a memory of the last few years of operation of the Van and by this time the Cerist siding was rarely, if ever, used. She thought it was unfair that the railwaymen would give her brother a ride up to Garth in both the van and on the footplate and she was envious. She lived in the house next to the Cerist crossing but in the late 1930s the guard or the fireman would open and shut the gate. Some said the line was like the river, dead. There was a ganger's hut and the children used to get into this and sit on the bench.

Gwilym Davies, known as Gwil Well Well, joined the army for World War II and returned on demobilisation to Llanidloes and Moat Lane so by the time he was courting Gwyneth, the Van line had gone. He trained as a fireman at Birkenhead then did time at Aberystwyth, on loan to Moat Lane and fired 'Castles' and 'Kings' from Wolverhampton. He qualified as a driver at Old Oak Common, and did the 'ups and downs' pulling carriages out for cleaning and pulling carriages in for the outgoing trains at Paddington. He returned to Aberystwyth and has driven on the Carmarthen line, the Aberayron branch, the Rheidol as well as the line to Shrewsbury including the 'Cambrian Coast Express'. From 1967 until retirement he drove the diesel multiple units (dmu) and diesel-electric locomotives from Aberystwyth to Shrewsbury. Gwilym can remember that one of his older friends, Llew James, fired the last Van train in 1941 that collected the rails.

The remains at Van lead mines in August 1952

J.I.C. Boyd

The Van Sidings

Hywel Evans was born in 1925 and has lived at Y Fan since he was five years of age. He recalled his childhood memory; the line closed as he left school for work in 1940.

The Van Terrace is just above the Garth Road station. The track crossed a gated road, went past the station house and then there was a combined storage and run-round loop. A single line ran further up to the foot of the Van mines. There were some complex shunts to get everything sorted out. There may have been more sidings earlier. The track ended in a tunnel, which had three holes in the roof at the foot of the incline. Loading was by tipping through the roof holes, which continued until closure. The material being carried out was lead sand, a sort of slag waste, which was used as fine ballast to control weeds. Two wagons were hauled out full and two empties were pushed back, so maybe up to 40 tons was leaving every week.

There was an additional loading bay at Garth Road in the loop; this was used for loading blende, crystalline gravel with a shiny sparkle. This was hauled in from the Penwar Mountain drift mine by lorry, a distance of just over a mile. Maybe two or three wagons were loaded each time, so the little train hauled out four to five wagons in total until the late 1930s. Hywel was not certain if the loop had shut before closure. If so, two or three wagons would be pushed all the way from Caersws to collect the final loads of lead sand ballast or rwbel.

There was still a small paint works in operation by the railway between Garth and the mine using local lead and baryte. Hywel can remember the machine noise and dust as the barytes were ground. He is not certain but the crushers and mixers were driven by belt pulleys and this would have been by a stationary steam engine earlier but could been a stationary water-cooled Lister-type engine by the late 1930s.

Most days, Hywel and his friends would have walked to the Van school through this little industrial complex. The engine could be heard pushing the wagons to the Van tunnel as the Van school was only about 200 yards further up the Cerist Valley. Some goods traffic was still coming in the early 1930s; there would be the occasional coal truck and a covered wagon. The bakery shop was opposite the Garth station and certainly Hywel has helped to unload and wheel sacks of flour across the road. The shop also sold maize, wheat and chick mash to those that kept a few back yard chickens. By the mid-1930s, a lorry carrier had taken this traffic. The other memory is of the inspection trolley coming in with the ganger pushing the see-saw handles to get the drive.

Hywel had some papers of the Arwystli Society (Arwystli is the Llanidloes Deanery similar to Cedewain for Newtown and Kerry) and the research of the late Cecil Vaughan Owen. This gives some idea of the Van lead mine. After about 10 years, a rich lode was found in 1865. Within the year the company had sold 40 tons, crushing machinery etc. was brought in and by 1868 100 tons per month were being produced. This had to be transported by road up and down some steep gradients to the Llanidloes railyard. Expansion continued and so a private railway was built from Caersws. The peak was in 1876 when 6,850 tons of lead ore was produced. Hywel's home, the Van Terrace, was housing for the

The remains of Van mines as a tourist attraction in 1996. This was the west side of the lower complex, the upper one being still hidden by trees. *R.W. Kidner*

The terminus and loading tunnel at Van in 2002. Much of the derelict mine was landscaped in the 1990s but certain features have been renovated. *B. Poole*

miners. The labour force peaked at over 700 and then the lead price fell. If the price or availability of lead lodes had remained, 700 miners plus their families and service staff would have created a township of 4,000-plus, and this could have justified the passenger service. So the line struggled on based on the lead waste ballast of up to 12 wagons a day. The mine re-opened in 1899, employed up to 160 men and finally closed in 1920 and so again reverted to taking out wagons of the lead sand ballast until closure.

When Lewis Cozens visited this site in the mid-1960s it would still have been a huge industrial scar of derelict buildings and lead waste. Llyn y fan (Van Lake) is still there. In 1946, Hywel can remember a partial burst and the flood carried much sediment and killed fish further downstream. There were several attempts to re-open but nothing was viable. The site became a nuisance with the noise and dust of scramble motor bikes. There were several accidents including drowning. A decision was made around 1990 to landscape, to fill in, to cap shafts and block drift mine entrances. Hywel knew the site so well that he had an extra job after retiring; first of all helping the planners measure and identify and then helping the contractors. The lead waste had been enclosed in huge plastic sheets, the site was scraped and topsoil was taken off several of the Garth fields. The result is that it is now greening over and blending back into the countryside.

Certain sites have been left such as the incline and the explosive storage shed. The octagonal chimney stacks have been repointed and the round dressing buddles and ore slide bases where galena was washed from the crushed gangue can still be seen. Part of the short rail track to the Van sheds is now the road and the Nant Cerist has been re-aligned. Settle beds of reeds assist in removal of toxic material and the stream now has plant, insect larvae and fish for the first time for 140 years. A visit to trace the remains of these mines is worthy of anyone's time. Another legacy is a number of virtually unknown footpaths used by the miners.

Further explanation will help with some of the terms:

Drift	Mine cut horizontally into the hillside.
Barytes	Barium sulphate used in paint, paper and photographic material.
Blende	The common ore of zinc.
Galena	The common ore of lead.
Gangue	(Rwbel in Welsh) Mixture of rock, calcite and galena as mined.
Lode or seam (coal) or Vein (gold)	Combination of ore and valueless material.
Shaft and level	Shaft to lodes where working level chambers were created. Needed pumps and winding gear, therefore stationary steam engines with need for coal traffic.

David (Dai) Jones was born in 1912 and has clear recall of the last few years of the mine operation. He can recall walking from Top Shaft (Brynlludw) to school both through and on the edge of the complex. Dad worked in the mine on maintenance and other duties and Dai has gone down one of the shafts with his dad. Edward Davies operated the steam winding gear for the cage; it really seemed to plummet down.

Dai can also remember walking to the Office House where the cashier Mr Edward Jones gave dad his wages. Dad died at the age of 50 of lead mining diseases. Men would move to the face soon after blasting with no respirators and poor ventilation. The poor men soon had lung problems compounded by the toxicity of lead.

There was not a daily train during the latter part of World War I. There were at least two and maybe three a week. The lead was loaded from a tunnel (still on site) and between 40 and 50 tons left each week. There were two sidings in parallel. Coal and anthracite trucks parked in the second.

Another long siding was on the Garth Farm side and this is where the blende stone from Penwar quarry was loaded. This was also where the ballast rubble was loaded until the pit closed. Then it was loaded at the tunnel. There was a run-round at Garth siding and any farm traffic such as farm food or lime would be parked here. The result was a loading of 12 to 18 wagons plus brake van would enter and leave most trips.

After leaving school, Dai worked at the paint factory for several years until it closed. Hydrated lime, coal and empty drums came in and the paint was dispatched by rail all over Britain. Maybe two to three trucks left every week either in a covered van or in a wagon covered with a tarpaulin. Humping full 10 gallon drums of paint on to the trucks was hard work. There was no siding by the paintworks, the last thing that the locomotive would do before heading back to Caersws was to place the trucks on the single line by the factory and pin the brakes down. After the mine closed, blende stone continued to come from the quarry. The change was from horse and cart to a lorry owned by Sidney Jones. Smaller parcels came from Llanidloes station ex-passenger train and there was a carrier service.

When the line closed, the rails soon were removed for scrap for World War II but the sleepers were left. These were pick-axed out and used for firewood. They had really set like rocks in the lead-based ballast. Ieuan Davis now lives in the Garth Cottage. He recalls the Cardiff University Medical School would test the blood of children of Y Fan every seven years to monitor any accumulation of lead and no one gave cause for concern.

First World War Letters from the Mining Company

The Llanidloes Museum had the bound copies of the correspondence of the Van Mine between 1915 and 1916. Much is routine ordering and selling; requests to settle bills and problems of labour supply because of military recruiting. The following is a sequence of letters between the mining company and the Cambrian Railways.

20th November, 1915, to Mr Fryer, Station Master, Caersws
We cannot understand why your engine has been up the line today in view of the fact that we particularly requested you that our ore is collected from here on Wednesday and we point out to you that this is Government work.

We urgently ask you to collect our ore tomorrow (Wednesday) and at the same forward and bring up the following:

1 truck of anthracite ex-Swansea Pwllbach Colliery
10 boxes of candles ex-GWR Bristol
2 Stone breakers (writing?) ex-Leeds H.R. Marsden Ltd
2 Barrels Oil ex-Liverpool

23rd November, 1915, to S. Williamson, Cambrian Railways, Oswestry
Notwithstanding our urgent request to your stationmaster at Caersws following our letter that our ore is collected from here on Wednesday, the engine has been here today and the guard says he does not know when it will be up again.

We enclose copy of letter sent by this office to the Caersws Station Master and instruct you that the engine comes up tomorrow as the forwarding of our ore is most important.

26th November, 1915, to S. Williamson, Cambrian Railways, Oswestry
I have your letter of the 24 instant. The point of my previous letter seems to have escaped you. I wish to draw your attention to the fact that your engine came up here on Tuesday whereas I have previously advised your stationmaster at Caersws that we require ore to be collected from here on Wednesday.

There is surely sufficient traffic to warrant your sending the engine up here two days per week and the request is that Wednesday should be one of these days and that we are supplied with a ten ton empty so that we can have it loaded for your engine each week on Wednesday.

[Whether the problem was resolved or not, the following letter shows a happier man at Van:]

10th January, 1916, to Mr Fryer Stationmaster, Caersws
Would you see that our coal supplier can forward on time to deliver here on Wednesday and that the trucks are brought up that day. The following goods are also on the line and we are in immediate need of them:

1 barrel cylinder oil
1 barrel tram grease
1 cylinder of detonators

Please send us an extra ten ton wagon and tarpaulin on Wednesday and we will arrange to load it while the engine waits.

19th July, 1916 to Mr W. Fryer, Stationmaster, Caersws
The TVR [assume Taff Vale Railway] wagons which left here yesterday are not suitable to load as the sides are much too high for loading.

We will have 8 ton wagon of loaded lead ready so please collect and at the same time please deliver any coal, oils etc. which you may have on hand as are in urgent need of oils.

Please arrange to let there be one empty wagon and sheet left at the mine to facilitate arrangements for loading up lead ore. At the moment we have no empty wagons on hand and are relying on you sending up two.

[There were two sources of coal. One was anthracite from Pwllbach, Swansea and the other was coal from a Liverpool wholesaler. The anthracite was for the suction gas plant. One letter requests the Liverpool Company not to supply for two weeks, as the mine would close for general maintenance. So the little railway did the best to supply materials and to take away the ore for smelting during World War I.]

A Railway Walk in 1938

Mrs Pat Gibson has purchased a bungalow which has been built on the track of the Van Railway as it entered the Carnedd Pastures on the outskirts of Caersws. For many years, she had wanted to live in the area. When her father called, he could immediately recall a holiday in the area in 1938 and found a photograph taken. This photograph is now enlarged, framed and is hung in the bungalow. The first field with a length of maybe 150 yards is part of the property and the track can clearly be seen. Her partner, Lawrie Woodhall, notes the way that sheep will rest on the old track rather than the dampness of the pasture. He has seen severe flooding where the higher ground of the bungalow virtually becomes an island as the flood water of the Trannon and the Carno backs up from the Severn.

Ted Lardner, her father, now retired at Dulverton in Somerset, remembers the walking holiday back in 1938. The walking part was a rump group from the Birmingham University Club and this was a year-end event about two weeks after degree day. The train brought them to Church Stretton and they walked, or caught a bus or took a train between various hostels in a circular tour including the Elan Valley near Rhayader. There are many interesting points in Ted's letter on the walk but the following concerned the Van only:

The Caersws-Van railway never quite got lost in my memory. We would often travel through Caersws on the way to holidays in Snowdonia. It is astonishing that our daughter, Pat, has a bungalow on the line that we walked so many years ago. We took a bus from Montgomery to Newtown and stopped in the Youth Hostel. Next day we walked to Caersws and from there took the railway track to the hostel at Van. This had looked like a very attractive alternative to a lot of road walking but by the time we arrived at Van, we were heartily sick of it. There was no way of finding an easy walk way on the track. The ballast had shifted badly and both sides of the so called permanent way had crumbled away and it was nearly impossible to walk on. The obvious alternative was to walk on the sleepers; taking care not to drop between where there were often deep gaps filled with water. To walk over six miles on such a track was fatiguing and extremely boring. No one had looked up anything about the railway but we did speculate about whether it was still in use and there was no sign of any wagons. As the metallurgist in the group, I was expected to make some judgement on the surface condition of the rails. I recall that I said it seemed that some very light traffic must be used occasionally because of the marks on the rusted surface; it must have been a very light weight motive power and I suggested it way be horse drawn. It had been a very wet few days and our leader consoled himself that we had kept our feet dry for some of the adjoining fields were waterlogged. After the night at Van, we walked to a little country station (Dolwen?) and caught a train to Rhayader.

It would be difficult to repeat this walk in 2002. Much of the bank of the line is intact as it follows the Afon Cerist all the way to the Van and has become field boundaries. However it is now farming land; it is not a permitted path. Lanes and roads closely follow the route. The purchase of a local OS map would enable anyone to observe the line. The few bridges and level crossings are no more; however, the station building is still in the yard at Caersws. Ceiriog's house, a short distance on the B4569 from Caersws station, has a plaque on it and the three keepers' cottages at Pwllglas, Cerist and Garth are well preserved as private houses. Brick culverts can be found often heavily silted up. A walk from Garth to the mine at the Van can be taken; the road and the stream have been realigned but the final 100 yards curves into the tunnel where loading took place; and these are the remnants of the Van Railway.

Firing the Van Engine

Ewart Gruffydd Jones (Griff) was born in Caersws in 1920. He passed the scholarship to Newtown County School and completed his education in 1936. He had been accepted for both the railway and the RAF. Most railway jobs went within families and he decided, with some advice, to be the first of his family to be a railwayman. He joined the GWR as a cleaner at Moat Lane Junction. His first duties were working nights preparing, cleaning and coaling up. This would include the Kerry and Van engines as well as the early goods to South Wales, the Brecon Mail and the school train plus several other locomotives such as a banker working back to Machynlleth. The chargeman was Bert Davage, a Bristol man, and he was quite hard on young staff. Bert was a very keen cricketer. Engine shed work could be very cold so Griff and his pal would get Bert to talk about his beloved game so they could spend more time in the warmth of the mess room.

The Van engine was then No. 819. There was also No. 824 on standby for both the Van and replacing the stationary steam engine which was used to pump water into the large tower. Coaling the stationary steam engine was a miserable job. Therefore No. 824 was kept cold and only brought into use if No. 819 had to go to Oswestry works. The Kerry engine was a pannier, an ex-Dean saddle tank and there were several that could be used. The daily duty was to clean out ash, light the fire and build up heat ready for the morning, load coal then clean and oil the engine. The firemen would take over and complete the filling of the water tanks, check and take out for duty. The Van engine was normally left cold on the day not working but the Kerry pannier was normally steamed each day as it was used for shunting. It would shunt at Caersws early in the morning prior to Kerry duties.

After several years, a junior cleaner could cover for a fireman due to absence or illness. One could be upgraded for a week and finally permanent upgrading occurred. Griff is almost certainly the last man in this country who would have worked the Van line for the twice-weekly service. After World War II, there was an offer for drivers in South Africa or Rhodesia and one of his friends took up this option and may still be alive.

Caersws was a railway village, the parish was Llanwnog but the bulk of the population had been in Caersws since the opening of the railway. Maybe 80 were employed at Moat Lane Junction with engine crews, cleaners, gangers, clerks, etc. while the Bridge Department was based within the Van junction and former engine shed and station. The Bridge Department served a wide area of Wales and the Marches and maybe a further 80 staff were employed here as well as sub-contractors. The Bridge Department in 1939 was still responsible for several bridges between Llanidloes and Llangurig, this line* was never completed, and so only contractors' engines ever used it.

The journey with No. 819 would start at Moat Lane, bunker first with empty ballast wagons, and empty wagons for pit props and on rare occasions, coal, lime or slag. A guard's van would be attached; this could be any from Moat Lane. Only the Kerry line had a specific van stored at Abermule with extra braking, weights and strong linkage. The train would cross the level crossing by the Llanidloes-Caersws road junction, then over the Severn bridge to the Caersws junction. A token was required for this short journey and the brake van had to be at the rear.

* The aborted Manchester & Milford Railway running from Penpontbren Junction.

The signalman at Caersws gave permission to enter the Van branch. The locomotive would shunt as required at the Bridge Department and then make up the arrangement to go up the Van line. The run-round loop was on the right-hand level side as the train entered the lower Van mine complex but most of the sidings had gone. The ballast, the sleepers and everything was decrepit and falling apart. Even this loop had ceased to be in place or functioning in the last few months in 1940, so the engine pushed and pulled as necessary to the siding.

The train proceeded over the River Carno bridge to the Carnedd crossing where either the guard or fireman opened and shut the gates. All gates at Pwllglas, Cerist and Garth were now operated by the train crew; there were no longer any gatekeepers. It would now be rare to use Trewythen or Red House siding, it was also uncommon to use Pwllglas. The remnants of a low platform could be seen at Garth but Griff cannot remember using the siding. The little engine proceeded slowly up the valley with the Cerist brook parallel to the track, sometimes on the left, sometimes on the right as bridges no bigger than large culverts were crossed. Cerist was used for loading pit props. Sometimes this would be the only goods in the final months of operation and this is as far as the train would go that day and would then propel back to Caersws. The line was on a very slight gradient with the fall of the valley from Cerist until Caersws. It did not tax the engine and it could glide back. The gradient started just before Cerist and continued to the Van terminus. Stops would have to be made at Cerist and Garth to open and shut the gates. The Van was still being used to collect the lead ballast but, by 1939, this loading was being phased out. Sometimes only two empty wagons were taken up and two full ones brought down. No one was seen at the sidings and sometimes the train crew wondered whether ghosts unloaded and loaded the wagons. The return was made back to the Caersws bridge section where the train was formed with engine, goods and brake van; the token obtained and permission was given to work back on the main line to Moat Lane Junction. Some days, the train would not run, as there was nothing to take up or collect. Traffic was so light, it was far easier to deliver by lorry from either Caersws or Llanidloes, and therefore the railway company had little choice but to close the facility.

Griff also took his duties on the demolition train. This is a memory of over 60 years ago and it is difficult to recall. The engine propelled all wagons to the point where the track was being lifted. The train went up according to demand and could be more frequent than twice a week. On some days, the engine stayed with the trucks so the gang was taken up by train. The steel was used for resmelting for munitions. The guard's van was placed between the engine and the wagons at Caersws and the whole lot was pushed up. Sometimes the van was left and all the demolition gang had to do was unscrew the brake and move a little further down to Caersws consuming the steel behind them. Sleepers were brought down by trailer to each of the sidings in turn for loading. It was all done by hand and some sleepers were almost soldered to the ballast and were left. The train waited when the sleepers were loaded. Dismantling only took several months. The little engine was stored at Moat Lane and never heard of again. The gang completed demolition by removing the structure of the three bridges of the Carnedd pasture levels.

The little Van locomotive was very restricted with a very small grate area. There was not much space in the cab and the small outside coal bunker fed into two boxes either side of the cab. It was not a good steamer and not a good ride; it truly was a vintage engine. Griff has been on it up to Kerry when there was non-availability of a pannier tank. Two full wagons and the brake van was all it could manage on steep gradients. The only reason for its longevity was the low weight which was necessary for the light rails and poor condition of the Van. The usual guard was Ewart Thomas. The line was unstaffed which was such a contrast to the warm welcome from Mrs Fryer that awaited the crew when the train arrived at Kerry.

Griff can remember Mr John Spoonley who gave some reminiscences to the local paper in 1940 when the Van closed. John had retired as Head of the Bridge Department in 1934 and was a well-respected railwayman. Another name associated with the Van was the Aldridge family. Griff's mother told him that John came in from Kent when the Van opened and drove the first train up. His son became one of the main drivers in the early part of the 20th century and finally, his son, a Tom Aldridge, would have been one of the last drivers. Three generations served the Van.

Griff knew the Van line which was just across the fields as a young boy. He and his pals would walk the line on a Sunday heading and kicking a football between them. It was the only dry place to practise during a very wet spell. Caersws altered as the railway expanded in the 1860s. It has left a legacy of surnames for not only are there the common Welsh names of Davies, Jones, Humphreys with Christian names such as Gruffyd, Emrys, etc. but also Claffeys, Shones, Aldridges, etc. came in during this period of expansion. Gruffydd retains lovely memories of Caersws, when it was a working railway village, from his childhood and his early railway career.

The Aldridge Family, three generations driving the Van

Bill Aldridge is the sole surviving grandson of John Aldridge. Bill was a close friend of Gruffydd Jones when they were children in Caersws. Bill was born in 1921. He opted not to join the railway but worked in local government. He is now retired and lives in Welshpool. His daughter, Margaret, kindly helped with the interview.

The family bible shows that Charles Aldridge, born around 1810, had married Sarah. Both were from Great Wigston, Leicestershire. There was a large family of eight or nine children. The first was born at Leicester in 1835, and then others were born in Kent, Solihull, and Hereford and finally the last child was born in Suffolk in 1857. John was born in Nettlestead in Kent. Great grandfather Charles had started as a yeoman farmer but was thought to have diversified into railway construction at foreman/manager level.

There is no evidence that Charles came to Caersws but his son had learnt the skills of railway construction and came to Caersws around 1869 and one of his duties would have been to drive the contractor's engine. Therefore John opted to join the Van company and became their first engine driver and also trained others. John married Mary Gough and they moved into Carnedd Villa (Ceiriog's house), after the death of Ceiriog. They had five children including Thomas Henry

Right: John Aldridge and his wife, Sarah. John came to Caersws with the contractors and stayed to drive the first engine in 1871. Their children included Tom and Charlie, who was one of the guards. John worked for both the Van Railway and the Cambrian Railways.

Above: Tom Aldridge (senior) followed his father's footsteps as one of the Van drivers, first based at Caersws Van shed and then from Moat Lane Junction. He worked for the Cambrian Railways and then the GWR. He married Mary, they had three daughters and six sons. Five of the boys joined the railway.

Right: Tom Aldridge (junior) would have been one of the last drivers at Van in 1940. He became a regular driver on the Kerry branch throughout the 1940s until closure in 1955. He married Beryl late in life and they had no children. His career spanned the GWR and British Railways. All these family portraits are from Bill Aldridge of Welshpool, the sole surviving brother and the only one not to work on the railway.

Aldridge (Tom Senior) born in 1878 and died in 1934. Tom worked for the three companies of the Van Railway, the Cambrian and the GWR. Bill can remember the childhood story of Tom being involved with the train that took royalty to the Van before World War I. Another brother, Charles, may have been a guard.

Tom Aldridge and his wife had nine children, six boys and three girls. Five of the boys joined the railway at Moat Lane. Tom Aldridge (Junior) was born in 1913 and died in 1985. He would have been one of the last drivers on the Van and was also associated with driving on the Kerry in the 1940s until the conclusion. Sidney worked in the Bridge Department; Jack became porter/clerk etc. at Caersws. Charlie became a station master on a number of stations in Mid Wales and Arthur became fireman at Moat Lane and continued to live at Caersws after the Mid Wales Brecon line closure when he became a river bailiff. The mother of this large family died at the birth of Arthur in 1930. Bill recalls that the older boys and sisters all helped to keep the family together. Dad had taken on the railway tenancy of Carnedd Villa. Bill can remember being scolded for throwing a ball against the wall where the plaque for Ceiriog was fixed. Bill confirmed the tragedy of Aunt Edith born in 1873 and died on 16th November, 1929. Poor Edie was drowned in the Carno Brook when attempting to collect water in a bucket when the river was in full spate.

Bill did go with his father on the Van donkey. He has travelled both in the cab and in the guard's van with Ewart when he was a boy of around six years of age. He would not remember any details except the excitement of the treat. There were photographs within the Aldridge family history showing grandad and dad with the Van train but they have been lost. A lady had called many years ago (1930s) and collected copies from one of the aunts and these may be some of the photographs shown in railway history books. Bill kindly lent the family portraits so the three generations can be recorded for posterity.

The Van engine shed at Caersws is now a listed building, it is seen here in 2002. It is now on the premises of Powys Farm Services. *B. Poole*

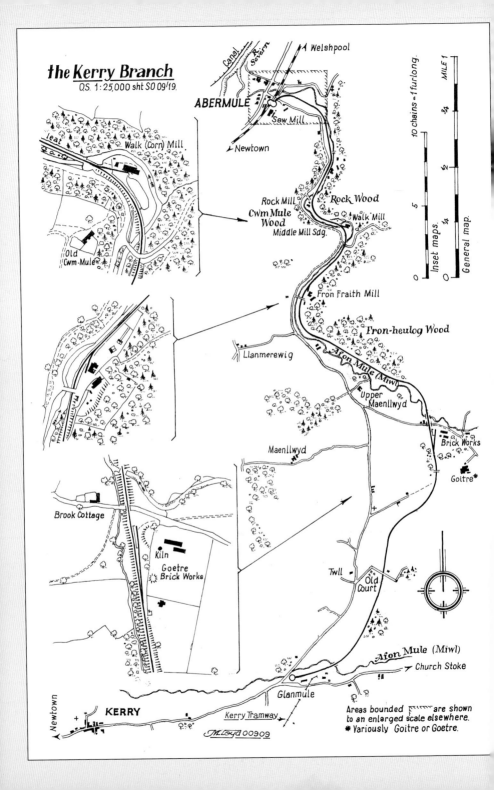

Chapter Eight

The Kerry Railway

The opening of the Llanidloes & Newtown Railway in 1859 was followed by further early local railway construction, the Newtown & Machynlleth Railway (opened in January 1863) and the Oswestry-Newtown Railway, authorised by Act of 26th June, 1855, and opened through out in 1861. This caused Mr John Wilkes Poundley, of Kerry, to press for rail connection for the village, and the construction of such a line was authorised under the Oswestry-Newtown Railway Act of 17th May, 1861:

> To enable the Oswestry and Newtown Railway Company to construct additional lines of railway to Llanfyllin and Kerry.
> It shall be lawful for the Company to make and maintain the following railways, with all proper stations, works and conveniences connected therewith, respectively, that is to say:
> A Railway commencing by a junction with the Oswestry and Newtown Railway, at or near the Abermule Station of that railway in the Parish of Llanmerewig and County of Montgomery and terminating at or near the village of Kerry in the said County of Montgomery.

It was largely due to Mr Poundley's enthusiasm and ability that he should have succeeded with his plans to secure rail communication in an area which to this day is thinly populated. The famous Kerry Flock sheep were started by Mr Poundley and thus Kerry is well known in all parts of the World. A yearling ram, 'Winsbury Joyful', secured the record figure of 405 guineas at the Kerry Hill sheep sale at Kerry on 6th September, 1952.

Construction of the railway through the narrow confines of the Mule gorge and so to more open countryside beyond was completed early in 1863 and led to the opening of the line to public traffic on 2nd March of that year.

Monday 2nd March, 1863, witnessed the inaugural train with a locomotive hauling a single carriage up the steep incline from Abermule to Kerry. The promoter, Mr J.W. Poundley, was of course an important passenger, whilst accompanying the driver on the footplate was his son, Mr John Edward Poundley. After several stoppages to make steam, Kerry was reached, where the train was received with cheers and the promoter offered personal congratulations by the assembled guests. On the following day a truck of coal was attached at Abermule for distribution amongst the poor of the Kerry district.

In July 1864, the Cambrian Railways Company came into being by amalgamation of the following railways: Llanidloes & Newtown, Newtown & Machynlleth, Oswestry, Ellesmere & Whitchurch, Oswestry & Newtown.

As part of the last named railway thus did the Kerry line lose its identity. The Cambrian in its final form successively secured, in addition, the Aberystwyth & Welsh Coast Railway (in 1865), Mid Wales Railway (1904), Vale of Rheidol Railway (1913) and Tanat Valley Light Railway (1921).

0-4-0ST No. 36 *Plasfynnon*, with the branch train, poses for the photographer on the bridge over the River Mule just outside Kerry station c.1903. Glanmule weir is in the foreground.

R.W. Miller Collection

In these early days Abermule main line station boasted four up trains and three down trains daily, with two in each direction on Sundays. The provision for trains on the Kerry Railway was of similar weekday proportions: no Sunday passenger trains ever ran to Kerry.

Traffic has always been dealt with by a single main running line with run-round loops at Abermule and Kerry. The stations, Abermule and Kerry, together with the halts, Fronfraith and Goitre, were provided with siding accommodation.

Chaired track was in use and the services were operated on the principle of one locomotive in steam or two coupled together. The train staff was triangular in shape, red, marked 'Kerry Branch', and equipped with Annett's key for operating the several ground frames.

Until 1931 Kerry boasted a station master, but on closure to passenger traffic the branch was placed under the supervision of the Abermule station master.

In passenger days trains were subjected to a speed limit of 9 mph: from 9th February 1931, the limit for freight trains was 5 mph.

The failure to attract passengers was due primarily to the tedious roundabout rail journey to Newtown via Abermule as compared with the direct and cheaper approach to the market town by bus. Services between Newtown and Kerry (and beyond) were operated by the Mid-Wales Motorways Limited (of Newtown) on both weekdays and Sundays. This company was formed in 1937 by the merging of local operators: bus services have run between Newtown and Kerry since about 1930. There are no bus services between Kerry and Abermule.

Normally trains were 'mixed' with a single four-wheeled carriage meeting passenger requirements, for whom two classes only were provided - first and third. This carriage had four compartments (one first and three third; both classes were upholstered) and it was lit by four oil lamps. The words 'Kerry Branch' were painted above the waistline between the central compartments. The carriage was numbered 84 in the Cambrian list (built by Midland Carriage & Wagon Co. in 1872, withdrawn in 1922). First class travel ceased during World War I. The guard used a separate van, which bore the legend 'Cambrian Railways Kerry Branch' in two lines.

Passengers at Abermule and Kerry obtained their tickets at the booking offices, but the guards issued tickets to those joining at intermediate halts. Passengers at Fronfraith were provided with their own signals for stopping trains.

The railway settled down to a quiet, steady existence for the first quarter of a century of its life until the owner of the Brynllywarch Estate, Kerry, Mr Christopher J. Naylor, who was a keen and very successful forester, visited Canada in 1887 and returned to add considerable revenue to the line.

The station masters at Kerry from the 1880s to 7th February, 1931, were successively:

Messrs Eagles, F. Newell (1890 till the early 1900s), W. Rowlands, Edwin Jones and finally R. Bennett (June 1917 till 7th February, 1931).

A posed photograph of 0-4-0ST No. 36 *Plasfynnon* at Kerry in the 1890s. Coach No. 23, behind the locomotive, was built by Ashbury in 1860 and was withdrawn by 1900. At the rear is brake van No. 37, this vehicle survived into GWR days and was withdrawn in 1926. The guard's van was always attached to the passenger train because of the steep gradients on the line.

R.W. Miller Collection

Plasfynnon with a mixed train at Kerry in July 1904.   *J.I.C. Boyd Collection*

The timetable for July, August and September, 1903, was as follows:

	Weekdays						
Down	Mon. & Sats. only			K	Tues. only		
	Pass.	Mixed	Pass.	Pass.	Pass.	Mixed	Pass.
	am	am	noon	pm	pm	pm	pm
Abermule	7.25	9.40	12.00	1.20	2.40	4.45	8.55
Middle Mill Siding	–	–	–	–	–	–	–
Fronfraith Siding	–	–	–	–	–	–	–
Goitre Siding	–	–	–	–	–	–	–
Kerry	7.50	10.05	12.25 pm	1.45	3.05	5.10	9.20
Up	am	am	am	pm	pm	pm	pm
Kerry	6.50	8.40	11.20	12.45	2.05	3.50	7.00
Goitre Siding	–	–	–	–	–	–	–
Fronfraith Siding	–	–	–	–	–	–	–
Middle Mill Siding	–	–	–	–	–	–	–
Abermule	7.15	9.05	11.45	1.10	2.30	4.15	7.25

Notes: K   From 25th July to 12th September inclusive.
Pass.   Passengers only. (Officially. In fact usually 'mixed'.)

Middle Mill Siding disappeared from the Working Timetables shortly afterwards.

The leisurely progress of the trains naturally caused the railway to be the butt of local ribaldry and it became known as the Kerry 'Express', the Kerry 'Donkey' and the Kerry 'Jimmy'. In a series of photographs *Plasfynnon* is shown at Kerry with the caption 'The Kerry Express No Hurry or Worry', whilst the same locomotive is hauling a mixed train to the title 'Kerry Express Full Steam Ahead'.

In 1905 *Plasfynnon* followed *Mountaineer* - an occasional Kerry visitor - to the scrap heap and was succeeded by No. 35, an 0-6-0 side tank purchased from the Lambourn Valley Railway (Berkshire). No. 35 was relieved from time to time by the second No. 22.

In the early 1900s Kerry witnessed the removal of a remarkable old frame type point indicator situated at the Goitre end of the station: a movable blade at some distance above the ground gave indication whether the points were set for the sidings or platform line. It was of a type favoured by the Great Northern Railway (of England).

The 1903 Timetable quoted represents high water in the passenger services and by July 1912 only three trains daily in each direction were being run, viz:

	Weekdays		
Down	am	noon	pm
Abermule	10.15	12.00	4.30
Kerry	10.40	12.25 pm	4.55
Up	am	am	pm
Kerry	8.55	11.20	3.50
Abermule	9.20	11.45	4.15

Above: Abermule station in March 1948 looking towards Welshpool. The Kerry branch veers away to the right.
J.I.C. Boyd Collection

Right: A slotted-post signal just outside Abermule on the Kerry branch in March 1948.   *J.I.C. Boyd Collection*

World War I witnessed increased activity, particularly in freight traffic. The resurrection of the Kerry Tramway (*see Chapter Ten*) in 1917, with its attendant timber felling for the provision of pit and trench props, brought additional revenue. Passenger traffic at this period was mainly comprised of parties of schoolchildren on their way to and from Newtown. Market days (Tuesdays) witnessed the weekly journeys of many of the local inhabitants.

An 0-6-0 tank, No. 26, was by now at work upon the railway. A photograph of 1918 shows this locomotive at the head of a train of nine wagons on the transhipment siding at Kerry. The following railways are represented by the wagons: Great Northern; Great Central; London, Brighton & South Coast; London & North Western; and the Midland.

During the years 1917-1919 an interesting working was in force, to be repeated for a spell after the 1926 General Strike. On Mondays and Thursdays (the days on which the Van Railway was then in operation) the Kerry locomotive worked the first passenger train to from Kerry to Abermule, then going to Caersws, there to make the return journey to Van before returning to work the 4.30 pm to Kerry.

The March 1920 Timetable disclosed that third class travel only was then available and the service provided was becoming progressively less:

			Weekdays		
				F	
Down				am	pm
Abermule				10.25	4.15
Kerry				10.50	4.40
				A	F
Up		am		am	pm
Kerry		8.55		11.15	3.30
Abermule		9.20		11.40	3.55

Notes:	A	Tuesdays Only
	F	Wednesdays and Saturdays only

Physical Description (as in 1930)

The traveller from London, having passed through Welshpool, the principal town of Montgomeryshire, suddenly finds himself in the Severn valley with periodic views of that beautiful river. First Forden and then Montgomery stations are noted, to be followed by a narrowing of the valley as the single line pushes southwards.

Running into Abermule the main line splits to form a passing loop and having crossed a minor road on the level the train pulls up at the down platform, on the further side of which is the Kerry Railway. The junction with the main line is at 43 miles 72 chains (distance from Whitchurch, Salop).

The Kerry Railway is provided with a run-round loop and sidings. Passing the signal box on the left and leaving the station in the direction from which we have just entered, i.e. north-east, the same minor road is crossed by a further level crossing (at 9¼ chains).

'Dean Goods' class 0-6-0 No. 2516 just north of Middle Mill with the branch goods on 2nd December, 1955. This engine has survived into preservation and can be seen at STEAM: Museum of the Great Western Railway at Swindon. Notice that it carries its number on the buffer beam in GWR style as well as on a cast BR smokebox door number plate.

G.F. Bannister

This March 1948 view shows the tight curves on the Kerry branch north of Fronfraith. Notice the check rail which would reduce the risk of derailment or the track spreading. *J.I.C. Boyd Collection*

The home signal for Abermule is to the left of the line as it curves sharply right-handed prior to a short straight stretch, at the end of which is the fixed distant signal for Abermule. The line again curves right-handed and climbing at 1 in 75 enters the Mule Gorge, where rail, road and river keep close company. This is a particularly beautiful stretch with oak, larch and beech woods predominating.

We pass the site of Middle Mill Siding (with level crossing) and at rather over ¾ mile from Abermule the River Mule is crossed, followed by a short cutting and then a further river crossing just before the first milepost. Shortly afterwards the river is crossed yet again and immediately the line passes below the first overbridge.

At 1 mile 28 chains Fronfraith Siding is reached. A short disused siding protected by a ground frame (two levers) is thrown off left-handed in a facing direction: this siding formerly served a mill. The platform is shortly beyond and lies on the left-hand side between the siding and the main running line. It is without any shelter and of diminutive proportions, being 27 feet in length, 2 feet 6 inches in height and having an average depth from platform face to rear of platform of only 2 ft 6 inches. A curiosity of Fronfraith Halt was that though the track was curved the platform was straight.

Leaving Fronfraith a road is carried over the railway and a stream dashing under the railway here was formerly diverted by means of a chute to provide water for the locomotives.

At 1½ miles the railway turns sharply left-handed before a short distance of straight running is encountered. A further river crossing is followed by an overbridge and with the countryside now more open in character the railway climbs at 1 in 43 past Goitre Siding (2 miles 19 chains). Here, too, the platform is on the left-hand and without buildings of any kind. Three feet in height it is otherwise much larger than that at Fronfraith, being 81 feet in length and of full depth. On the further side of the platform and at the level of the platform edge lies a siding serving Goitre brickworks. This siding joins the main running line by a trailing junction a short distance beyond the further platform ramp.

The railway continues to climb and at approximately 2 miles 43 chains passes under a bridge. The summit is reached at 3 miles 2 chains, after passing under a small modern bridge, at which point a Stop Board requires all up (i.e., Abermule) freight trains to stop dead before proceeding. This incline, one of 1,467 yards at 1 in 43, was the most severe gradient over which the Cambrian operated passenger trains until that company undertook the working of such trains on the Golfa Incline (1 in 30 for 1,738 yards) on the Welshpool & Llanfair Light Railway from that line's opening on 4th April, 1903.

The Kerry terminus (3 miles 61 chains) can now be seen flanked by its trees: the platform - of conventional type - is lengthy and, together with Fronfraith and Goitre, unusual in that it was, before the GWR, without station nameboards. This station is without signals though equipped with several sidings and a locomotive shed. The shed is 35 feet in length, 15 feet in width and 17 feet in height (to eaves) with sides of galvanised iron sheet over a wooden frame; a slate roof is provided. The station boasts two ground frames - East and West (each of two levers), whilst there is a loading gauge over the main running line near the East frame.

Road, river and railway share the Fronfraith Gap. The Captains Pitch bridge, one of two on the line now 'listed' is in the centre. On the brow of the hill to the left is Fronfraith Hall. The pond in the foreground was *not* a feeder for Fronfraith mill, it may have been an amenity pond for Fronfraith Hall. The pond has long since gone and this area is now wooded.   *Valentine Series*

Fronfraith Halt in 1904 looking towards Kerry; the short platform is not curved to match the railway.   *F.E. Fox-Davies*

Above: Fronfraith Halt looking towards Abermule in February 1948. *J.I.C. Boyd Collection*

Left: The point indicator which stood outside Kerry station indicating whether the points were set for the platform or the sidings in 1904.

R.W. Miller Collection

The station throat at Kerry in March 1948 with the small ground frame to the right.
J.I.C. Boyd Collection

Kerry station in 1935; *left to right*, station platform, sidings, and engine shed; the coal stage and water tank were behind this.   *R.W. Kidner*

The terminus station at Kerry viewed towards the buffer stops in March 1948.

Kerry station goods yard viewed from the buffer stops in March 1948. The engine shed can be seen between the wagons, notice the replacement water tank, provided in GWR days, at the rear of the engine shed.

The station building at Kerry in 1904.   *R.W. Miller Collection*

Kerry station building in 1948. Notice the significant tree growth that has occurred in the intervening 44 years.   *R.W. Miller Collection*

The station approach leads to the main Craven Arms-Newtown road, and the village of Kerry one mile distant. To a visitor in the 1930s the large yard at Kerry seemed out of proportion for such a small line, and it seems probable that some of the long sidings were added by the Board of Trade in 1917 when there was very heavy traffic in pit props and trench timber coming from the re-opened Kerry Tramway (*see Chapter Ten*). T.R. Perkins who visited the line in 1904, refers only to one siding. A sector table for the engine to run-round would have been replaced by points when the four-wheeled engines ceased to be used.

Perkins stated that the trees in the gorges were very close to the tracks, and supposed this was the reason that windows were barred. Safety was very much to the fore, with the 9 mph limit strictly observed; the goods brake used was later piped; for some reason it carried at one end a white panel with a black cross; lettering on the side restricted it to use on the branch. The heaviest trains before the Great War period were annual Kerry Sheep Fair specials, double-headed to conquer the gradients and provided braking, seeing that the sheep trucks would not have continuous brakes.

1922-1956

The railway was to be saved from extinction by the absorption of the struggling Cambrian Railways Company by the GWR on 25th March, 1922.

When the GWR obtained control they relaid the track throughout and erected a new water tank at Kerry. They worked the line with their locomotives Nos. 819, 821, 1196 and 1197. The interesting 2-4-0 tank locomotive, *Lady Margaret* (formerly Liskeard & Looe Railway No. 5) joined the stud for a while.

GWR six-wheeled carriages with the comparative luxury of gas-lighting were introduced and through excursions ran to Aberystwyth during the years 1923-1926, as many as 400 passengers being carried on occasions.

Under the GWR the carriage livery was brown with cream upper panels.

Normally the passenger trains were mixed, but a special up freight left Kerry about 5.30 pm when traffic was heavy. The Timetable for the Summer Service of 1929 read as follows:

		Weekdays only		
Abermule	dep.	10.10 am	12.15 pm	4.30 pm
Kerry	dep.	8.55 am	11.35 am	3.30 pm

Two sets of enginemen were stationed at Kerry during the passenger years, and the locomotive shed there was in use until the cessation of passenger services after the last train on Saturday 7th February, 1931.

An 0-6-0 pannier tank with a single GWR four-wheeled carriage worked mixed trains on the last day. Messrs Cooper and Roberts were the driver and fireman respectively with guard Ewart Thomas in charge.

Following the closure to passenger services on 7th February, 1931, Abermule was provided with new nameboards, 'Abermule Change for Kerry', giving way to 'Abermule'. The GWR announced that they would continue to carry parcels, merchandise and minerals over the branch.

'Dean Goods' class 0-6-0 No. 2516 with the branch goods in sidings at Kerry on 2nd December, 1955. The water tank is just visible on the extreme right.   *G.F. Bannister*

This view was taken in the last week of operation from the bridge that links Goetre Farm to Hoddley. A 'Dean Goods' has just passed the Goitre sidings and is entering the cutting on the steepest gradient on the way to Kerry. The driver in the centre of the cab is Charlie Claffey, the fireman may be Neville Bound. Barely visible is Ewart Thomas leaning out of the brake van.

Don Griffiths Collection

With the passing of regular passenger traffic, Mr Bennett removed from Kerry to Abermule, where he was station master until 2nd January, 1937, and, in addition, supervised the Kerry line. An annual Sunday School excursion was worked over the line until the summer of 1939 inclusive.

Until the outbreak of World War II a brickworks at Goitre Siding gave much business to the railway, as did the movement of sheep in connection with the Kerry sheep sales held annually on the first and third Fridays in September. This traffic was now lost.

Working tables showed that a freight train ran if required on Tuesdays, Thursdays and Saturdays only. These trains were worked to Kerry by the locomotive off the down midday main line freight train, usually a standard 0-6-0 type.

A visit in 1934 showed a large variety of wagons, open and closed, in the sidings, possibly there 'out of the way'. Perhaps the only one being used was an open wagon lying at the station platform. The timber Court Pile overbridge near Kerry was replaced by a concrete one in 1935.

The branch was finally closed for freight traffic on 1st May, 1956.

Locomotives

The locomotives listed are those which have most commonly worked the railway. The earliest recorded Cambrian Railways Company's locomotives that worked this railway were *Plasfynnon* and *Mountaineer*. Both of 0-4-0ST type, their principal dimensions were as follows:

Cylinders:	14 in. diameter x 20 in. stroke
Driving wheels:	4 ft diameter
Boiler:	10 ft 6 in. long x 3 ft 4⅞ in. internal diameter
Heating surface:	669 sq. feet
Tank capacity:	480 gallons
Coal capacity;	12½ cwt
Weight in working order:	22 tons 6 cwt 2 qrs

Plasfynnon and *Mountaineer* were both built in 1863 by Sharp, Stewart & Co., their works numbers being 1431 and 1432 respectively. *Plasfynnon*, Cambrian No. 36, was the more regularly used and was scrapped in 1905. *Mountaineer* was numbered 37. These locomotives were never re-boilered, but cabs were added in 1897 - these cabs were unusual in that they had six spectacles, four 'forward' and two to the rear. The regular driver during the period 1880-1900 was one Jimmy Harding.

With the passing of *Plasfynnon* the Cambrian worked the railway with No. 35, an 0-6-0 side tank, which they had purchased from the Lambourn Valley Railway. No. 35 was built by Messrs Chapman & Furneaux, Gateshead-on-Tyne, in 1898, their works number being 1162. It bore the name *Aelfred* when working the Lambourn Valley line: on the GWR it became No. 821, and later passed to a South Wales anthracite colliery.

No. 26, a sister locomotive of No. 35, came from the same source (Works No. 1161). It, too, commenced its life at Lambourn, where it bore the name *Ealhswith*:

A beautifully atmospheric view of No. 36 *Plasfynnon* at Kerry *circ*a 1900. Notice the original water tank in the background.   *R.W. Miller Collection*

Plasfynnon prepares to leave Kerry station with the passenger service *circa* 1903.
R.W. Miller Collection

on the GWR it became No. 820, and in 1931 went to a colliery near Radstock, Somerset, before being withdrawn in 1945. Nos. 35 and 26 were named in honour of King Alfred and his Queen respectively.

No. 22 (from the Van Railway) occasionally relieved No. 35.

Cambrian 0-6-0 Nos. 14 (re-numbered 898 by the GWR), 22, 24 (GWR 819), and Cambrian 2-4-0 tanks 58 (GWR 1196) and 59 (GWR 1197) also made appearances. No. 24 was built in 1903 and should not be confused with the earlier Cambrian Railways locomotive of the same number which saw service on the Van Railway. No. 59 was built by Messrs Sharp, Stewart & Co. in 1866, their works number being 1683. It was formerly named *Seaham* and was rebuilt in 1894 at Oswestry when a new boiler was fitted. Under the GWR a new chimney, top feed arrangement, safety valve covers and larger bunker were installed. (Principal dimensions are shown on page 55.)

On the GWR obtaining control the 2-4-0 tank, *Lady Margaret*, saw service on the line. This locomotive was built by Andrew Barclay, of Kilmarnock, in 1902 for the Liskeard & Looe Railway (Cornwall) by whom it was numbered 5. the GWR purchased this locomotive in 1909 and re-numbered it 1308. In addition to the Kerry Railway it also worked on the Tiverton Junction-Hemyock branch (Devon) and finally on the Tanat Valley Light Railway (Montgomeryshire): it was condemned in May 1948.

Principal dimensions:

Cylinders:	14½ in. diameter x 22½ in. stroke
Wheel diameters:	2 ft 7½ in. and 4 ft
Boiler pressure:	160 lb. per sq. in.
Heating surface:	650½ sq. ft
Grate area:	11.6 sq. ft
Weight in working order:	28 tons

GWR 0-6-0STs Nos. 2032, 2068 (saddle-tanks fitted with pannier tanks in the 1920s), 0-6-0ST No. 2075 (fitted with pannier tanks in 1934) and 'Dean Goods' class 0-6-0s Nos. 2343, 2408 are amongst others that have worked the railway. Locomotives of the '2301' 'Dean Goods' class are of the following dimensions:

Cylinders:	17½ in. diameter x 24 in. stroke
Driving wheels:	5 ft 2 in.
Boiler pressure:	180 lb. per sq. in.

0-6-0T No. 26, formerly Lambourn Valley Railway *Ealhswith*. This locomotive saw use on the line after the demise of *Plasfynnon* as the regular branch engine.   *R.W. Miller Collection*

Ex-Cambrian Railways 2-4-0T No. 1197 at Oswestry in 1935.

Chapter Nine

Kerry Railway Memories

The Shunter

The first of the retired railwaymen to be approached was Vic Corfield of Newtown. Vic suffers poor health and his wife Joyce kindly arranged for the interview to take place. Vic was born in 1921, the final year of the operation of the Cambrian Railways and the year of the Abermule crash. On leaving school, he commenced work with Pryce Jones at Newtown. Their warehouse is close to the station; it was famous in both rail and retail history, for Pryce Jones pioneered the concept of mail order in the Victorian period, generating much railway business. Vic joined the railway in early 1941 but, by the end of the year, he commenced service in the RAF, until 1947. On demobilisation, he returned to join the GWR at Newtown when transfer to British Railways was already underway. He became the shunter at Newtown; this would be his main duty until the Beeching cuts stopped single wagonloads in the 1960s. He retired in 1986. He has many valued documents and records of railway operation in this area, the most intriguing being the rulebook of the 1860s for the then Oswestry & Newtown Railway.

Vic's mother was born in Caersws and worked in service at the Kerry vicarage. Dad was born in Kerry and he was the waggoner at the Cloddiau. It would be almost certain that both would have travelled on the branch line as paying passengers early in the century. By the time of Vic's youth, bus services were far more frequent and quicker from Newtown to Kerry and he never travelled the line as a passenger. Vic travelled on occasions to Kerry either in the guard's van or on the footplate.

The daily pick-up goods left Oswestry at 9.30 am. It would have had any Kerry wagons on only three days of the week; he thought it was Tuesday, Thursday and Saturday. The locomotive on these days would always be one of two 'Dean Goods', which were the only locomotives with permission to enter the Kerry branch. The cousin of Joyce, Vic's wife, was one of the firemen who worked the line in the final years, Neville Bound, who lives in Shropshire.

There was a limit on the number of wagons that could be taken up, the exact number or weight cannot be remembered. The 9.30 ex-Oswestry was due at Newtown at 2.00 pm. Newtown was the most important station and staff would have been waiting in the goods sheds to start unloading parcels etc. from the covered wagons. The problem was the day of the Kerry branch. The engine would stable the bulk of the train at Abermule and then proceed up the Kerry branch. By this time it was never economic sense to move one or two wagons using driver, fireman and guard. A morning and afternoon train operated from Machynlleth for Grammar School and Technical School children. It arrived at Newtown before 9. 00 am, and returned after 4. 00 pm. On Saturday it was the shopping special. The carriages would be stabled in the bay platform at Newtown and the locomotive was then available for yard shunting. Vic would arrange with the station master's authority that this engine would proceed to Abermule to collect the main section of the goods so that unloading at Newtown could proceed at 2.00 pm. The 'Dean Goods' locomotive would then return from Kerry, proceed to Newtown with return Kerry wagons and then collect the bulk of the goods and proceed to Moat Lane Junction. Any Kerry wagons would then be attached to the goods train from Machynlleth (Newtown around 5.00 pm) or the 9.00 pm goods to finally arrive at Oswestry. The usual guard for this roster was Ewart Thomas of Moat Lane and he retired on the closure of the Kerry line.

By 1950 very little traffic was being carried on the branch. It would be mainly coal to Kerry with an occasional wagon of non-perishable agricultural goods such as fertilizer. The only goods back would be pit props from Kerry and products from the Goitre brickworks. The older railway men in Vic's youth would talk about the importance of the Kerry Sheep sale, but there was little stock trade long before closure.

There were shunters only at Moat Lane, Newtown and Welshpool, all shunting at Abermule and on the Kerry branch was done by the guard. A train staff was given at Abermule to unlock points for access to the branch; the same staff would also have unlocked the points at Kerry station.

Vic was uncertain of the operation of the branch before and during the war. After the mixed goods/passengers finished in 1931, he believed that a small locomotive was kept in steam at Moat Lane to cover the Van line two days a week and a Dean pannier was available for Kerry. These may have worked on both lines during an emergency.

The Fireman's Story

A tape was received from Neville Bound of Wem in late June 2002. Neville now suffers from emphysema and has difficulty with his sight so both he and his wife thought that sending a tape would be far less stressful than an interview.

Neville joined the GWR towards the end of World War II as a cleaner at Moat Lane Junction. After several years he was asked to move to Old Oak Common, Paddington. He then did National Service and in 1950 he returned to Moat Lane as a fireman. Soon after the Kerry line closed, he became a driver and moved to Shropshire.

His first connection was at Moat Lane when his duties would have included cleaning and servicing one of the duty 'tankies' which would be on site for about three weeks before going to Oswestry for a wash out. These were Nos. 2032, 2068, and 2075. He remembers one driver had been sent from Shrewsbury and another was Jack Hatton from Croes Newydd (Wrexham) and Jack wondered 'where on earth was Kerry'. The drivers would often be men close to retirement for the Kerry trip was an easy day job between 9.00 am and 4.00 pm and soon the fireman would be ready for promotion to driver. One senior fireman was Tom Aldridge and he was the last driver with Neville firing the Kerry in 1955.

In Neville's words:

On one occasion, we had to put a new lead seal in one of the Kerry panniers. All steam was let out. The engine had to be cooled down and the chargeman told us to tidy up the cab as well. We filled with water right to the top, oiled and fired ready for duty and we had washed the cab out with a pipe from the hydrant. We decided to move her but forgot the pipe so we ran over it. Cleaners were not supposed to move engines so we knew we would get a telling off, but the duty fireman said 'Tell the chargeman I did it' so we were lucky. The pannier would work the cattle shunt to Welshpool every Monday and was available for Kerry the rest of the week. There would be enough water for the day so the water tank at Kerry would rarely be used. Before the war, these engines had been saddle tanks instead of panniers with less water and may have been replenished during the day.

So I returned to Moat Lane as one of the rota firemen for the last few years of the Kerry. The panniers had gone, the Monday cattle shunt had gone and the Kerry was now operated on three days a week only. We would work the 10.15 goods from Moat Lane, sometimes with another engine tender type (usually a Jones, but also a Collett or light Ivatt), shunt at Newtown and then change crews at Montgomery station with Oswestry men. The train coming from Oswestry had to be a standard 'Dean Goods', the Jones Westernised Cambrian engines were not allowed because of axle weight. So we would now start working back on the 'Dean Goods'. We would put the wagons in the yard at Abermule, sort out the Kerry wagons and add the brake van marked 'Abermule'.

We had to go up tender first. The line was worked with one engine in steam so we received the key, which operated the entry to the branch and all ground frames. The rail could be bad, especially in the autumn. There is nothing new about leaves on the rails. The sanders were at the front except for No. 2484 which for some reason also had a sander on the tender, but this sand could often be damp. We would have a successful go but we had to lift the fall plate, between the tender and the engine. This hinged on the engine and was designed to slide on the steel floor of the tender. This plate would fall in the gap caused by the severe curves, snag and the force would bend it. We would pass the Fronfraith Mill. Here there was an embankment and a millstream with a wooden sluice, which could be swung across for emergency water, but we never had to use it. The first stop was the Goitre siding to put down coal and pick up land drains. We could move away from the Goitre all right. It was on a gradient but out in the open so the worst part was at the Court in a damp cutting with frost pockets. There was a most odd high bridge (rebuilt in early 1930s) and the road was concrete and the sides of wood pales. The bridge department had tarred (creosoted) these and spill on to the line stopped the engine. This steep section would often cause a slip and I had to leave the cab to shovel, scrape and put down ash and sand to keep going. Soon after clearing the bridge, the line levelled and we were soon at Kerry. We went into Kerry beside the platform, stop, unhook and then draw forward, unlock the ground frame with the key and then run round the loop. Every shunt needed one of us to operate the ground frame, so either the guard or myself climbed up and down like a yoyo. The usual loads were placing full coal trucks in and collecting the empties. There would be an occasional covered van and there were loads of pit props. Because of the petrol shortage, the Co-op would also send a wagon up from Newtown yard and the lorry would deliver for several days around the Kerry area. This was done to save the lorry crawling up the Vastre hill with full loads. Every year we would take a horsebox for a farmer who took a prize Hereford bull to the shows. The horsebox had been designed for racehorse with one end for the groom to feed and look after the horses. So we would take a stockman and a bull down to Abermule, Newtown or Moat Lane where a truck would be attached to a passenger train. I have also loaded other stock at Kerry into livestock wagons, just odd wagons. I was never on duty on the sheep sale day, but took the empty wagons up

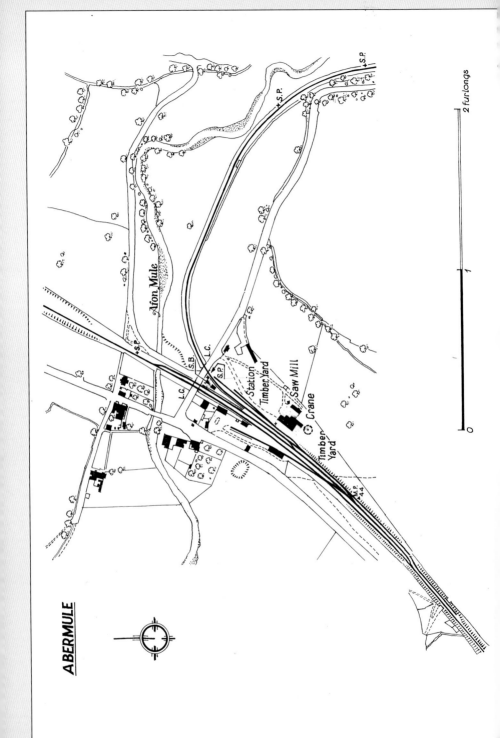

ABERMULE

Afon Mule

Station
Timber Yard
Saw Mill
Crane
Timber Yard

S.P.
S.P.
S.P.
S.P.
L.C.
S.B.
L.C.
L.C.
M.P.
44½

2 furlongs
1
0

on the previous day. It was an odd feeling taking a long train up because the guard's van would keep disappearing from view on all the sharp curves.

There was no water problem with a 'Dean Goods'. When shunting had been completed we would then connect the train to the goods which was marshalled by the station platform. We would then lock the ground frames and then glide down to Abermule. We would then form the train if still at Abermule, however, it would often have been moved to Newtown so that parcels could be unloaded from the covered wagons. At Newtown we should have all the train together again and could then proceed to complete the shift at Moat Lane.

On the Kerry there was no hurry so we cut pea and bean sticks, collected mushrooms and hazel nuts in season and local farmers would always allow us to have a few swedes from fields close to the line. I had an allotment by the Kerry Road Bridge in Newtown so I would drop these items off and when I got home again to Newtown I would carry them across the track. It was a real Rock Island Line,

Ernie the platelayer looked after the Kerry section, hedges, track etc. and he had three cabins. He would often come down with us from Kerry. Once he was short of coal at one so asked us to stop. I was up on the tender throwing coal down to him to put in the cabin. I suppose I was young and foolish because I tried to land a lump down the chimney. Ernie had put a glazed pipe extension to try and get a better draw for the fire. This pipe split and Ernie was very cross. Obviously, with such light traffic, the whole line was struggling so no one was surprised when the service finished in January 1956. No. 2516 had been at Moat Lane for many years and she was a better steamer than No. 2538. These were the last two Deans by 1955.

Neville has also been on the Van Line, a distance of about 200 yards to shunt for the Bridge Department. One of the drivers in 1945 when Neville started was a Jack Jarman. Jack was a cleaner at Llanidloes in 1922; the foreman came and told him to prepare a locomotive quickly, this was connected to the breakdown crane so Jack, as a young lad, had gone to the Abermule smash. The Abermule crash must have had a deep effect upon many railwaymen of the Upper Severn Valley.

Abermule Station

Ron Jones was born in 1921 at Newtown. He was always interested in trains as they could be seen across the valley from his house. Dad was a postman and often Ron would go with him when the 8.06 pm mail train was loaded.

Ron joined the GWR on leaving school and became junior clerk at Abermule. After a year he was moved to Moat Lane Junction and in early 1939 he transferred to Oswestry. He was called up during the war, serving in the RAF and was demobbed in 1946.

This is his memory of 1936 to 1939. The Abermule station master was Mr Richard Bennett, the ex-Kerry man. A Mr Reg Fryer was retained at Kerry to look after freight unloading and loading for several years after passenger closure. Ron's duties would include issue of invoices after any goods had left the Goitre siding or Kerry. Most trade came from the Goitre. It was bricks or clay pipes and much was sent west to Aberystwyth. Invoicing out of Kerry was not common except for sheep sales. There would be an occasional wagon of round timber.

'Dean Goods' class 0-6-0 No. 2343 has just arrived from Kerry in the branch platform at Abermule with a brake van in tow *circa* 1949. The Cambrian main line is to the left.

Stephenson Locomotive Society

'Dean Goods' 0-6-0 No. 2538 with the goods train from Kerry approaches the level crossing on 4th April, 1956. In May 1956 rails were removed near this location, isolating Kerry and bringing to a close any prospect of further rail traffic on the line.

G.F. Bannister

The sheep sale days in September were very busy. Clerical staff came up from Newtown Goods to invoice sheep loads out. Also livestock loaders came down from Oswestry. The trains would be shuttled down with the tank engines. Three to five shuttles would make a train of up to 50 livestock wagons, which would head out to England. The usual locomotive would be a 'Dean Goods' which were turned at Welshpool and ran tender first to Abermule. Up to 100 wagons would be moved on the main sale, needing three trains out. The other sales were not quite as busy.

The line slumbered the remainder of the year. There were three goods only per week using pannier tanks Nos. 2032, 2068, or 2075 stabled at Moat Lane. These were pre-Grouping locomotives and were already being phased out and only a few passed into BR ownership. These were not allowed to be used on the Van railway, which retained an outside-cylinder Manning, Wardle. One of the regular guards for many years for both lines was Ewart Thomas, but engine crew were drawn from the roster at Moat Lane. The traffic was mainly coal for Goitre brickworks and the coal merchant at Kerry yard; there was also some feedstuffs and fertilizer. Certainly firms such as Bibby's and Silcocks (Oil Cake and feed firms at ports such as Merseyside) shared a large depot at Newtown, so that Kerry agricultural traffic was receding. If there was a limit on the journey up, it would rarely have to be applied for it would never be more than six wagons. This little Welsh line would rarely carry Welsh coal apart from some anthracite. The rest of the coal came in from the Cannock collieries. He cannot, in 1936, remember any wagons working to or from the Fronfraith Mill siding.

Ron can remember the 1936 Sunday School Special to Aberystwyth. Four- or six-wheel carriages were used. Some may have come from the Tanat Valley Line and there could not have been many left on the stock book. At Abermule, the kids and parents changed to corridor bogie carriages with a tender engine for the hour and a half journey so toilets were available.

After the war Ron returned to the railway as booking clerk at Newtown. He became clerical officer in charge in 1970. There was no longer the post of station master, and an area manager based at Shrewsbury controlled the station. The power base had moved from Oswestry when the Buttington Junction line north closed.

There could he no more Sunday School trips, as there were no longer any short wheelbase carriages available. One of the small 2000 series pannier tanks continued to work the freight until around 1950, one of the last of the once numerous Dean saddle tank rebuilds. On Mondays, it would take cattle or sheep wagons from Caersws and beyond to Welshpool Market but by 1950 this had dropped to two wagons. From 1950 to closure, the Kerry line was worked from Oswestry by a 'Dean Goods'. These 'Dean Goods' were solely retained for the Mid Wales line to Brecon and the Kerry Line.

Ron cannot remember a passenger farewell service for groups such as the Stephenson Locomotive Society before the line was lifted. There may have been a service using guards' vans, but he thought safety in the narrow section of the dingle may have prevented such a venture. However, he can remember the special notice for the lifting trains which would have worked down from Kerry recovering rails, sleepers and anything else that could be sold leaving just the ballast. Unfortunately he never travelled the line to Kerry. Like most, he never could understand why it was built with no hinterland of minerals, slate or quarry. It was more of an extended siding than a branch line.

The main line was full to capacity on Saturdays in late July and August as holidaymakers returned to the coast after the war. The single line between Welshpool and Newtown was a bottleneck. This story may have been either 1947 or 1948. The Kerry line was still being worked by a Dean pannier tank. One Saturday, the Kerry branch duty had taken a little too long and on return to Abermule the train had missed the allotted slot. It had the choice of a four hour wait or the signalman offered the chance of it being attached to a Churchward tender engine that was returning from Oswestry with the Aberystwyth breakdown set that had just been serviced. The Churchward came through Newtown with the poor little tank behind appearing to go so fast that the six wheels looked like spinning catherine wheels. The driver was glowering but the fireman was laughing. Anyhow, they did not have to simmer for a four-hour wait in Abermule siding.

A Local Man's Story

John Maurice Arthur (Jack) was interviewed with his son David. Jack was born in Kerry in 1915. His grandfather farmed The Court, which is just west of Abermule station. Jack would often stay with his grandparents and his great joy was to spend any spare time in the Abermule signal box. A chair was provided for him in the corner, he always had to leave with the signalman.

Jack would often travel the train from Kerry. It always was a thrill; it would just coast down but had to work hard on the gradient returning. The specials were truly special; there was an annual Sunday School Trip to Aberystwyth seaside. When very young, maybe seven or eight years of age, there was also a trip from his chapel to the home of David Davies, Llandinam. David Davies was the entrepreneur who did much to finance the Montgomeryshire railways, he then developed coalmines in South Wales and built Barry Docks. Both he and his family became local benefactors.

The engine was stabled at Kerry overnight until passenger closure in 1931, afterwards the goods engine was held at Moat Lane Junction. Kerry station was fully equipped with a waiting room and booking office; the remainder of the building was the residence of the station master, Mr Richard Bennett. An engine cleaner/general hand worked here, he was a young man called Smith who later went to Oswestry and became a driver. A pair of drivers, firemen and guards were also based in the village. All moved on passenger closure.

Kerry station could be a beehive of activity. The adjacent area to the east of the station was the transfer siding for the narrow gauge timber railway (*see Chapter Ten*) and there would be huge stacks of timber. The now B4368 to Clun was built soon after the first war from above Kerry to the Anchor and much road stone came up the line for this purpose. A coal merchant worked from the yard with horses and wagons and there was an office store of the old

Montgomeryshire Farmers. Up to 20 men could be working at this now deserted railhead. Goitre brick works struggled during the recession, but coal came in and bricks and clay pipes went out when there was active trading.

Acute bends in the dingle always limited engine size, they were always small tank locomotives and loading was light. The busy days were that of the sheep fair and there could be two or three engines in the Kerry yard including tender locomotives. The foreman lengthman was called Richard Pryce, there were three others including his son Bob. The line and hedges always appeared well kept. The guard was Ewart Thomas and he must have served the line for 35 years because he retired on closure in 1956. He would carry his bike in the van and if there was an hour to spare at Kerry, he would cycle for a pint in the village. There was a small weighbridge at Kerry and certainly Jack can remember helping Dad take a wagon across for a tare ticket. There was a water tower at Kerry; he cannot remember one at Abermule. The engine would not use much coal or water gliding down from Kerry so there would certainly be enough to return.

Passenger service was sparse after World War I, one train down in early morning and a return about 4.30 in the evening. Extras were run on Tuesday (Newtown market) and Saturdays, these would be mixed and goods only on the other days. Jack really cannot remember the carriages, there had been a change from four-wheelers to six-wheelers and two were stabled at Kerry. Full-length bogie carriages would not have cleared the rock face on some of the severe bends. The main loading was to get scholarship and fee-paying children to Newtown County School (boys and girls) opposite Newtown station. There would be between 12 and 18 pupils, otherwise the remainder, including Jack, stopped at either Sarn or Kerry all-age schools until fourteen. Sometimes only one coach was used but always with the guard's van for brake insurance on the steep gradient. The Monday train would use both coaches for the extra passengers en route to Welshpool Market. Jack could remember that the coach was comfortable, after all 'Kerry people would not put up with rubbish' even though the bus service was far quicker.

John left school in 1930 and joined Dad and two brothers on the family farm. He often received no income because of the recession so he joined the RAF in 1937 and he lost contact with the enchanting little branch line of his childhood. After the war he lived in Aberhafesp and had his own livestock haulage business.

Jack can remember the narrow gauge forest railway, which closed soon after the first war. He can remember riding the end wagon with an older lad called Martin Edwards. Martin was the gatesman, he would run ahead of the tram engine to either open gates or wave a red flag, allow the train to pass, shut the gate and then run to catch up.

Right: William (Bill) Pryce with his grandson Vaughan taken around 1922. Bill was the senior ganger on the Kerry line, retiring in 1927. His railway career would go back to the 1890s.

Bob Pryce was a lengthman in his father's team. Later, Bob became the senior ganger between Moat Lane and Newtown. This photograph is taken from Bob's Railway War Pass issued in 1940. Bob died when still employed on the railway in 1951.

Ewart Thomas was often the duty guard on both the Kerry and Van lines. Ewart retired in 1956 and this photograph would date from that period.

The Ganger's Grandchildren

William Richard (Bill) Pryce was the senior ganger on the Kerry line. He retired in 1927 and died in 1930; he may well have commenced his railway career with the Cambrian in the late 1890s. He also took on the tenancy of Cefn Maenllwyd and purchased 60 acres when the Naylor Estate was sold. The railway took all his time and grandmother and an employed man worked the farm.

This can be recalled by his three grandchildren, Vaughan Pryce, Nancy Price and Mary Evans. Their father, Bob Pryce joined the railway before World War I and rejoined the Cambrian on demobilisation. He worked from 1919 until his death in 1951. In the 1920s when the three children were young, Bob worked with grandfather on the Kerry; he then became senior ganger on the single line between Newtown and Forden for a few years before promotion to the double section between Newtown and Moat Lane. He twice won a prize for best-kept section on the Oswestry division.

Both Bob and Dad were called immediately to the Abermule crash, as it was a Tuesday, they half expected granny to be on the local train to Newtown market but she had changed her mind and had gone to collect faggots for heating the bread oven. Both men were stunned by the event of that day.

All three children have travelled on the passenger service; they were between seven and eleven when it closed. First of all Mum would catch the train at Goitre when they lived at Lletygelli. After they moved to Maenllwyd, Fronfraith Halt was more convenient. Dad had free or reduced rate travel so they continued to use the train when other families were switching to the more frequent bus service. All went on every Sunday School Trip from 1925 until the last one in the late 1930s. The trip to Rhyl was a very long day and all can remember cycling on hired pushbikes.

In the 1930s, Dad was a heavy smoker, and then he did give up the habit. The others in the gang decided that Ewart Thomas, the guard, would look after his 'fags' and give him some when the train passed. The train did not stop and Ewart, with a great grin, waved the cigarette at Dad. The next day, Ewart was on the Van line so dad had no fags for two days.

Vaughan and his two sisters would often travel with Dad and Ewart in the brake van up to Kerry. Sometimes during the school holiday, Vaughan would travel down or up until Dad was seen and the train would stop to let him off. He would share some of the contents of Dad's budgett (straw food box). He has sat with the men in all three gangers' huts near Rock Mill, the Goitre and the Court Cutting; the latter is just about standing. Rail staff were entitled to one ton of coal free per year and Dad told Vaughan to deliver this free coal with a horse and cart to three Abermule staff, Charlie Baylis, Alec Wood and Mr Gilbert who were all signalmen.

Vaughan had several treats such as being on the footplate when shunting at Kerry. One of the coal merchants was Bertie Williams. He was a very tall man and they would pass him as they walked to Kerry School and he was walking to the coal yard. The Montgomery Farmers had a store and next door was a covered wagon, which was the office, and Vaughan can remember the staff member, Mr Ray Francis, being paid for goods sold. Dad walked with a bit of a gait; this may well have been the result of years of walking the lines. All the railway ladies would put some extra dough mixed with currants on baking day. Mary Fryer's buns at Kerry were delicious. Ewart would always remember his flags and his whistle but would often forget his teeth. He would put a whole bun into his mouth and start chewing; he had a gigantic appetite. He was a great friend and character.

The Pryce grandchildren started to make their own way in the early 1940s and would have lost the frequent contact with the Kerry line which was so much part of their childhood, although Nancy's first job was clerical officer in Newtown goods shed.

The bridge with three arches in the middle of the gorge is reputed to be haunted with a headless horseman or something similar coming down the Captains Pitch (Hill). On a cold winter late evening, Bob heard a chain rattle coming down the hill, he jumped over hedge from the rail line and landed on a donkey. The cause of the phantom was a local farm dog which broke from the kennel and was dragging the chain along. The ghost licked Bob's hand and he took the apparition back to its owner.

Middle Mill Siding

Hilda May Ryder (previously Mills) was born in Abermule in 1912 and was brought up in the cottage beside Middle Mill in the dingle section of the railway line. Hilda's father was killed in World War I when her mother was heavy with child, the little girl died at birth. It is a sad thought that many young country lads from the Vale of Kerry saw their last view of this little border paradise from the carriage of the Kerry 'Jimmy'. Every branch line in Britain and Ireland, every small country station from Russia, from Saxony, from Brittany, etc. carried loyal citizens to the carnage of Belgium and Eastern France. It must remain a stain on European history. The German prisoners of war that came up the Kerry line to help cut the forests and load the tramways were the lucky ones to be repatriated in 1919 with limbs and lungs still intact.

Hilda did her best to recall her childhood and the railway, but her memory was poor so her story can only give a sense. The cottage by the mill was almost on the line. Hilda would stand by the door of the cottage and the driver, fireman and guard would always wave to her. The train would whistle as it came close to the cottage. The trains were then quite frequent, maybe every hour one would rumble past from early morning to darkness. Several had only a passenger coach, but most had mixed goods and passenger (around 1918-1919 traffic was at its zenith). There were long timber trains coming up the valley empty, and then returning with pit props or long timber. They always travelled very slowly because of the gradient.

There was a siding at Middle Mill but Hilda was uncertain whether it was used much, the next siding at Fronfraith would still be used for unloading coal and chicken and pig feed. (Both steam mills and the railway delivery quickly made many water mills uneconomic.)

Hilda would sometimes help the lengthmen with such tasks as pulling weeds; the line always seemed to be very tidy. Trains would not normally stop at Middle Mill and Hilda would walk along the line to Kerry station, this would be with a girl friend. They would help at Kerry station such as unloading coal with a shovel; it was very hard work. The station yard was very busy with piles of timber coming in on little trains from the forest. There was a small hut with a fireplace and a chimney and Hilda would help make tea and toast sandwiches for lunchtime. This was all when she was under was under 10 years of age and railwaymen were always very kind. Hilda can remember men speaking German.

She certainly would have travelled in the passenger coach and in the guard's van and would have been taken to the footplate of the engines. It is a pity that Hilda could not give more detail, she truly was one of the railway children of this little line.

The Fronfraith Mill Siding

As in Chaucer, we now have the miller's tale. Dan Evans, retired agricultural merchant, now aged 74, inherited the long established business of D.C. Evans. The Fronfraith Mill in the Abermule Dingle was one of seven water mills owned by the family firm.

In some ways, this is a story of energy. The early business would have brought in imported grain by canal, maybe taking five to seven days from Liverpool, later rail would have taken at least a day and finally, a bulk lorry would deliver straight to the farm with no transhipment within a few hours.

Dan recalls the mill from his childhood to closure in 1948. The second war prolonged the working life of the mill and the railway siding by at least 10 years. The siding was placed at or soon after the branch opened in 1863. The siding entry faced down hill; there was a gate to enter level with the mill wall. It was a private siding, but Dan has no idea who owned the rails and the sleepers. The siding was very short, only three to four short wheelbase wagons could be stored. No traffic went out but coal, basic slag, fertilizer and feedstuffs came in. The company already had light lorries in the 1920s for delivery to farms, so trade concentrated at the large depot in Newtown railway yard. The traditional trade of farmers coming to collect their supplies at a rail source was in rapid retreat. The company were agents for both Crosfield, Calthrop, and BOCM. These companies were oil crushers of imported material to make vegetable oils and the residues were blended with imported cereals to make complete livestock foods, which were called compounds. The first large diesel lorry was purchased in 1936 and it was far more economic, especially with large loads, to deliver direct to farms rather than rail. Coal was delivered to the siding as a full load (10 tons plus) and farm customers collected themselves in a minimum of about three tons for their own use and for the threshing contractor, smaller loads including household were done by coal merchants. It was often summer delivery to get maximum discount from the colliery wholesaler.

One of the three arches of the Captains Pitch bridge that leads to Fronfraith Hall *circa* 1905. Fronfraith Halt and bridge are further up the line. The two river arches are hidden within the trees on the right-hand side. The line crosses the River Mule in the foreground as the river flows down to power the long closed Middle Mill.

Fronfraith Mill and Halt in March 1948.   *J.I.C. Boyd Collection*

Siding space was narrow between the mill to the east and the Fronfraith single carriage platform to the west. There was a fence on the platform with a wicket gate. Dan can remember the water sluice for engines in an emergency and the story of the passengers operating the signal. George Sneade was the miller; it really was not economic. For example, the water mill would only grind five to six cwt a day while the electric mill at Newtown would grind one ton an hour and modern hammer mills with automation will handle six tons plus per hour. Dad had bought a Bamford Roller mill for Fronfraith but the water power was not good enough so it was moved to Newtown where it worked for a further 20 years. In some ways the mill was very clever with pulleys, belts, hoists and grinding stone feeding ground grain by gravity to bins on the ground floor. Farmers would bring their home grown grain for grinding or rolling.

By the time Dan could remember these memories of childhood, the siding was not often used. The train had to stop and do the shunt on the way down from Kerry. The engine would leave the trucks above the siding held by the brake van, then come below the points. The train would enter the sidings, pull the empties out, then out on to the branch, empties above the points, return with mill trucks, out again, lock gates and siding then push up to couple up with the remainder of the train and then down to Abermule. It sounds complex but it did not take long. It could also be worked by a tank engine pushing two wagons up from Abermule.

The working mill was extended by the Ministry of Supply paying for storage space. Grain silos were damaged in the Liverpool blitz in 1940 and the mill became a strategic store for imported milling wheat. The technical word was a buffer depot but the actual buffers were wooden sleepers fixed to a turned up rail. The grain was replaced, the older grain going for bread flour and a new delivery came in, turnover maybe only once a year so most of the time little happened. All this came in and left by rail. A number of covered wagons would be stabled at Abermule and the tank engine would push the two wagons up so within two to three days the mill was emptied and refilled. There were two doors for the mill entrance so the covered wagons were placed opposite, four-bushel (2 cwt) sacks were wheeled in and hoisted up to store in the upper floors. This ceased around 1948 when rationing was still in place; the storage in the mill was an insurance against bombing. When the Ministry of Supply contract finished, the mill ceased and the siding closed. It was about this time that Dan entered the family business to take over from his widowed mother.

Living at Fronfraith Mill

George Sneade, born in 1918, was a Kerry lad who went to the all-age school. He never went on the scheduled passenger service, there really was not much money to spare and Kerry village had shops supplying most needs in the 1920s. However, he did go on the Sunday School trips and can remember these before passenger services ceased. 'There would be two or three coaches at Kerry and it would be a heck of a squeeze to get on.' Extra coaches would be on the normal train from Whitchurch to Aberystwyth so they changed at Abermule. The first bus owner was a Mr Cecil Bebb at the Saw Mill and his bus would shuttle down to Newtown and return through the day. It was replaced by a Bedford in 1930. George left school around 1933 and worked for J.E. Corfield at Abermule. This was then a garage and lorry business. George cycled down from Kerry around 5.00 am and returned about 8.00 pm. It was a very hard task cycling home up the gradient in a winter gale. He started as a lorry driver's mate and the usual route was to Liverpool Docks for stock feed to deliver around local farms on return. When old enough, he was taught to drive. Somewhere around 1939, Dad became the Fronfraith miller and the family moved to the tied house at the Mill. George cannot remember the name of the previous miller. There had been a shop run by a Mr David Davies but this had closed maybe 10 years previously. Within the year, George was called up and served throughout the war in the Royal Army Service Corps as a driver. He therefore would not have seen much of Dad's duties at the mill. The mill was coming to the end of its economic working life and much of the equipment would soon be cleared out so that it could be used for an emergency bread wheat store. Dad continued to live in the tied house but worked at D.C. Evans store and shop at Newtown.

The mill had three levels; the top floor stored the whole grain etc. Grain was lifted by a hoist and rope that pulled the sack up through a double trap door. The second floor was the milling floor with grinding stones and roller mill. A huge spindle came in from the outside water wheel. Much of the drive was through oak cogs or spur gears. These changed the vertical drive of the waterwheel to the horizontal needed for the mill stones. Dad would go up to the weir first thing in the morning to allow water to enter the leat. A wooden trough was swung into position so water finally hit the top of the wheel so it was an overshot drive. The mechanism would creak and groan but it was really quiet. Material flowed by gravity to the bottom floor where it was bagged. Pig and poultry food was mixed with a shovel and then bagged up. There was a portable weighing machine and sack trucks. Farmers would come in with their horses and carts to collect the processed grain. Many farmers provided their own grain to he ground. The leat was also used for washing sheep. Grease or lanolin could be close to the skin of the sheep, making hand clipping difficult. Modern powered shearing handpieces shear the sheep with little problem, also sheep are in far better body condition now. Dad would return from the mill looking like a white phantom with flour in every seam of his clothes and every pore of his body. Such things were not understood then, but Dad died of lung problems almost certainly related to this work. A dressing man would come about once a year with a chisel and hammer to renew or dress the face of the mill stones. George spent much of the war overseas. He would return on leave and walk home from Abermule. There was now no chance of a travel warrant to Fronfraith Halt to drop him off a few yards from the front door. Once he arrived at Abermule station about 2.00 am on a dreadful night so he slept in the waiting room. Charlie Baylis came on duty and woke George up and they had a cup of tea in the signal box about 6.00 am. George made several comments, which have also come from others who were manual workers. People remember the friendship, the Sunday School trips etc. with great pleasure. However, there was a black side of primitive living and working conditions. A workplace had no toilets, no washing facilities, no mess room, no safety clothing etc. and George commends all who ensure that things are much better now.

Commuting on the Kerry 'Jimmy'

Catherine Corfield, née Sneade was born in 1919 and lived at Hollybush, Llanmerewig. She started school when she was six walking over two miles to Kerry. Cath passed the scholarship and started the daily journey to the County Girls School at Newtown. Now she only had to walk about a mile to Fronfraith station for a full year and a term until the train service stopped in February 1931. Then she was again faced with a walk of nearly two miles to Abermule station for the main line train. The Kerry and Sarn children travelled by bus after February. There would now be very few alive who used the Kerry 'Jimmy' for school. The County Boys School, although adjacent to the girls at Newtown, was a separate school so Cath cannot remember the boys so well. She can remember her peer group. Kathleen Sneade and Olwen Rogers, joined her at Fronfraith, Medina Jones boarded at Goitre and Ethel Robinson and Rene Jones came from Kerry. All are sadly deceased except for Ethel and herself.

The Education Authority issued a brown-coloured season ticket for each term that was free to scholarship children. There were also fee-paying students and their parents had to buy the ticket. Maybe there were over 20 boys and girls and certainly another 20 from Abermule and Llandyssil joined at the junction. The coach was very comfortable, it was a compartment coach, but Cath was uncertain if there was a corridor, there certainly was one on the main line because they would change seats for a chat.

The journey was only about eight minutes from Fronfraith to Abermule and another 10 minutes to Newtown. The morning train was timed for connection and the main line train was either waiting or came in within a few minutes. On arrival at Newtown, everyone would cross the footbridge and then cross the road into school. The afternoon trip was a little longer as there was a short wait for the Welshpool train to come in which was timed for the connection at Abermule (passenger trains passed at Montgomery about eight minutes time away).

On arrival at Abermule, everyone had to wait on the Welshpool platform side until the main line train had left. The level crossing gates were opened, the signalman now allowed us to cross and we could go to the island platform where the Kerry train was waiting. Soon the Welshpool train came in and passenger's were exchanged. The Kerry level crossing gates were opened and away we went. Catherine remembers everyone having lots of fun on the train, it was an adventure. The duty guard was often a man with a large grin and always telling jokes and teasing them. Catherine, when prompted, confirmed the name of Ewart Thomas. Once when the three girls ran down the slope to Fronfraith when the train was already waiting, Ewart told them to hang on tight because he would have to take a short cut across the fields to catch up. However, if everyone was a little too boisterous, he could become strict. He would check the carriage doors and then he would go to the brake van which was always attached because of the gradient. There would often be adults waiting for the train at the halt, especially on Monday (Welshpool market) and Tuesday (Newtown market). The guard would issue tickets to these people at the halt. The Fronfraith platform was very narrow and a siding was squeezed

Goitre Halt and siding in 1948. The remains of the Halt can just be discerned in the distance. The siding is on the level and the gradient on the line to Abermule can be clearly seen. The coal wagons were parked by a pier and embankment. Coal was unloaded and wheeled to be placed in a circle around the brickwork kiln. *J.I.C. Boyd Collection*

'Dean Goods' class 0-6-0 No. 2538 passes Goetre Brick and Pipe Works with a short goods train bound for Abermule on 4th April, 1956. The brickworks' chimney can just be seen on the extreme left. *G.F. Bannister*

between it and the mill. Usually the siding was empty. There was no shelter if it was raining but by that time everyone was already soaked from walking from Llanmerewig.

Catherine can still picture and hear the engine leaving Fronfraith at around 4.30 pm as it battled up the gradient through the dingle to Goitre as she started to walk home. Her mother would help her dry her clothes but could not help her conjugate Latin verbs. Cath thought such tales must now seem very distant to young people with school buses or parents taking children door to door in a car.

Goitre Siding

Dennis Jones was born in 1933 and brought up in Llandyssil near Abermule. Dennis left school in 1948 to work on local farms. Later he worked at the Goitre including firing the kiln. The Goitre siding was still being used and some bricks and pipes were still going out by rail but much was already leaving by lorry. All coal still came in by rail, unloaded by hand into wheelbarrow and taken to the top of the kiln area ready for firing. Usually only two coal trucks would come in and they were often still wooden-sided, maybe former private owner wagons. The pipes and bricks were dispatched in two-plank-side wagons and a coal wagon would rarely be used as their destination was back to the colliery. The train only operated a few days each week and sometimes there was nothing to collect or drop at the siding.

There was only one siding on the left-hand side facing up the gradient. There was the remnant of a platform and the siding trailed off curving slightly so to be level, the junction was just beyond the platform edge.

Shunting could take two forms. If the train was light, the guard's van and the Kerry section would be pinned down on the branch gradient. The engine would draw out wagons from the siding, then reverse these to the remainder of the train, draw forward and then reverse the goods for the siding, draw out again, then collect the rest of the train and proceed to Kerry. The gradient after the Goitre was the stiffest section of the line; if there was a heavy load or the line was slippery because of frost or rain, the train would go straight through to Kerry where there was a run-round. It would then bring the few wagons down to Goitre and sort out the returns. Once one wagon which was empty must not have had the brake pinned down enough because it disappeared down the branch and went through the Kerry branch gates at the Abermule level crossing. Only the guard's pride was hurt. The engine always worked tender-first up to Kerry (it must have been the 'Dean Goods'); even though Dennis thought that there had been a turntable at Kerry, it was never used. The engine arrived at Abermule from Oswestry and then reversed up. On wet days, a canvas hung from the cab roof to the tender to try and get some weather protection. The Goitre wagons should always have been next to the engine. The train ran non-stop back from Kerry to Abermule. There were some small fires in dry weather on the banks set off by the steam engine; there was one substantial blaze within the wooded section of the dingle, but it was contained. It was a difficult area for a fire engine to have access.

In 1958, after the line had closed, Dennis joined British Railways as a lengthman from Newtown to Forden and helped relieve at the Abermule crossing gates. Everyone was very proud of the Cambrian line. Dennis was made redundant with the Beeching cuts and worked in the building and timber trade but hurt his neck and returned to British Rail for lighter duties around 1978, working as a crossing keeper, mainly at Abermule, but also Caersws, Carno and Llandre (near Aberystwyth). These gates were all hand opened, the only one controlled from the box was at Westbury, which was not ex-Cambrian but ex-LNWR. As these crossings became automated, Dennis became based at Machynlleth on station maintenance as one of two cleaners. He worked at Machynlleth cleaning dmus until retirement in 1995. Dennis also helped on the Vale of Rheidol narrow gauge until it transferred to a private heritage company, both at the end of season and in the spring securing and checking all the fittings such as benches etc.

Dennis has a most interesting collection of lamps, oilcans etc. which also includes the Caersws station bike, which may have gone up the Van! All this material was on the way to the bin as the local stations closed in the mid-1960s. Scrap of one decade, collectors' delight 40 years later.

The level crossing work could be very lonely on the main line by the late 1970s. There was, at virtually every level crossing, an inherited allotment going back a century, so there were always plenty of vegetables; the Abermule plot also had a chicken run. Many an inspector must have gone back to Oswestry with fresh vegetables and eggs.

Goetre* Brick and Pipe Works: Operation in the early 1950s

Impure clay came from the pit by tramway. It was dug and loaded by hand. The clay could vary even within the same vein and the human eye could judge that which was porous for footing bricks and agricultural drains or was of a different quality for facing bricks. The tramway was continuously being re-laid at the pit face and for the temporary sidings to exchange filled and empty trucks. At the brickworks, the trucks were drawn up an incline into the works by winding gear driven by the same steam engine that drove the shafts and pulleys via belts to each of the machines.

Because of the high rainfall etc. the clay was slightly acid and there was no need for souring pits to lower the pH. The clay was tipped into a feed mill that fed into the grinders or pugs. This worked the clay until it was plastic. The clay moved directly to a roller (the trough mixer rarely had to be used) and then to the extrusion press with dies for bricks or pipes. The clay came out in columns and was then cut into lengths. The green bricks were now stacked on a trolley so that air could move through and taken to the drying sheds with heat from the boiler that also drove the stationary steam engine. Fresh green bricks would crack if placed in the kiln and therefore had to dry slowly. Once dry the bricks would be ready for the kiln. The kilns were 14 chambers and therefore the cycle took 14 days from loading the kiln, firing, slow cooling and unloading and

* Goetre is the correct spelling of farms and brick works. It is also anglicised to Goitre or Goytre. It derives from Coed-tref, meaning a woodland settlement. The name is found in all areas of Wales. The railway used Goitre.

cleaning. After the fire was lit, coal was fed by gravity from the top of the kiln for a number of days, the sealed kiln was then allowed to cool slowly. The bricks were then stacked either under cover or outside awaiting dispatch by rail or lorry.

The coal was loaded into a wheelbarrow from the rail truck and taken directly to the top of the kilns waiting their turn to be fired. Dennis Jones recalls that in winter he moved from snow and sleet of an Icelandic storm into a Sahara dust heat within a few yards, he would then tip the barrow and then out again. The loading pier was fixed, the siding was on a minute gradient so the truck was moved down to the pier by hand, releasing the brake with care, because there would be no shunting engine for two days. The brick and tile wagons were closer to the points and were loaded there. The works were at full capacity until around 1955 because there was a shortage of bricks throughout the country as recovery took place from World War II. Builder's lorries would sometimes be waiting to take the bricks straight from the kilns before they had hardly cooled. Much of the equipment was replaced in the early 1960s with electric motors and controls, oil-fired boilers, pallets and forklift trucks, etc. There was again heavy demand in the 1960s for both construction and farm drainage when clay pipes still awaited the competition from plastic reels and lengths. Work in the brickyard was physically demanding. Not only was there much hard physical work, it took place either in freezing wet outside or baking heat inside. Also most men walked or cycled three to four miles daily from their homes. The only consolation was that there were immense spaces to dry out any wet clothes and to germinate spring garden seeds. Maybe up to 30 men were employed at the 1950 peak and it was down to around 15 with modern equipment. Although not a large employer, it made a valued contribution to such a rural area. Every brick was handled by hand, green cut, loaded to the kiln, unloaded from the kiln, loaded on to rail wagon, loaded off rail wagon, taken to builder's site, unloaded and would finally end up in the brickie's hand.

Modern automation with pallets etc. can give a situation where a footing brick or block is loaded on to a pallet that is then placed adjacent to the footings and is only handled once or twice. No wonder a traditional brickworks was such hard work. This description of working conditions was given by George Baylis.

There has been concern on transport from the Goetre Quarry and brickworks. Did it close for the duration of the war or during the war? It closed towards the end of the war, the exact date is not known but it would have been in late 1943 or early 1944. The then Kerry children confirmed stories from their dads that worked in the brickworks. Demand for footing bricks for the Army and RAF camps being built in the Marches and Wales was so great that bricks were being loaded when still hot and that the floor of the flat wagons was being charcoaled. The quarry did not re-open again until 1950 when new owners sent most bricks/drainage pipes out by road and coal was the main item coming in by rail.

Goetre Brickworks large local labour force in 1930, all would have lived within walking or cycling distance. The main regular goods on the Kerry line were the two products of Goetre Brickworks, bricks and drainage pipes. The clay was not of the highest quality and bricks to facing standard would be a special order. Goetre's bricks were used for foundations, cavity etc. The weakness of the clay for bricks was the strong point for agricultural drainage pipes. The clay would have slight porosity, this enabled water to flow into the pipe always lowering the water table to the depth which the pipe had been placed. The highest quality clay layer was found as the works came to closure, clay was being brought in by lorry in the final years. Automation, pallet loading and flexible lorry transport would have made it very difficult for a small rural brickyard to trade by 1970. Clay pipes were being replaced by plastic ones which could be laid by large drainage machines. There was a small narrow gauge tramway taking clay from the pit or qaurry to the clay grinding machinery. The tipping trucks were loaded by hand, hauled out by winch and hand pushed on flat sections. The track was moved as required.

Right: An aerial view of Goetre Brick & Pipe Works *circa* 1970. After the closure of the brickworks, George Baylis, who was licensed to use explosives, moved to Penstrowed Quarries. Steeple jacks had repaired the Goetre kiln chimney and removed the top 10 feet in the mid-1950s after a crack developed as a result of a lightning strike. By the mid-1980s the chimney was in poor condition and the new owners of the yard asked for George's help. George and the representative of the company supplying explosives worked out what was necessary to fell the chimney. Holes were drilled, explosives fitted, police stopped traffic on the road and everyone cleared the area. There was a bang, the chimney toppled, the cloud of dust cleared and the line of bricks was in the predicted spot.

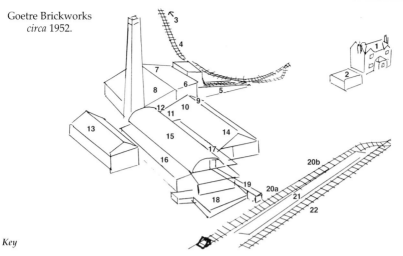

Goetre Brickworks
circa 1952.

Key

1. Goetre Villa, Manager's house.
2. Offices and garage.
3. To impure clay in pit.
4. Tramway.
5. Incline.
6. Feed mill and grinders.
7. Steam engine with drive to main shaft and belt pulleys, also incline winch.
8. Boiler serving engine and drying chambers.
9. Rollers and mixer.
10. Extrusion press and dies.
11. Tile and pipe cutters.
12. Stacks of green bricks/tiles.
13. Drying shed.
14. ditto.
15. Fourteen chamber continuous kiln.
16. Bays for loading green and unloading finished bricks/tiles and ash removal from kilns.
17. ditto.
18. Ramps serving lorry loading and unloading bays.
19. Pier from siding to kilns (coal).
20. Rails siding (a) coal in, (b) brick and tiles out.
21. Goitre passenger halt (disused).
22. Abermule to Kerry line.

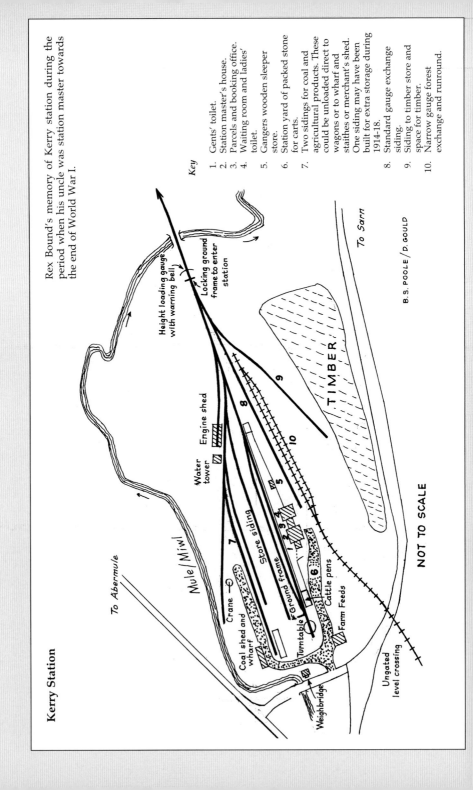

Kerry Station

Rex Bound's memory of Kerry station during the period when his uncle was station master towards the end of World War I.

To Abermule

Mule/Miwl

Coal shed and wharf

Crane

Turntable

Store siding

Ground frame

Weighbridge

Cattle pens

Farm Feeds

Ungated level crossing

Engine shed

Water tower

Height loading gauge with warning bell

Locking ground frame to enter station

TIMBER

To Sarn

NOT TO SCALE

B.S. POOLE / D. GOULD

Key

1. Gents' toilet.
2. Station master's house.
3. Parcels and booking office.
4. Waiting room and ladies' toilet.
5. Gangers wooden sleeper store.
6. Station yard of packed stone for carts.
7. Two sidings for coal and agricultural products. These could be unloaded direct to wagons or to wharf and staithes or merchant's shed. One siding may have been built for extra storage during 1914-18.
8. Standard gauge exchange siding.
9. Siding to timber store and space for timber.
10. Narrow gauge forest exchange and runround.

Kerry Station

Rex Bound was born in 1911 at Llandinam but moved to Kerry when very young. His mother's oldest brother was Richard Bennett, station master at Kerry. He would often visit the station either with his mother, or when a little older, by himself. He has clear memory of both the tramline and the German prisoners of war; his uncle became good friends with a naval prisoner and they continued correspondence for many years. Rex would have travelled the Kerry 'Jimmy' as a passenger; however his memories are of the yard.

He would walk round with uncle on inspection and can remember the warmth of the little engine shed and became friends with the young cleaner. He is sorry that he cannot remember his name. He can remember the last cleaner called Hilary (George) Smith. A Mr Cooper, one of the engine drivers, held Rex to man height and he can remember the thrill of moving the engine from the shed to the sidings. Some days Rex would be in the booking office when a train arrived or departed, but uncle was never rushed, as there were few customers; freight was the main business.

The turntable would sometimes be used but usually the small tank engine came in chimney-first and then ran back cab-first. The turntable was installed as the earlier tank engines would not have had a full cab. One of Rex's tasks would be to use a hand pump to get water to the cisterns of the station toilet; you stopped when the overflow shot water out.

Much of Rex's story was similar to that of Jack Arthur. His description of the station yard was a wonderful preview of the Kerry station map. There was a loading gauge just before the first points. This was for timber and a bell would ring if the gantry was touched, The first siding went to the east of the station and was the transfer siding for the tramway timber trains. The next points took the train into Kerry station where the train could run round either goods or passenger stock. The turntable was at the blind end of the station. The first building on the station was the platelayers' cab and then there was the main station and a warehouse for both distribution and dispatch. The final building by the entrance was the weighbridge and shed. This shed had a fireplace so it is where Hilda Mills would have made the tea. There were long sidings parallel to the station and it was here that covered wagons would have held farm feed. Montgomeryshire Farmers had a depot here and also a Bibby's and a Silcocks' agent worked from here. He thought that sheep and cattle loading also took place here. The next two sidings were the coal wharves; there were two coal merchants, a Mr Owen and a Mr Williams. Mrs Owen was one of the teachers at Kerry School and she could not walk very well because she was quite lame. The two final sidings were against the Glanmeheli Brook; the longer siding had the water tanks and a crane, which was used for any heavier loading and unloading. The short siding went to the engine shed. All trains leaving Kerry travelled about a mile to the summit close to the Court Bridge where they had to stop to pin down brakes before starting down the gradient.

The Anchor Road was built after the first war. Much of the stone came by rail and a Mr Bowen was the contractor. He had a team of horses and wagons and it must have been very hard work for the horses on such steep gradients. (Kerry station was 600 feet above sea level and the crossing of the Kerry Ridgeway within a distance of about four miles would have been 1,500 feet.) Traction engines and trailers were also being used. Rex can remember picking bilberries with his grandmother high on the moor and watching the traction engines on the pitch (gradient).

Mr Edwin Brown was the carter who had a pony and gambo and carried parcels, passenger luggage and sundries to and from Glanmule to the village. Only the wealthy had a pony and trap; everyone else walked or cycled from Kerry. Rex often had a lift back for his dinner to the village with Mr Brown; his uncle was an important man!

Rex joined the GWR in 1927 and worked for them for nearly 50 years. He started at Welshpool as lamp lad looking after oil lamps which would work for up to eight days but needed attention after five days as the wick would harden. He spent most of his working life at Welshpool as relief worker, anything from parcels to ticket office to porter. He lived at Abermule and he purchased Kerry station from BR Property and lived there for about 15 years until moving to Newtown. He put a door frame from the booking office to access the main house. He kept a pitch pine bench from the ladies waiting room, but it has now gone.

Rex has very poor sight now but this is a remarkable recall for a 90-year-old man remembering his childhood with his uncle at Kerry station. A visit would often be made to see Rex Bound and read him some of the material that was being collated. Over these visits, he would add some gems.

Every Friday, during the latter part of World War I, the meat wagon would come up from Newtown for the German prisoners of war and three or four of them would be at the station to take the meat to the camp. There would always be six carcasses of mutton and a large leg flank of horse, sometimes there would be several pig carcasses or a half side of beef. Some would be salted, most would be roasted that weekend. Some was eaten hot and the remainder would be cold cooked meat. This helped to keep the maggots away.

The tramway (*see Chapter Ten*) was virtually operated by the Germans. They did the forest extraction; they drove and looked after the little engines and loaded at Kerry station exchange. Towards the end of the war, there really was not a problem. Many had become friends with local people and guard duty must have been the easiest of tasks. Many were good craftsmen with wood; maybe it was all they could do with their free time. Mum would work in the station pump house, which also had an oven to bake bread. She gave one huge chunk to a German working at the exchange siding. About three days later he had made a wooden shovel for her to help get the bread out the oven. Several stayed on after the war, but Rex can remember the final train out. It was a special of covered vans and cattle trucks to take them down to Abermule to change to a special train which took them to somewhere like Harwich and then home. Many came to wave them goodbye; they all had carved walking sticks etc. to take home as gifts. This would be somewhere around 1919.

The passenger platform was used for sheep loading on fair days in the early 1920s; there was only an early and a late passenger service. The platform was filthy with sheep droppings and as the last pen was loaded, the pens were dismantled and every one attacked the filth with brush, shovel and barrow and the platform was then washed down.

The GWR bus operated after passenger closure, on sheep fair days. This bus was driven by one of two Rowland brothers and normally operated as an extra to the very limited railway passenger service from Welshpool to Llanfair before 1931. He assumes that Llanfair bus services may have been cancelled on Kerry Sheep Days.

Rex knew Ewart Thomas well and knew the contrast between the Kerry line with strict instructions on use of the brake van and wagon pinning down compared with the Van line where wagons were unloaded or left virtually on request because there was such a limited service. It was, in effect, a siding albeit a very long one.

The Engine Shed

George Smith, now 89, was an Abermule lad. He started work in the Abermule village shop then joined the railway on 7th April, 1930. He was sent to Oswestry. His christian name is Hilary, but his landlady decided George was better, so George he has been since. After six to eight weeks he returned to become the last cleaner in the Kerry engine shed. When the passenger service closed in February 1931, he was given the choice of Moat Lane or Oswestry, so he chose Oswestry. Slowly he worked his way up the hierarchy of the railway system, fireman, engine driver, locomotive supervisor, seeing out his career at Machynlleth. He has a manuscript of his career, in some ways he would know more about the Llanfyllin and Llangynog branches and the Porthywaen quarry than the eight months spent at Kerry.

He can remember seeing the little Van engine at Oswestry, maybe after line closure in 1941. The engine was waiting for the breakers or maybe it was just before the war when the engine was at the works for repair, he cannot remember which. When at Kerry, he lived at his home in Llanmerewig. His duty commenced in the shed at 4.00 am and he finished at 12.30 pm. The fireman at the end of the previous day had to place the engine in the shed and dowse the fire. George's duties would be to clean out the ash and start with a fresh fire, building up the coal and filling the coal bunker. It was important to check water was at the right level to start to raise steam; some engine tanks would leak. The driver and the fireman would expect the engine to be fully operational by around 7.45 am so that they could take it to the platform and hook on to the passenger coach. The rest of the morning was spent cleaning the shed out, removing the ash and transferring coal from a wagon to the coal stage ready to fill the bunker next shift. He would go home just after midday so he would see little of the activities in the yard.

There were two Dean saddle tanks Nos. 2032 and 2075, changing maybe every month when one went to Oswestry for washing out. There was little trouble with scaling with Kerry water. George took considerable pride and he was very disappointed when one of these engines (2075?) returned in a filthy condition. George has fired on the Kerry line, certainly for an extra excursion,

Kerry engine shed on 20th May, 1937. There are a good number of wagons in the sidings. Notice the yard crane in the distance.   *R.W. Miller Collection*

Kerry shed with the doors closed in 1948. Notice the broken windows by this time. This picture gives a good view of the GWR-built water tank at the rear of the shed.   *R.W. Miller Collection*

and he would be reserve cover if someone failed to turn up. This would be a rare event; time discipline was enforced and a railwayman would have to be really ill before taking any time off.

When far younger, the then Hilary would visit Fronfraith Mill to collect ground grain; there was a small area almost like a shop where ground flour for baking and smallholder feed could be purchased.

George enjoyed his railway career, which commenced with the humble but vital task of engine cleaner at Kerry.

The Kerry Sheep Fair

George Jones of Weston Farm, Kerry was born in late 1932 after the line had closed for normal passenger services but he can remember travelling on a special for the visit of George VI and the Queen to Aberystwyth in the Coronation year of 1937. This may have been the last excursion special (apart from the Sunday School trips). His family with his mother travelled in small coaches to Abermule where they changed to what looked a huge long train.

George was so excited that he pulled the leather strap as the train was travelling down through the dingle; the window opened and a grain of soot went into his eye and smarted all day. At Aberystwyth, the passengers were escorted to the promenade and there was a line of the military in front of the crowd. A guard lifted George on his shoulders so that he could see the procession. George can remember little of the journey back; he suspects that at the age of under five he slept in his mother's arms.

George visited the station often with his father in the 1940s; it was always a place of magic. He can give some idea of how just one village farm made use of the station. It was a bonus for Kerry that the line served the community with freight for over 90 years.

Some 20 sheep feed racks were delivered direct to the station from Corbetts of Oswestry and several are still on the farm over 50 years later. Until 1950, many agricultural products would be quoted with price inclusive to the nearest station. An International Tractor Model 10/20 was delivered from Picketts of Ilkeston, Derbyshire, bought from an advert in *The Farmers Weekly*. He can remember it on the flat truck, roped down and the yardman, Reg Fryer, discussing how to unload it and nobody was certain how to start it.

The Weston Farm chose to sell the wool direct to the Smiths Wool Merchant of Shrewsbury. Other farmers sent their wool by the train to auction at Newtown. A representative of Smiths would be at Glanmeheli (farm nearest the station) and all people selling wool to that firm would be asked to deliver on a said date. After weighing and labelling, the wool sacks were taken straight to the sidings and loaded into covered vans. The selling of wool in this way ceased around 1946 when the Wool Marketing Board took control of purchase.

His father was a founder member of Montgomeryshire Farmers (now Wynnstay Farmers) and bought most products from that firm. The salesman was Mr William Lewis and the goods were stored in the covered vans. Before the war, farmers would have to get their own wagons to collect within the day.

.. NEWTOWN ..

MONTGOMERYSHIRE.

....

CATALOGUE

OF THE ANNUAL

Wool Sale

COMPRISING ABOUT

50,000 FLEECES

Of Kerry Hill, Cross-bred, Shropshire and Welsh Wool

TOGETHER WITH

The Clip of Several Thousand Lambs

To be Sold by Auction by Messrs

MORRIS, MARSHALL & POOLE

On Wednesday, July 19th, 1922.

☞ The Wool has been Warehoused at the Severn Valley Mills, close to Railway Station, where the Sale will be held at **12-30 p.m.**

THE WHOLE ON VIEW DAY PREVIOUS TO SALE
AND MORNING OF SALE.

A wool auction notice for 19th July, 1922. Wool prices were good until man-made fibres became available after World War II. The Wool Marketing Board purchased all wool against a price list of grades through an approved merchant after 1947. Pre-World War II wool from Kerry would have been transported direct to a merchant such as Smiths of Shrewsbury or be sent to Newtown for auction. Wool would have come in covered vans from branches such as Kerry and Van, plus all stations from beyond Welshpool in the east to Llanidloes and Llanbrynmair in the west. There would be about 30 fleeces to a sack and around 15 sacks per van so these would require between 100 and 115 van loads, all local traffic which would transfer to lorries within 20 years.

This continued after the war but the feed firm would also deliver to the farm in a lorry. All fertiliser and compound cakes were delivered, often in one cwt hessian sacks; cereals came in railway sacks which weighed 1½ cwt for oats or 2 cwt for wheat. There was much humping done at both the station and the home farm.

The Kerry branch must be unique in Britain in that a sheep fair dominated by one breed, the Kerry Hill, was the only time the branch operated to full capacity.

For centuries, drovers moved sheep and cattle out of Wales. From 1750 to the railway building, this trade expanded as urban areas such as London and Birmingham grew. Kerry Ridgeway was the eastern part of Hir Hen Ffordd (Long Old Route) starting from North Ceredigion, South Merioneth and West Montgomeryshire. There are still traces in the clumps of Scots Pine on hill points acting as visual beacons; there is a drovers' milestone near Bishops Castle with '157 miles to London', and names such as Sarn City and Little London east and west of Kerry may be drovers' humour.

In the early 1800s, progressive farmers started to understand livestock breeding principles and used both local breeds and some infusion to fix standards. Sheep had survived on the Kerry Hills, which straddle parts of Radnorshire, Shropshire and Montgomeryshire; these high hills are colder but drier than much of Wales. So the Kerry Hill breed evolved from local Clun, Long Mynd and Kerry Mountain with some Cheviot and Ryeland to fix characteristics. The wool trade and manufacture of Welsh flannel boomed, in Newtown and the Kerry fleece was very important for this. Expanding population increased demand for mutton, so around 1850, profitability looked good. No one yet knew the effect the Argentine, the Australian and the New Zealand sheep industries would have from 1870 onwards. Pressure from one of the pioneer breeders, John Wilkes Poundley, helped the Oswestry & Newtown Railway to make the decision to build the branch.

In 1871, a major change occurred linked to the opportunity of the railway. Instead of dealers (ex-drovers) buying by private treaty and a handshake at the farm, an auction for the sheep fairs was established. This became the basis of the modern market where an independent auctioneer provides a service between buyer and seller. The Kerry Sheep Sales marks a very important concept in both agricultural and railway livestock transport history because many auction sites were established close to railway centres.

Kerry Sheep Sales with rail dispatch boomed and would have peaked in the 1920s and 1930s. Such was the demand that other larger important sales of draft and store stock centred on rail facilities at Craven Arms and Welshpool and other areas of the UK came about. The sale took place in the Glanmule/Glanmeheli fields adjoining the station. Some of the older people can still remember earning the shilling for helping with watering and droving.

At the peak, there were three sales on Fridays. The pedigree sale of ewes and rams took place in late August; this would have been a smaller volume but with higher prices.The main sale in early September generated huge rail traffic. This was the draft ewe sale. Sheep were kept on the hill for between two to four lamb crops depending on lambing percentage. These ewes were sold to lowland farms when six tooth to full mouthed, where better grass enabled the full

Larger locomotives were sometimes used on the branch during the sheep sales to deal with the additional traffic. This view shows Cambrian Railways No. 21, which, as GWR No. 1118, had been used for the sheep sales traffic in 1928, and then continued to be used on the branch for sometime afterwards. Due to the tight curves on the line No. 1118 had a detrimental effect on the permanent way and this prompted the memo below to be sent which threatened withdrawal of traffic on the Kerry branch if the engine was not removed!

31st October, 1928.

48271/7. B.

O. 9101.

Dear Sir,

ENGINES WORKING ON KERRY BRANCH.

In August last I gave authority for an engine of the 1112 type to work specially on the Kerry Branch during the Sheep sales, but as engine 1118 has been working daily on this Branch for some time and is causing considerable damage to the permanent way I wrote to Mr Warwick on the 19th instant asking him to arrange for this to be withdrawn at once. I find this engine is still working, and unless it can be withdrawn immediately I shall have to consider closing the Branch to traffic.

Yours faithfully,

E. COLCLOUGH, ESQ.

'Dean Goods' class 0-6-0 No. 2411 at Abermule with a train of empty cattle wagons for Kerry on 19th September, 1952 during that year's annual sheep sales. The engine was based at Oswestry and had been turned at Welshpool and so unusually arrived at Kerry smokebox first.

G.F. Bannister

No. 2411 has just arrived at Kerry with the empty cattle wagons on 19th September, 1952. Notice the penning on the platform in use as a sheep race to temporary loading pens.   *G.F. Bannister*

fertility with many twins (often Suffolk crosses) to be exploited for a further three to six lamb crops; good fleeces were clipped and finally the old ewe could be fattened for mutton.

The final supplementary sale was for yearling ewes and store male wether lambs. Lowland farms had stubble regrowth, arable by-products, rape kale grown to smother woods and autumn flush meadows to take these stores to finish. The urine and dung (the so-called golden hoof) from these sheep helped the soil fertility.

Both hill farmer and lowland farmer found these systems of stratification profitable. Estimates vary, but older people thought around 40 rail vans were used for the pedigree sales, over 100 for the draft sales and up to 80 for the store sale, huge rail traffic for this little branch. Dealers and farmers generated extra passenger traffic.

Until 1931, special pens were placed on the south end of the platform in addition to the cattle pens. After passenger closure, the station platform was used and as the platform was the same height as van entry, loading would be very quick. After World War II lorry transport quickly made inroads into this traffic; the final sheep fair train took place in September 1955 with one train of less than 15 vans. After 1960, mixed farming became less common in England and Wales, so farms specialised in arable or dairy etc. The draft ewe and store sales still existed but with nowhere near the same volume.

The Vale of Kerry also sold fat cattle and lamb through the year. Street sales had ceased for sanitation reasons so there was weekly traffic to both Newtown and Welshpool markets. There were small loading pens close to the turntable. This small volume traffic would not have survived the late 1940s.

So, for three days between late August and mid-September, the sheep fair would have seen the branch full to capacity. Sheep would have walked from all over the Kerry Hills to the central point by the railhead. Local farmers provided overnight lairage, rail staff ensured wagons were in place, the auctioneers would have arranged food and lodgings for buyers so in all it was a major operation. This could not have operated with the traffic density of today; the lanes and main road became packed with sheep, men and dogs as everything moved to the auction pens and the railhead. One yearly sale now meets the local vendors' demand on another farm in the area so there is still a link with the time when Kerry, over 130 years ago, provided the model auction systems which are now the basis of the modern professional livestock auction.

Kerry Driver

Sometime during the war, Griff Jones (*see Chapter Seven*) was sent to Swindon for the driver course. Afterwards, his rota would sometimes have him either firing or driving up to Kerry. The Dean pannier was a powerful little engine designed for such industrial branches from Cornwall to Wrexham but especially for South Wales. The shift would commence by going to Caersws to do any shunting, then back to Moat Lane which was then a double line as far as Newtown. Travel would normally be as a light engine with the guard in the cab but sometimes it could have a brake van and several trucks. The goods to and from Kerry were normally marshalled at Abermule sidings. The wartime trains could be substantial; the goods up would have three or four coal wagons for Goetre brickworks. Autumn and winter would have three or four more coal trucks for Kerry and, in summer, coal was taken up to store ahead. There would be empties for bricks and pipes to be loaded at Goetre. Many military camps must have had Goetre footing bricks for their Nissan huts. There would be several covered vans with cattle feed, empty cattle wagons and wagons of fertiliser, lime or slag. Often there was a flat wagon with either a tractor or piece of farm machinery allocated to the Kerry area by the War Agricultural Committee. The Forestry Commission loaded much small timber, especially pit props at Kerry. A Mr Francis of Montgomeryshire Farmers was still based at the station. It needed concentration and skill to keep all this moving on the gradients as it was not a saunter like the Van line.

The sheep sale days required special operation. They were on a Friday so the Van service would be cancelled. A train of cattle trucks would work up late on Thursday after the regular goods had returned the staff to Abermule. On the Friday the staff working was replaced by train staff and ticket. The first train took a ticket and the inspector up to Kerry. Several trains would now follow up the line and were issued with a ticket up only, the last one taking the staff. Griff assumes the inspector was in contact with the Abermule signalman by phone. The inspector would issue a return ticket and the locomotive would set off with up to 40 cattle wagons. The train would stop just above the Court and pinning down would take place. People like Ewart Thomas had become very skilled in judging the number of wagons to pin down. There was an interval of about 25 minutes before the inspector would allow another train to leave. The final locomotive and goods would bring both the staff and the inspector down and, the following day, the line would revert to single train staff in use again.

Horse Sales

Freda Sanders became one of the wartime lady staff, first at Afon Wen and then back to her home at Newtown. Male staff were being called up for military service. Cyril Davies continued as booking clerk at Abermule but certain tasks were taken on by Newtown station for the Kerry branch. Freda became very skilled at the morse code. This was very important for horse sales. Montgomeryshire was very important for the supply of young horses for the cavalry and the urban horse-drawn trade. The war delayed the run down of this supply and horses were still being sent all over the country for milk floats, brewery delivery, local rail delivery, etc. There were three big horse sales each year at Glanmule (Kerry station). These sales were in March, April and October.

The wagons were loaded at Kerry and then sent out from Abermule but the paper work was done from Newtown. After each sale Freda would be working late into the night advising stations that horses were on their way.

At the end of the war, most ladies had to finish but Freda was retained until 1967. She can recall the special workmen's train running to Rhayader each day between 1945 and 1950 taking workmen to Claerwen dam construction. She can again remember the extra traffic of bulk cement wagons for the Clywedog dam in the 1960s.

One of the lovely trips of her childhood in the early 1920s was to travel to Kerry. She has done every combination possible but an example would be Newtown to Abermule, change to Kerry, then walk to Kerry village with her uncle and aunt. Uncle would buy a beer, Freda would have a lemonade, Auntie would have a cup of tea and then they would walk down the Vastre hill back to Newtown. She must have done such a trip many a time and when they were teenagers they would go by themselves so she can remember how disappointed she felt when the passenger service closed in 1931.

The Kerry and Van Guard

A name that is frequent within these stories is that of Ewart Thomas. Some people of Newtown can still remember Ewart. Gwilym, Penri and Aldwyth Thomas were neighbours to Ewart at Bryn Street when they were children in the early 1930s. Ewart would always have a smile and a greeting for the two young brothers and their sister. Their father, Robert Thomas, had started his postman's career in the village of Llanymawddwy before moving to Newtown. He would have travelled on the Mawddwy branch. He died in 1932. He would return from Newtown to see his family at Mawddwy by catching the early mail train, which would arrive far too early for the branch train at Cemmes Road. He would have his bike on the train and cycle to his old home. He would race the train back from Dinas to Cemmes Road. The branch line had closed by the time Gwilym and Penri can remember a rare journey to see the old family when they would have travelled from Newtown to Cemmes Road on the train and then by bus to Dinas.

Ewart would leave Bryn Street early on his bike to cycle to Moat Lane Junction for his shift on either the Van or the Kerry. He would be in his uniform with his whistle, his red and green flag wrapped round the cross bar but most important of all, his lunch box. He had married late in life to Elsi from the shoe department of the Co-op. Elsi was famous for her rice puddings. They had no children. They had a disaster, which hurt both of them very much. They took two young brothers, Brian and Jack, as evacuees from Birkenhead in World War II. Brian was drowned in a deep pool one warm summer's day when swimming in the River Severn which was close to Bryn Street.

Ewart was a charismatic man, a generous character who was well liked by everyone. He is immediately recognised by everyone when shown the photograph with such comments as 'That's Ewart, bless his soul' and 'It's lovely to see his smile again'.

An article in the *County Times* was published on 13th February, 1971 retelling the drama of the Abermule railway disaster. Ewart was one of the survivors and was unhurt; he was travelling on the train actually on duty but not in charge of it. Guard Shone had charge of the train as far as Welshpool where it was divided and he continued with the Shrewsbury & London section while guard

Thomas continued in charge of the Manchester section as far as Whitchurch. He was therefore riding in the rear end of the last coach sitting in the boxed-in guard's seat with its padded sides. This stopped him being thrown cross the van when the impact happened.

There was very little noise and until he got out of the train he did not realise how bad a crash had occurred. Then naturally his first thought was how to start getting the passengers out. Guard Shone was killed because he had gone along to the Paddington coaches to attend to his duties. Mr Thomas said, 'If he had stayed just that much longer at the back he would have been saved'. He remembers that the train carried a buffet at that time up at the front and two girls served refreshments. Miraculously, they were uninjured in the crash. Another thing that he remembers was that an injector from one of the engines was thrown across the road into a field near to the smallholdings. Two men who were working on the house were thrown to the ground by the blast of the impact.

The thing that impressed Ewart was the devotion to duty of the fireman of the express who found the tablet held by the other driver. He and his driver were cleared from any responsibility for the accident.

Ruby Cookson of Berriew and Ewart Roberts of Manafon remember their Uncle Ewart (their mother's brother) and his wife Elsi Griffiths with great affection. Ewart died in December 1983 at the age of 92. His mother was from the Van and his father was born at Trefeglwys. Ewart was born in the Van Terrace. The family moved to Abercynon in South Wales due to the first demise of the Van lead mine. Dad worked down the coal mines when Ewart was a young boy. The family were to return to the Newtown area to live at Abermule. Both parents then worked at the Royal Welsh Warehouse as tailors.

Ewart Thomas worked for 45 years for the Cambrian, the GWR and BR with the exception of serving in the Royal Welsh Fusiliers in the Great War. He started as a lamp boy in Newtown station. He told the story of being on parade for the through journey of the then new Prince of Wales, maybe in 1911. He recalled to his nephew that there was some dissent from certain railwaymen. Chartism still remained part of the fabric of the area.

Ewart's brother, Walter, also worked for the railway. He was a lorry driver at Montgomery station where there was much parcel traffic to Montgomery Town and the Churchstoke area. Ewart Roberts can remember rides up the Kerry line with his uncle. He cannot remember the journey in detail. All Ewart junior can recall was the hard work of shunting, especially the lifting of chains to the hooks. He also had rides with Uncle Walter in the GWR lorry that was noisy and a real bone shaker. These journeys would have been in the 1920s when Ewart junior stayed with Granny in Abermule.

The Concluding Kerry Story

Bill Jones, now of Kerry, has read the draft section of the Kerry reminiscences for any major error and he now completes the Kerry story. Bill started work at Moat Lane in 1946 as a junior cleaner, and then went to Old Oak Common. He did National Service and returned to Moat Lane in 1953. His career would be almost identical to that of Neville Bound.

Bill would sometimes cadge a lift back to Newtown from Moat Lane in the guard's van. In early 1948 for a few months, in the depth of the petrol shortage, the bottled, pasteurised milk from Central Dairies, Newtown was taken up for the Kerry School and the village by train. This train would load milk at Newtown; the guard was Ewart Thomas. The train would leave Moat Lane around 7.00 am just after Bill had finished a night shift. Ewart would have his breakfast cooked during the short journey on the brake van stove.

After return in 1953, Bill may have acted as fireman about 40 times on the Kerry branch with either Tom Aldridge, Reg Cwmbelan (Jones) or Tom Jones as driver. The engine would be a 'Dean Goods' changing crew at Montgomery as already described.

The longest load he can remember during this final period was three trucks! Sometimes, they only took one truck up so they would not bother with the brake van and Ewart would ride in the cab with them. The goods wagon would have the brake van tail lamp hung on the coupling so the Abermule signalman would know they had not left part of the train behind.

Ewart had the biggest leather lunchbox. The man was a trencherman for his food. During the final few years, the yard was looked after by Mrs Fryer as Reg went daily to another station, Bill thinks it was Forden. One day when they had completed the shunt at Kerry, Mrs Fryer said there was a cup of tea and a tart in the station kitchen for everyone. When Bill and the driver came to the kitchen, Ewart was already there and had eaten half of the very large plateful of the blackcurrant tart! Bill did not smoke but older men were wary of Ewart saying 'Hast'tee a bit of bacco boy?' because he would shovel half the pouch content into his pipe.

A few times Bill took a pannier tank from Moat Lane Junction. It would go head first up the line and come down with bunker first. It was a good puller on the gradients. The pannier was once low on water so the Kerry water tank was used. It must have been a museum piece from the Oswestry and Newtown railway for instead of unscrewing a valve, a chain was pulled against a counterweight sluice gate and water sloshed down a sluice. The yard was overgrown in the last summers; it was more like shunting into an overgrown allotment. All sidings were west of the station; any sidings for loading from the forest tramway had long gone.

Sometimes, the fireman would have to walk in front, scraping frost and leaf mulch off the rails but with the pannier, the sanders were in the correct place. The problem was that this slipping occurred on frosty mornings when the damp sand itself could be frozen. So until the last, the Kerry journey could be a challenge.

Chapter Ten

The Kerry Tramway

This tramway was constructed at the instance of Mr Christopher J. Naylor, of Brynllywarch Hall, Kerry. He was much impressed with the narrow gauge tramways used in connection with the Canadian lumber camps and, on his return from his visit to that Dominion, laid private lines in 1888. Built on a gauge of 1 ft 11½ in. (popularly known as 'the 2 ft gauge') they extended from Kerry station to his own saw mills and his various woodlands: his residence, Brynllywarch Hall, was not connected by rail. The contractor to the Kerry Tramway, as these lines were early termed, was a Mr Croom-Johnson, of Wrexham with Mr (later Sir) Henry Maybury in charge of the men. The rails weighed 22 lb. per yard; the single tracks were spiked to wooden sleepers.

For the opening Mr Naylor secured an 0-4-0 wing tank locomotive with outside cylinders from W.G. Bagnall Limited, Castle Engine Works, Stafford (Works No. 970) and built by them in the same year. The name *Excelsior* was prominently displayed on the diminutive water tanks. Dimensional details were as follows:

Cylinders:	5 in. diameter x 7½ in. stroke
Diameter of driving wheels:	1 ft 3¼ in.
Diameter of rear wheels:	10 in.
Wheelbase of driving wheels:	3 ft 0 in.
Total wheelbase:	7 ft 0 in.
Weight in working order:	3 tons 15 cwt approximately
Tractive effort:	1,290 lb.

This locomotive was equipped with a single step on either side of the cab, which was not fitted with a rear weather-board when new. It was built with left-hand drive, link motion between the frames, disc wheels, double-plate type smokebox doors, Salter safety valves, and probably a marine firebox.

Following the closure of the tramway in 1895 the locomotive was sold early in 1896 to Mr J. Nuttall, of Manchester, who used it in the construction of the Lynton & Barnstaple Railway, North Devon, work on which commenced in March of that year. It later saw duty in the Portland stone quarries of F.J. Barnes, Ltd [a company acquired in 1947 by Bath & Portland Stone Firms, Ltd (of Bath)]. In the early years of the tramway this locomotive was driven by Mr William Evans, who later became a driver on the Festiniog Railway.

Mr Naylor fitted one of his trucks with seats and a cover for use when taking his guests on picnics: the tramway was not otherwise used for passengers. Subsequently he inherited Haggerston Castle, a property in the North of England, assumed the name of Leyland and left Kerry, the tramway ceasing to operate in April 1895. The rails were sold to Messrs Thomas Beatson, of Derby. The locomotive, of which Mr Samuel Ware was the driver at the close, was disposed of in 1896 as previously indicated.

In its original form the tramway, including branches, returned a mileage of 5 miles 5 chains (tramway distances quoted are approximate only). From a

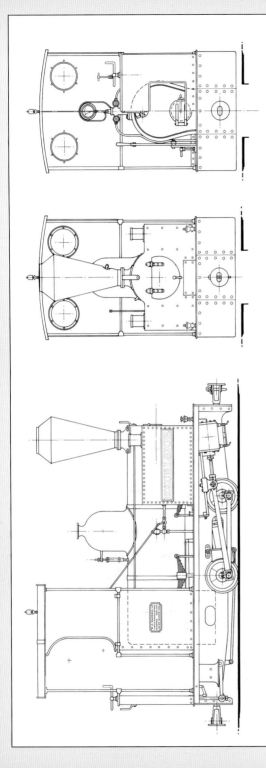

W.G. Bagnall
Works No. 970
Built 1888
0-4-0 Wing Tank
Excelsior

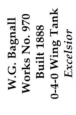

Excelsior in its original form as an 0-4-0 wing tank and fitted with a spark arrestor chimney at Kerry, with estate workers on the Brynllywarch Estate. This poor quality image may be the only one in existence of this locomotive at Kerry. The locomotive was sold on and photographs exist of it later in its career as an 0-4-2 on the construction of the Lynton & Barnstaple Railway (*see below*) and later in the quarries on the Island of Portland (see *Isle of Portland Railways Vol. 1. The Admiralty and Quarry Railways*, B.L. Jackson, Oakwood Press (OL106A)).

G.S. Chadwick Collection

By the time this photograph of *Excelsior* was taken during the construction of the Lynton & Barnstaple Railway the engine was in the ownership of contractor J. Nuttall of Manchester. Nuttall comenced work on the Lynton & Barnstaple Railway contract in 1896, by this time *Excelsior* had been rebuilt, where and when can only be speculated at. The form we see here is of an 0-4-2 wing tank. The locomotive's frames have been extended so as to accommodate an additional water tank. A temporary looking bunker extension has also been added to the top. The spark arrestor chimney has been replaced by one of 'stovepipe' pattern.

R.W. Kidner Collection

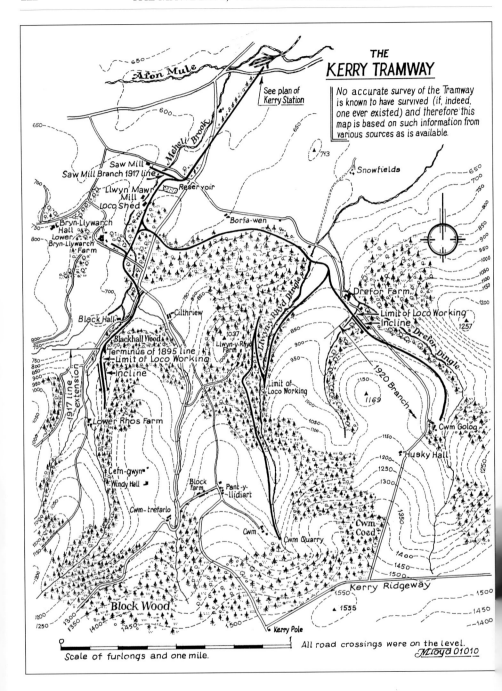

THE
KERRY TRAMWAY

No accurate survey of the Tramway is known to have survived (if, indeed, one ever existed) and therefore this map is based on such information from various sources as is available.

Afon Mule

See plan of
Kerry Station

Meheli Brook

Snowfields

Saw Mill
Saw Mill Branch 1917 line
Reservoir
Llwyn Mawr
Mill
Loco Shed
Bryn-Llywarch
Hall
Lower
Bryn-Llywarch
Farm

Borfa-wen

713

Drefor Farm
Limit of Loco Working
Incline
Drefor Dingle
1257

Black Hall
Cilthriew
Blackhall Wood
Terminus of 1895 line
Limit of Loco Working
Incline
Llwyn-y-Rhyd
Farm
1037
Llwyn-y-Rhyd Dingle

1920 Branch

1917 line
extension

Lower Rhos Farm
Limit of
Loco Working
1169

1150

Cwm Golog

Husky Hall

Cefn-gwyn
Windy Hall
Block
Farm
Pant-y-
llidiart

Cwm-trefarlo

Cwm
Coed

Cwm
Cwm Quarry

Block Wood

Kerry Ridgeway

1555

Kerry Pole

All road crossings were on the level.
M Lloyd 01010

Scale of furlongs and one mile.

The tramway engine shed above the saw mills by the Meheli Brook in 2002. This shed was built by the Naylor Estate around 1887, ceased use on first closure in 1895 and then became part of the forest tramway during World War I. The short branch to Brynllywarch was not restored during the second period of operation. The farm track was previously tramway formation heading to the Kerry Hills. *B. Poole*

terminus adjacent to Kerry station it crossed the Newtown-Craven Arms road on the level - in common with all road crossings - and passing to the east of Glan Meheli Farm entered woodlands before crossing first the Anchor Road and secondly Springfield Road, at which point a branch (4 chains in length) was thrown off right-handed to the saw mill. The main running line continued to climb the valley containing the Meheli brook, passing to the east of Brook Cottage and Llwyn-Mawr Farm. Here a lane was crossed and the brick-built locomotive shed came into view. This building was on the right-hand side of the main running line (at 69 chains). It is still in being and is in use as a cow-shed.

Shortly beyond this point the tramway split, one line turning left-handed to cross the Kerry station-Pentre Road (1 mile) before passing through Keepers Wood. On approaching Drefor Farm this line turned southwards and climbed Llwyn-y-Rhwd Dingle for some distance before gaining height by means of two reversing junctions which carried it past Llwyn-y-Rhwd Farm and Cwm Farm and on to a terminus at Cwm Quarry (3 miles): nowadays noteworthy only for its profusion of rhododendron blooms in due season.

The second line, which was regarded as the main line, pressed forward towards Black Hall. A line came in left-handed to form a triangle with that from Llwyn-y-Rhwd, following which the Meheli brook was crossed and a short branch (10 chains in length) from Lower Brynllywarch Farm - the home farm of Brynllywarch Hall - effected a trailing junction on the right-hand side. The gradient was sharply falling from the farm.

German prisoners of war at Black Hall, Kerry. They were from the German Navy, many were submariners. These were the men who rebuilt and extended the Kerry Tramway, cut the forests, operated the system and trans-shipped the timber at Kerry station when activity was at its peak. Local men took on the duties after 1919 until closure in 1925. *Jack Arthur*

Black Hall prisoner of war camp. This photograph would have been taken from the tramway as it started the climb into Rhos Dingle. There is evidence that the Red Cross had expressed some concern for the welfare of these men in such a cold and wet valley. *Jack Arthur*

The main tramway crossed a further road and running on a low embankment re-crossed the brook. With Black Hall on the right it crossed a lane and turning sharply right-handed made three further crossings of the brook before traversing the lane as it climbed to a field west of, and adjacent to, Lower Rhos Farm (1 mile 66 chains from Kerry station).

The present physical evidence is that the running lines were single, though no doubt nature has obliterated erstwhile passing loops and sidings. The two bridges over the Meheli to the north of Black Hall, together with the relative embankments, are still intact.

The tramway had a further lease of life when in 1917 it, was relaid on the 1 ft 11½ in. gauge under the joint auspices of the War Department, Board of Trade and Forestry Commission: it operated in connection with the prisoner-of-war camp situated in the natural amphitheatre at the foot of Cefn Gwyn, near Lower Rhos. The first batch of these prisoners, numbering about 150, arrived by rail at Kerry on 19th June, 1917, and were put to work on timber felling for the provision of pit and trench props. The weight of the rails used in this relaying cannot be ascertained: it is understood that the branch to Lower Brynllywarch Farm was not revived, though there were minor extensions elsewhere. Two standard gauge exchange sidings were built by the Cambrian Railways at Kerry station; the sites of these sidings, one of which was in a shallow cutting, are still apparent.

Initially the resuscitated tramway was worked by a 0-4-0 tank locomotive with outside cylinders built in 1917 by Messrs Kerr, Stuart (now the Hunslet Engine Company Limited), Works No. 1158. This locomotive which was of standard Kerr, Stuart type for War Department and other work, boasted the following principal dimensions:

Cylinders:	6 in. diameter x 14 in. stroke
Diameter of driving wheels	1 ft 10 in.
Wheelbase:	3 ft 6 in.
Length over headstocks:	12 ft 3 in.
Maximum width:	5 ft 8½ in.
Height, rail to top of boiler:	4 ft 8 in.
Height, rail to top of chimney	8 ft 2 in.
Height, rail to top of cab:	8 ft 0 in.
Length of boiler and smokebox:	8 ft 8 in.
Diameter of boiler:	2 ft 6 in.
Weight:	5 tons 12 cwt 3 qtrs

As built, the locomotive was equipped with a semi-open cab fitted with a front weather-board and roof only and a 'capped' chimney. The locomotive had outside frames and boasted Stephenson link motion working valves above the cylinders through rocking arms.

Since leaving the tramway this locomotive saw service at the quarries of The Oakeley Slate Quarries Company Limited, Blaenau Festiniog, North Wales, by whom it was received on 28th December, 1925, and given the name *Diana*, painted centrally on the tanks. By sale through an agent it passed, about late 1943, to the Pen-yr-Orsedd Slate Quarry, Nantlle, Caernarvonshire. At an unknown date during its sojourn in North Wales it was fitted with a totally

A picture of unknown date showing the overhead gantry at Kerry sawmill.
Millennium Collection, Kerry Women's Institute

German prisoners of war at the timberyard, Kerry. The forest tramway would have been to the left of this picture. The processed timber would be reloaded to go to the narrow gauge siding at Kerry station for trans-shipment. Note the flywheel of a steam roller being used for the pulley transmission.
Millennium Collection, Kerry Women's Institute

Right: Portable steam engines working in tandem sawing planks on saw benches at Kerry. Note the trestles and feeder on narrow gauge rails. The owner, Mr Evan Bebb, is on the extreme right.
Millennium Collection, Kerry Women's Institute

Left: A portable steam engine at work in the timber yard or sawmills near Lower Brynllywarch during World War I. The source of fuel may have been wood rather than coal.
Millennium Collection, Kerry Women's Institute

Delivery of the 'Haig' class locomotive. It is on a standard gauge flat truck in the course of transfer at the narrow gauge exchange sidings at Kerry. PC Pugh observes the proceedings, he was remembered as a very strict, but very fair, village constable.   *National Library of Wales*

All traces of the narrow gauge exchange, plus the two extra standard gauge sidings built during World War I have gone. This picture taken in 2002 looks at the approach to Kerry yard. This extra section was to the left beyond the line of now mature trees. It is now gardens and the large site for holding timber is now a row of bungalows, the roof of one of these can just be seen through the trees.   *B. Poole*

enclosed cab, sanding gear and a chimney of stove-pipe type. It went out of use in 1950, the boiler being considered beyond repair. It then lay shunted away in an old shed, intact apart from the cab.

Early in 1919 the German prisoners-of-war were repatriated, and after a spell of less than two months in the hands of a private individual the locomotive, rolling stock and woodlands passed to E. Longhurst & Sons Limited, timber merchants, of Epsom, Surrey, who secured an 0-6-0 tank locomotive built by Messrs Kerr, Stuart in 1918 (Works No. 3118). This locomotive was one of the makers' 'Haig' type, built both for the Canadian Forestry Corps for use in Great Britain (for several gauges) and in a slightly varied form for the French military railways.

Principal dimensions:

Cylinders:	8½ in. in. diameter x 11 in. stroke
Diameter of driving wheels	2 ft 0 in.
Wheelbase:	4 ft 7½ in. (no flanges on central pair)
Maximum length:	13 ft 10 in.
Maximum width:	5 ft 9 in.
Maximum height:	8 ft 6 in.
Boiler pressure:	160 lb. per sq. in.
Tractive effort:	3,683 lb.

This type of locomotive was capable of traversing a 60 ft radius curve. Two injectors were fitted and for picking up water on temporary tracks, a steam water lifter (as on road engines). One of the drivers was a Mr Pryce.

This locomotive saw subsequent service with the Surrey County Council, who numbered it GP 76, and utilised it in the construction of the Guildford by-pass in 1930-1934, thence it proceeded to the Charlton Sand & Ballast Company Ltd, Shepperton, Middlesex, and in 1941 to the Cliffe Granite Co. Ltd, Cliffe Hill Quarries, Markfield, near Leicester. One of the company's maintenance staff serving as an engineroom artificer lost his life in the sinking of HMS *Kashmir* off Crete on 23rd May, 1941, whereupon the locomotive received the name of that ill-fated destroyer.

Early in 1920 a branch was constructed from a point near Drefor Farm, where the Cwm Quarry line first crossed the stream in the Llwyn-y-rhwd dingle by a bridge. Turning left-handed this branch left the woods and crossing some open fields met the road up Drefor dingle about 280 yards above the farm. This was the limit for locomotive working. Immediately beyond there was a short winch-worked incline as the line dropped sharply before commencing the climb up Drefor dingle to Cwmgolog. A lengthy self-acting incline lifted the line to Bryans Wood (about 2½ miles beyond the limit for locomotives).

In the same year an incline was laid to secure timber from Cwm Wood, the junction with the Cwm Quarry line being effected just before the first reversing junction (i.e., on coming from Kerry).

About 1920 an incline was constructed beyond Lower Rhos to gain access to Rhiwdantin and Cefn Graig Wood, whilst the final extension was a line up Rhos Dingle to secure pit props from New Pool.

Additional motive power was provided in 1919 in the form of an 0-4-0 petrol locomotive built by Baguley of Burton-upon-Trent (Works No. 777) which is

The 'Haig' class locomotive with four loaded bogie wagons. The train has left the Drefor Dingle area. The timber may have come down from the Cwm incline which was this side of the dingle or from the Drefor incline which was trestled up the very steep-sided dingle.

National Library of Wales

The traces of the track bed that sweep across the field on the east side of the lane just above the Drefor farm can still be clearly seen in this 2002 view.   *B. Poole*

The Baguley petrol locomotive is seen on the flimsy bridge in the upper part of the Rhos Dingle.
National Library of Wales

The bridge would have been just behind the wood poles which mark a boundary. The track can easily be walked on a ledge cut on the dingle side on the left-hand of the picture. The earth slip where the horizontal timber embankment had been placed can be traced. After crossing the bridge to the right, there was an incline. This is now within the forest and is very difficult to trace.   *B. Poole*

The Kerry Tramway, The Western Branch

The trackbed can be clearly defined in many places. This 2002 view shows the steady gradient as the line commences to climb through the lower Rhos Dingle.   *B. Poole*

The tramway crossed the Meheli Brook twice, both bridges are still in place, this is the upper bridge just below Black Hall and the ex-German prisoner of war camp.   *B. Poole*

stated to have been used on one specific branch only, where it boasted its own shed. Its first driver was the Mr Pryce already referred to: when he graduated to the steam locomotives his successor was Mr Tom Gwilt. Initially but little used it was frequently in operation by E. Longhurst & Sons Ltd. Further details are lacking.

So far as can be ascertained the rolling stock in the early 1920s comprised about 30 eight-wheeled logging wagons and eight to 10 four-wheeled trucks.

Early in 1922 the tramway fell into disuse for the second, and final, time. The narrow gauge rails were removed and disposed of, together with the locomotives and rolling stock: the two standard gauge transhipment sidings were removed on 13th March, 1931.

Kerry Tramway Memories

Bryan Jones, born in 1923, was interviewed at Cwm-trefarlo Farm high up towards the Kerry Ridgeway. Bryan was born at Rhyddwr which straddles the ridgeway. He cannot think of anyone now alive who would have worked on the tramway. There are only a few older people that would even be able to remember it. He was one of a few of the Kerry parish that went to Bettws-y-crwyn school in Shropshire which was under three miles from his home while Kerry school was over four miles across high moorland.

He took on Cwm-trefarlo, the farm of his uncle, while his brother took on his parents' farm. Much of the western branch of the tramway to Rhiw-dan-tin and the Rhos dingle was within this farm. This line extension was built around 1917 and closed around 1922 when much timber had been extracted.

As a youngster, he can clearly remember traces of the line through his uncle's land but it was built with minimal earthworks, just laid on the ground with minimum ballast and there is no trace left in any of the pastureland. However, he could walk close to the exact route even now, although his feet are more willing than his lungs. All the fields have been ploughed and re-seeded and Bryan can remember ploughing out one rail in one of the higher fields in the 1950s. Until 15 to 20 years ago, the trace of the stumps of Rhos bridge across the brook could still be seen but weathering and rotting have now done their task. There are slight traces still on the edge of the dingle where a cutting was made on the steep bank. Bryan can remember traces of the winding gear close to Rhiw-dan-tin; he thought there were two inclines rather than one long one.

Bryan went on one school trip, maybe when he was about eight or nine, to Aberystwyth. He thought that it was organised by the school rather than the chapels and church for that year because there was some arrangement for him and several others because they went to school in Salop. It was the first time he travelled on a train.

As a very young boy, he can remember the completion of the five miles of road to the Anchor (now the B4368); previously there were just three or four tracks straight down the slopes. Some of the base stone was cut and carried but the finished stone was all hauled up from Kerry station by either horses and wagons or traction engine and trailer.

The Kerry Tramway, The Eastern Branch

The branch to Drefor crosses the Llwyn-y-rhwd Dingle. The culvert is a considerable length, maybe 20 yards and the embankment has been built over the brickwork.   *B. Poole*

A curve outline on the first section of the tramway climbing to the first reverse of the zig-zag beside Llwyn-y-rhwd Dingle can be clearly seen to the right of the farm track. The bridge and the junction to Drefor are just below this picture.   *B. Poole*

Both Bryan's father and his uncle were very fond of their shire horses. There was still much wood left after the tramway shut and this was extracted by his uncle with his shires and timber wagons and taken to Kerry station. This continued into the early 1930s.

Bryan has a clear memory of a World War II tramway that was laid close to his father's farm at Rhyddwr on the ridgeway. The soil here is very peaty and there was no good metalled road in the vicinity. One area is called Bryan's Wood and this is why Bryan received his name. The track really was just half pit props laid on the surface with very light rails. It was moved as extraction took place. The timber was taken to the metal road where there was a crane to load on to the lorries. The whole trees were taken by a Shropshire timber merchant; he would take up to nine trunks weighing about nine tons and Bryan can remember having a lift in the cab. Some of this went down to Kerry and then out to Shropshire via Churchstoke while the remainder went out on the Kerry railway. All the smaller timber cut for pit props went down on a Forestry Commission lorry to be loaded at the station. The regular driver was called up and a land girl (forestry section) received instruction on driving the lorry when empty. On one of her first full loads she missed the gears by Cwm-trefarlo; she controlled the lorry with the brakes until near the Pentre when they failed. The lorry went through the hedge but no one was hurt. The ridgeway locomotive had a small petrol engine but with no weather protection, it must have been bitter for the poor driver in the cold driving rain and snow.

John Morgan is now 77 and lives at Hodley. His dad worked on the forest railway from 1919 when the POWs left until closure. He then went farming. John can only tell stories from Dad. He did general work, loading, operating petrol engine inclines, greasing wagon axles, repairing track and transfer loading at Kerry station. He was not an engine driver. There were some accidents, de-railing and jacking back would occur and there were cases where loads could push on the gradients so that the wagons would tip on the bend and then throw the load off. His father can remember German prisoners of war singing in the camp before he joined the tramway. Their voices were excellent on an evening drifting across the valley. Dad said that the trains had to work very hard pulling empty wagons up the gradients before the inclines. The main problem coming down was braking with the heavy loads. There was only a run round at Kerry station and there were some sidings further back.

Llwyn-y-rhwd Junctions

Harold Jones moved to Llwyn-y-rhwd when he married Edwina Davies in 1945. Their son, now farming the land, arranged for his retired parents to discuss the tramway. Edwina was born just after the tramway closed so her memory is that from her father's tales. The reversing junctions were built in the 1880s by the Naylors to Cwm quarry and traffic was horse drawn with loads down by gradient with a brakeman. It was a folly.

The tramway used the same line when the track was re-laid in World War I but only went part of the way to the Cwm. She thought that the steam engines worked up the reverses but sometimes horse haulage was also used. Much of the timber was taken out at the first reverse where there was a siding. There was also space at the second reverse, which was near an old quarry. Edwina knew that locomotives and wagons could reverse at the triangle junction just above the farm house. A tramway chassis and a length of rail is still on the farm. The incline through the Cwm on the far edge of the farm had a big steam winch.

Harold was born in 1914 and brought up near Glanmule. He can remember the tramway with both the petrol engines and the steam engines. He remembers getting a real telling off by one of the tramway workers for riding down on the trucks.

His son broke up a large concrete plinth at the top of the Cwm Incline several years ago and the square can still be clearly seen with nettles on the disturbed ground. This is almost certainly the site of the large stationary steam engine. Harold would go with his dad with a horse and cart to Kerry station. His dad was employed by the auctioneer to unload sheep pens from the train then erect these pens around the Glanmeheli fields for the auctions. When sales had been completed the pens were dismantled and reloaded on the train and were returned to Abermule or beyond.

To walk the reverse junctions may be a unique experience in Britain. Virtually all is contained within one long field and the switchbacks can be clearly seen. It is almost like 'los zig-zags de los Andes'. It commences by curving up the side of Llwyn-y-rhwd dingle on a gradient where adhesion must have been difficult even with empty wagons to the large reverse. The second length sweeps round the middle contours into a wood. The final section again climbs the contours to a triangular junction and then climbs again to where the forest tramway line terminated. The track of the 1880s line climbing further to the Cwm quarry can still be seen.

The reverse incline at Lywyn-y-rhwd in 2002. The first section would have lifted the train up from the junction to Drefor. It can be seen falling downwards towards the trees in the dingle. The first reverse has much space and there was a siding here as much mature timber was loaded here. The second curve climbing to the next reverse can clearly be seen. To walk this zig-zag on a gradient of around 1 in 40 may be a unique experience in Britain.
B. Poole

Output from Van Mines
(from official figures)

Lead and Silver	Ore (tons)	Lead (tons)	Silver (ounces)	Value (£)
1866	240	186	1,176	n/a
1867	615	462	2,390	n/a
1868	1,170	894	9,257	n/a
1869	2,260	1,718	17,176	n/a
1870	4,525	3,451	32,785	n/a
1871	5,300	4,028	42,400	n/a
1872	6,230	4,672.5	49,184	n/a
1873	5,740	4,335	48,824	n/a
1874	6,050	4,840	48,400	n/a
1875	6,450	4,871	55,884	97,645
1876	6,850	5,136	59,000	102,905
1877	6,470	5,205	54,693	22,645
1878	5,800	4,524	47,200	64,590
1879	4,300	3,975	25,800	45,252
1880	2,700	2,174	26,105	12,451.7
1881	2,600	2,080	23,400	28,201.4
1882	2,602	2,081	16,652	27,771
1883	2,290	1,832	22,900	21,441
1884	1,187	950	10,458	9,631
1885	900	684	6,327	7,868
1886	900	684	8,829	9,047
1887	1,200	912	10,597	10,870
1888	1,110	844	9,779	11,231
1889	930	707	8,194	9,345
1890	450	342	3,965	4,277
1891	150	114	1,174	1,297
1892	137	104	1,068	1,063
1893	Not recorded			
1894	500	394.5	3,902	3,154
1895	1,500	1,140	11,715	10,210
1896	1,100	846	8,589	7,775
1897	1,400	1,091	10,927	11,919
1898	1,120	857	8,586	10,087
1899	600	467	4,683	6,302
1900	505	393	3,942	6,139
1901	710	553	5,542	5,920
1902	275	214	-	2,085
1903	296	231	2,310	2,245
1904	576	460	3,917	4,753
1905	732	577	6,444	7,000
1906	1,507	1,188.5	5,731	18,349
1907	1,171	934	7,966	15,865
1908	83	65	565	688
1909	547	426	3,723	4,457
1910	931	734	4,472	7,270
1911	888	692	5,155	8,397
1912	825	643	4,125	10,076
1913	862	671	4,310	9,800

This woodcut notes the most valuable mine in the county of Montgomeryshire in 1872 as it was rapidly being expanded and would justify the private construction of the railway line. *Powys County Council, Newtown Library*

Zinc	Ore (tons)	Metal (tons)	Value (£)
1870	450	-	1552.5
1871	1,260	-	3,087
1872	2,110	-	7,174
1873	1,400	-	6,160
1874	2,450	-	4,690
1875	1,950	-	3,225
1876	2,460	-	9,638
1877	2,404	-	9,315
1878	2,100	-	5,759
1879	1,750	-	4,562.5
1880	1,525	-	4,203.8
1881	1,414	610	3,231.4
1882	1,424	612.3	3,540
1883	1,805	722	4,148
1884	964	279	2,019
1885	746	273	1,779
1886	594	213	1,017
1887	300	131	606
1888	865	247	2,726
1889	746	291	2,582
1890	280	80	715
1891	127	24	321
1892	79	15	171
1902	45	18	77
1903	478	156	1,770
1904	441	15	158
1905	92	30	409
1906	166	54	458
1907	109	25	68
1908	28	10	90
1909	18	6	56
1910	20	5	23
1911	10	3	30

Appendix Two

Kerry Sunday School Trips in the 1930s and other Excursions

Many of those over 70 years of age can remember the Sunday School trips. A record of these is held in the Cedewain Magazine (Joint Church in Wales in the area) from 1930 onwards. Previously, the churches produced their own magazine, if at all. There is evidence that Sunday School trips had been organised previously by both Kerry Church and the chapels.

Monday 28th July, 1930. Special train from Kerry station to Rhyl for annual outing. Early rain cleared and it was a beautiful day.

Thursday 23rd July, 1931 (passenger service now ceased). Outing to Aberystwyth. Charabancs from Kerry to Newtown for special train leaving punctually at 11 am; the return train left Aberystwyth at 8.00 pm, making a lovely long day.

Monday 25th July, 1932. A special train was run from Kerry for the Sunday School and Choir accompanied by many friends and parishioners to Rhyl. It remained fine in spite of ominous clouds and it was an enjoyable day.

Monday 24th July, 1933. Special train from Kerry station to Aberystwyth; many took advantage and the train was packed.

Monday 30th July, 1934. Sunday School trip to Aberystwyth on a special from Kerry station. (No record can be traced for 1935.)

1936. (No dates given) Two Sunday School outings, Mothers Union and friends to Hereford (transport unknown) and Sunday School special train to Aberystwyth (in Ron Jones' story). After weeks of rain, we all had a lovely day.

1937. (No dates given) Two annual trips, the first to Chester and the second was a packed train from Kerry to see the new King and Queen at Aberystwyth. It was a day and an occasion that the children will long remember (in George Jones' story).

Excursions would have been a very important business. Research from the *Newtown and Welshpool Express* shows many advertisements for them, but poor Kerry missed out on many because of lack of connection in the early morning or no chance of return from Abermule in the evening. In 1886, Kerry people would have missed Bala Sheep Dog Trials, the National Eisteddfod, day returns to Barmouth and Pwllheli but could have joined the following:

Tuesday 27th April. Welshpool steeplechase Kerry dep. 10.05 am third class fare 1s. 6d.

Tuesday 4th May. Chester Race Cup Day - Kerry dep. 8.00 am third class fare 3s. Kerry passengers MUST return on 5.00 pm from Chester.

Monday 24th May. Kerry dep. 8.00 am for London Euston. *Tuesday 25th May* at Epsom Races. Return leaves Euston on *Wednesday 26th May* dep. 10.00 am. Third class fare 15s.

By 1894, some really exciting extras were available:

April. Day fare to Llanymynech Tanat Side Point to Point. Leave Kerry at 9.25 am 2s.

June. Handel Festival at Crystal Palace. Leave Kerry on Friday at 7. 10 pm, return from Euston at 9.45 am Monday.

18th August. The Royal Warehouse Special Train from Newtown with extra Kerry train, 5.50 am Kerry to Abermule; arrive Blackpool at 10.30 am leave Blackpool at 11.00 pm, connection at Abermule at 3.20 am to return to Kerry around 3.55 am. Fare 3s. 9d. A 22 hour excursion.

A further example where there was no connection to Abermule for Kerry people would have been the Congregational Union of Wales at Cardiff via Mid Wales line from Oswestry.

There were also special tickets, Rail and Coach on certain days finishing for the season on 1st October, 1894 to Dinas Mawddwy including Bwlch Oerddrws. This would have been on the daily train from Oswestry to Machynlleth with tickets from every station except Kerry.

Bibliography

Mawddwy

The Locomotive Magazine, February 1911
Railway & Travel Monthly, July 1911
Railway Magazine, December 1918, January 1919
A Guide to Dinas Mawddwy, J. & J. Gibson, Aberystwyth, 1893
The Slates of Wales, F.J. North, National Museum, 1946
DM ai Hangylchoed, T. Davies, Dinas Mawddwy, 1893
Narrow Gauge Railways in Mid-Wales, J.I.C. Boyd, Oakwood Press, 1954
Cambrian News, 11th September, 1908
Aberystwyth Observer, 8th July, 1909

Van

Railway Magazine, April 1926
Railways Vol. 2, p.68
Montgomeryshire Express & Radnor Times, 1st August, 1882, 29th March, 1941
Locomotive Magazine, 15th January, 1912
Railway Magazine, January 1941, February 1941
Llandinam Papers, National Library
GWR Magazine, December 1940
The Mines of Shropshire & Montgomeryshire, Roger Burt, 1990

Kerry

The Locomotive Magazine, November 1913
Railway Magazine, January 1907
Montgomery County Times, 23rd June, 1917
The Kerry Tramway and other Timber Light Railways, Cox & Krupa, Plateway Press, 1992
'Excelsior', *Narrow Gauge & Industrial Railway Modelling Review No. 53*, 2003

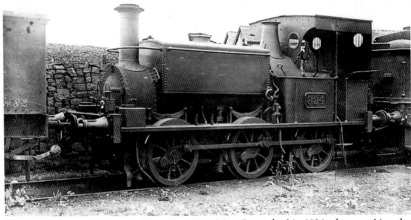

The locomotive *Mawddwy* as GWR No. 824 at Moat Lane shed in 1934 when working the Van Railway.   *R.W. Kidner*